GHOSTLAND

ALSO BY EDWARD PARNELL

The Listeners

EDWARD PARNELL

GHOSTLAND

IN SEARCH OF A HAUNTED COUNTRY

WILLIAM
COLLINS

William Collins
An imprint of HarperCollins*Publishers*
1 London Bridge Street
London SE1 9GF

www.WilliamCollinsBooks.com

First published in Great Britain by William Collins in 2019

1

A catalogue record for this book is
available from the British Library

ISBN 978-0-00-827195-4

Set in Berling LT Std and Albertus MT Pro
Printed and bound in Great Britain by
CPI Group (UK) Ltd, Croydon

For the ghosts

'And so they are ever returning to us, the dead.'
W. G. Sebald, *The Emigrants*

Contents

Always the ghosts.

Reaching into the past concealed behind the glow-in-the-dark cardboard apparitions that decorated my childhood bedroom, the fascination was there from the start: on a family holiday to Wales, aged four, asking the tour guide in Caernarfon Castle whether we might see the place's spectral lady; a few years later, obsessing over Borley Rectory – the 'most haunted house in the world' – which called out to me from my spine-creased *Usborne Guide to the Supernatural World*; or, at the Halloween party I begged my mother to let me have (long before such events were a commonplace British occurrence), dressing up as Dracula, my friends as the Wolfman and various grinning ghouls.

The writer M. R. James once wrote: 'For the ghost story a slight haze of distance is desirable. "Thirty years ago," "Not long before the war," are very proper openings.'

And if I think back through three decades of self-obfus-
cation, a host of recollections give confirmation.

With me, always the ghosts.

Yet even with hindsight no disquiet comes to me from
these memories; they are reassuring, I can find shelter
within them. Only later were we to become a phantom
family – a host of lives lived, then unlived. The disquiet
comes when I realise there's no one left to help me reconcile the real and the half-remembered.

So, I must do it myself.

I must attempt to explore that sense so many before me
have felt. The shadows they too have glimpsed among the
fields, hills and trees of this haunted land.

To lay to rest the ghosts of my own sequestered past.

Chapter 1

LOST HEART

It was, as far as I can ascertain, on Christmas Eve of the year 1994 that a young man drew up before the door of his childhood home, in the heart of Lincolnshire. He looked about him with the keenest curiosity during the short interval that elapsed between the fumbling of his keys and the opening of the front door. Inside, he began to study the four programmes available on his television set, pausing before a presentation that caught his eye. The time was five minutes before one o'clock, he realised. Christmas Day itself …

This, more or less, was how I first became acquainted with the work of M. R. James, my favourite – and arguably Britain's finest – writer of ghost stories. I was home for the

holidays during my third year at university and had been
into town to celebrate the festivities. A little the worse for
drink, I was alone in the living room, as my brother Chris
– nearly six years my senior – was still out with friends. In
the morning the two of us would open our presents
together before spending the rest of the day at my aunt
and uncle's. In an attempt to compensate for the house's
emptiness and our parents' absence, we'd started a tradition of labelling our gifts to each other as if from various
half-remembered figures from our past: obscure family
acquaintances, disliked former teachers, or people who we
had given nicknames to – like Porkpie, the middle-aged
man in the pork-pie hat who was a constant fixture in the
pub we frequented, boring anyone who'd listen about the
supermarket where he worked.

   Not ready for sleep, I lay on the sofa and flicked through
the TV channels. On BBC Two a grainy drama from the
seventies was beginning. What I'd chanced upon was an
episode of the classic 'A Ghost Story for Christmas' strand:
Lawrence Gordon Clark's adaptation of M. R. James's
supernatural tale 'Lost Hearts'.

   There's a fearful symmetry to this, I've come to learn,
because this particular film was first shown on BBC One a
little before midnight on Christmas Day 1973, less than a
fortnight after I was born. Had I already witnessed it before
as a crying baby – perhaps my mother had happened at
that very point to switch on the TV set to try and calm my
tears? If she had, I doubt she would have found much
respite, because the BBC version is a frightening piece of
work; I was to find this out some twenty-one years later,

when the ghost of a razor-nailed boy and his dark-eyed companion appeared on the screen in front of me.

Through the white gate at the back of the graveyard the ground changes abruptly, the approach from the rectory with its aged, ivy-clad trees replaced by a squat jumble of shrubs and sedge, punctuated by paths that run aimlessly to the water. The 'lake', as it is called, seems out of place in the west Suffolk countryside, reminding me of one of the shallow, ephemeral coastal lagoons you find in the Camargue. Lifeless trunks point upwards from its greyness like rigor-mortised fingers. The division between land and water is tenuous; there are no banks as such, just a dirty shoreline of mud over which the waves lap, adding to the feature's temporary feel. This is not a giant puddle left behind by a flood, or some deliberately drowned world,

but a spring-fed mere that has given its name to the neighbouring village.

Livermere Lake. 'The lake where rushes grow', from the Old English *laefor-mere*. I've known about this place for a long time too: since my brother saw a vagrant black-winged pratincole here in 1993, a rare hawk-like wading bird. I couldn't join him to see it, which, as a keen birdwatcher, riled me for years (until I finally caught up with one myself on the Norfolk coast) and lent the location an enduring mystique in my head. Only later did I become aware of the connection between Great Livermere and M. R. James.

Montague Rhodes James – known to his close friends as Monty – was born in Goodnestone, a small Kent village midway between Canterbury and Deal where his father was then curate, in August 1862. After three years the family moved to Livermere, six miles from Bury St Edmunds, when Herbert James took up the rectorship of St Peter's Church, whose gravestones I passed between on my way to the mere. This section is Broad Water, with the narrow tree-lined southern arm, Ampton Water, snaking off somewhere behind me, obscured by a screen of trees. The rain slants sparsely down as I scan the surface and shore: there are no rare waders today, though a typically noisy pair of black-and-white oystercatchers flies past, splitting the silence with their piping.

Across the water stands a second church, the now-ruined St Peter and St Paul of Little Livermere, derelict since the first half of the twentieth century. The tower, according to James in his 1930 work *Suffolk and Norfolk: A Perambulation of the Two Counties with Notices of their*

History and their Ancient Buildings, was heightened so as to be seen from Livermere Hall, itself long gone, demolished as superfluous in 1923. Its owner, Jane Anne Broke, was a relative by marriage of Herbert James, which was how he came to be offered the role of attending to the spiritual needs of the village – a serendipitous move in terms of its influence on young Monty's future ghost stories. Stately homes and their surrounding parkland appear in a number of those tales, reflecting James's upbringing as the son of a well-connected rector and the privileged circles in which he was to circulate during his later career as provost of both Cambridge's King's College and Eton's famous public school.*

In 'Lost Hearts', the young protagonist Stephen Elliott stands at his open window listening to the strange noises coming from across the mere: 'They might be the notes of owls or water-birds, yet they did not quite resemble either.' The lake is rich with bird life, and it's easy to picture the youthful James kept awake by their sounds – distorted by the space between mere and rectory – as he lay in his bedroom searching for sleep. Monty, however, appeared fond of his childhood home – various surviving fragments

---

* There are, perhaps, wider sociological factors as to why grand houses and their surroundings feature so prevalently in the stories of James (and other writers) – historically, ghosts have seemed largely a concern of the two extremes of British society, with belief in them concentrated among the upper and working classes. Roger Clarke's *A Natural History of Ghosts* makes a neat case for these polarities: 'Your middle-class sceptic would say that toffs like ghosts because it is a symptom of their decadence, the plebeians because they are ill-educated.'

of juvenilia extol the virtues, and to an extent the eeriness,
of the local landscape. In the undated poem 'Sounds of the
Wood' he begins:

> From off the mere, above the oaks, the hern
> Come sailing, and the rook fly cawing home.

The scene in front of me is little changed from that the
young James took pleasure in over a century ago. Sure
enough, a heron is present this afternoon ('hern' is an
archaic form of the word), roosting in the alders beside
Ampton Water. A striking adult bird, its blue-grey plumage
is broken up by its black-feathered shoulder and the thick
stripe that extends above its eye.

I walk back towards the church of James's father. A
small deer – a muntjac, I presume – peers at me from
through the sedges, sliding beneath the cover of a sallow
before I can get a proper look. In the churchyard I wander
among the headstones, one ghosted with the faint outline
of a cherubic face, another with a lichen-covered skeleton.
The commonest surname I find is Mothersole, the name
James bestowed upon the witch from his story 'The Ash
Tree'. The horrifying Mrs Mothersole goes on to enact a
spidery revenge on the descendants of Sir Matthew Fell,
the man responsible for her hanging, delivering a chilling
rebuke as she stands on the gallows awaiting her fate:
'There will be guests at the Hall.' 'The Ash Tree' is set in
Suffolk, and a mere features in the grounds of the fictitious
Castringham Hall; it's not unreasonable to suppose that
the now-vanished house across the park from James's

childhood home might have been the model for the story's location.

Alongside the grave of Charles and Ann Mothersole I find the remains of a blackbird, dead a week or so and becoming one with the surrounding soil and oak leaves. Banding its leg is an identification ring from the Natural History Museum. Later, I learn the bird's melancholy fate: ringed in Great Livermere as a fledgling the previous spring, barely moving from its place of birth.

Towards the back of the churchyard, beyond a dark rectangle of yews (which bring to mind the whispering grove from James's story 'The Rose Garden'), stands a spindly cross. This might be the memorial to his mother and father that James had erected. I look for the word 'PAX', which is meant to be inscribed on it, but can only make out the letters IHS at its apex: *Jesus, saviour of mankind*. The stone is crusted with pale-green moss,

obscuring the writing on its base. I start to flake off the
material with my fingernail in an attempt to expose further
clues. There is an inscription, though it's not easy to read
– and something about the act of uncovering it feels wrong,
like the sort of foolish feat an inquisitive scholar in one of
James's stories would do and later come to regret.

I decide to leave it a mystery.

Returning to where I parked my car by the front gate of
the churchyard, I peer over a wall, through the rhododendrons on the other side, at a cream-coloured building. It's
James's childhood home – a square, solid-looking place
rising to three storeys, with plenty of rooms for the young
James to have lost himself in on the occasions he was here
and not away at Temple Grove prep school, on the outskirts
of London between Mortlake and Richmond Park. This
was followed by Eton, where in 1882, and already writing

his own ghost stories (as well as indulging in more serious sixth-form study, including a love of the classics, ancient manuscripts and the architecture of churches), he passed his scholarship exam for King's College, Cambridge.

I contemplate the chances of being allowed to take a closer look at the rectory, restyled as the new Livermere Hall and used as accommodation for expensive game-shooting trips, but decide that rocking up unannounced is unlikely to gain me a warm welcome and an offer of the full guided tour (I tried the same earlier, without success, at the farm neighbouring the derelict church of Little Livermere). Besides, the daylight is waning and the rain now falling more keenly. As I drive from the village, past the dark earth of countless ploughed-open fields, the final words of James's last published story, 'A Vignette', resonate:

Are there here and there sequestered places which some curious creatures still frequent, whom once on a time anybody could see and speak to as they went about on their daily occasions, whereas now only at rare intervals in a series of years does one cross their paths and become aware of them?*

---

* Written in 1935 and printed posthumously in 1936, 'A Vignette' is the only one of James's works to reference Livermere and his childhood home directly. The apparently autobiographical tale tells of a malevolent, haunting face glimpsed through an opening in the rectory's wall.

'Lost Hearts' was probably the second of James's published ghost stories to be written (after 'Canon Alberic's Scrapbook'), finished at some time between summer 1892 and autumn of the following year. It appeared in print in the *Pall Mall Magazine* in December 1895, then in *Ghost Stories of an Antiquary*, his first collection of supernatural tales, in 1904.

By this point, James had been made a dean (of King's) and, from 1893, the director of Cambridge's Fitzwilliam Museum. In addition to an expert command of Latin, Greek and French, he also had a familiarity with German and Italian – and even a modicum of Hebrew and Danish. These formidable linguistic skills served him admirably: he was a noted scholar of the medieval, and of esoteric branches of study such as biblical apocrypha – the sorts of subjects the lone middle-aged protagonists of his stories specialise in. Now in his early forties – though always, perhaps, appearing a little older than his years – James was a tall, well-built man with dark hair (parted to the right) and rounded spectacles. His features were soft, apart from a strong, square jaw. He spoke quietly, often chuckling, often drawing on his curved tobacco pipe.

I knock and enter the opaque-paned door to the Founder's Library of the Fitzwilliam. Inside the architecture appears largely unchanged since James's time, when the room acted as his office. Built in 1848, it houses ten thousand fine volumes in carved oak bookcases that stretch more than twenty feet up to the white, geometrically patterned ceiling. An imposing marble-surrounded fireplace dominates the room. It's a place of work and study where today the museum's manuscript department is based – something James would approve of, I'm sure. A young woman at a table is leafing through an oversized

illuminated book of musical scores, the only sound apart
from the occasional swish of turning pages being the background hum of a dehumidifier. It is a soporific, comforting
space that sends me back to another time, another world
– and it's easy on this darkening winter's afternoon to
imagine the director at his desk, squinting through his
glasses in the pooled light at one of the antiquated tomes
that line the vast shelves.*

---

* It's tempting to think the room inspired 'The Tractate Middoth'.
But the primary setting of James's story (published in 1911) is
Cambridge University's old library – today the library of Gonville
& Caius.

James himself appeared rather indifferent to 'Lost Hearts', writing to his friend James McBryde in March 1904 that 'I don't much care about it.' The same was not true of Monty's feelings for the man who was to become the illustrator of his first collection of ghost stories, his affection rising from the page as he later described McBryde in glowing terms: 'no one who, even when he supposed himself out of spirits, brought so much enjoyment into an expedition. A smile will never be far off when his friends speak of him ...'

James McBryde was a decade younger than MRJ – the three initials were how James usually signed his own name, and how he was referred to by many acquaintances – arriving at King's College, Cambridge from Shrewsbury in 1893 to study medicine ('Natural Sciences' as it was then known). The dashing McBryde came to be a close companion to James, joining him on summer cycling trips, including those to Denmark and Sweden that provided the setting for the stories 'Number 13' and 'Count Magnus'. After completing his medical studies in tribute to the wishes of his late father (though caring little for the subject), McBryde took up a place at the Slade School in 1903 to commence his formal artistic training – a calling for which it is clear he had a considerable talent. Early in the following year, however, he became seriously ill with appendicitis, and a second attack followed in March.

During his friend's recuperation, James welcomed the idea that McBryde should illustrate some of his stories for the book that was to become *Ghost Stories of an Antiquary* – stories James had previously read out on Christmas Eve,

by the light of a single candle, to the assembled King's
choristers and his fellow academics and acquaintances of
the Chitchat Society. In carrying on a loose tradition popularised by Charles Dickens, the Cambridge don became
the unwitting new keeper of the seasonal, supernatural
flame. In folklore, ghosts had long been linked with
Christmas Eve – a night, like Halloween, in which the
boundary between this world and the Otherworld, the
realm of the spirits, is said to be thinned. And though the
festive telling of ghostly stories clearly took place before
Dickens – dark winter nights lend themselves to it – the
Victorian writer had brought the practice into the main-
stream through *A Christmas Carol* and the tales he
published in his own weekly magazine, *Household Words*.

Perhaps the most effective of these is 'No. 1 Branch
Line: The Signalman'. It too was produced specially for
Christmas, as was the 1976 BBC version directed by
Lawrence Gordon Clark, the first of the 'Ghost Story for
Christmas' films not to have been adapted from one of
James's stories. *The Signalman* features a superb performance from Denholm Elliott, whose terrifying vision of his
future may well be the most frightening sequence in the
entire strand. The story features three supernaturally foretold railway accidents, and it seems no coincidence that it
was written the year after Dickens was himself an unwilling participant in such an event.

On 9 June 1865, returning from France through Kent en
route to Charing Cross, the train he was travelling in came
to a low viaduct at Staplehurst that was in the process of
being repaired. Several carriages plunged off the tracks,

killing ten people and injuring fifty, although the structure stood only around ten feet above the muddy stream below; at the moment of derailment Dickens was reading through the manuscript of *Our Mutual Friend*. As the writer and his mistress, the actress Ellen Ternan, were at the front of the vehicle in first class, they got off relatively lightly. However, Ternan suffered physical injuries that incapacitated her for weeks, while Dickens, who helped to comfort other passengers, was traumatised, and nervous of train travel thereafter. And, in an odd twist, his own death (resulting from a stroke) was to coincide with the fifth anniversary of the accident.

James McBryde completed only four drawings for *Ghost Stories of an Antiquary*. He died in early June 1904, five days after having his appendix operated on. James's book was published at the end of that year, with his friend's illustrations embellishing 'Canon Alberic's Scrap-book' and 'Oh, Whistle, and I'll Come to You, My Lad'. In his preface James paid tribute to its illustrator: 'Those who

knew the artist will understand how much I wished to give a permanent form even to a fragment of his work.' Despite his Victorian, repressed reluctance to display his emotions, Monty was devastated by the death of McBryde, picking rose, honeysuckle and lilac blooms from the Fellows' Garden at King's, and taking them with him on the train to the funeral in Lancashire.* He cast them into his friend's grave after the other mourners had departed.

James's sexuality has long been the subject of speculation – he was a lifelong bachelor, and surrounded himself with close, often younger, male friends. Those searching for Freudian clues about his personal life might point to the

---

* That same month McBryde's wife Gwendolen gave birth to a daughter, Jane, with James taking up the role of her guardian; he wrote his sole children's book, the Narnia-esque *The Five Jars* for her, and remained in close contact with the pair for the rest of his life.

lack of female protagonists in his stories, or note that when women do appear they regularly take the role of the fiend, like Mrs Mothersole in 'The Ash Tree'. The academic Darryl Jones refers to the 'mouth, with teeth, and with hair about it' inside which Mr Dunning in 'Casting the Runes' unsuspectingly places his hand, in the nook beneath his pillow, as a *vagina dentata* – a nightmare image of the monstrous-feminine'. A similar horror could be ascribed to the mouldy well-cavity and the guardian-thing it harbours ('more or less like leather, dampish it was') in 'The Treasure of Abbot Thomas'.

Both of these examples may indeed, possibly, point to a fear of (or at least unfamiliarity with) women, and therefore may be indicative of James's clandestine fears or desires. Undoubtedly, having spent his life in all-male academia, he was far more comfortable in the company of men. This stretched to an enjoyment of the rough wrestling-games of 'ragging' and 'animal grab' that he played at Eton and continued to engage in while at King's – at the meetings of the TAF ('Twice a Fortnight') society, or at college Christmas Eve parties. James's friend Cyril Alington, later the headmaster of Eton (while James was its provost), provides surprising evidence contradicting the image of James as a stilted academic who we might expect to shun such physical contact; he recalled another friend, St Clair Donaldson – the future bishop of Salisbury – rolling on the floor during one of these games 'with Monty James's long fingers grasping at his vitals'.

James's tactile nature is reflected in his stories, in which the protagonists often experience the touch or feel of something that causes them revulsion, or, in the case of Stephen in 'Lost Hearts', wake to find his nightgown has been shredded in the darkness by the raking fingers of the ghost-boy Giovanni. However, it would be presumptuous

to assume that these horrors result from some subconscious psychosexual terror experienced by James – they may have been chosen simply for their unpleasantness, or for their resemblance to the medieval visions of Hell garishly on display in the paintings of Hieronymus Bosch and Pieter Bruegel the Elder, and also prevalent in the manuscripts of that period and the biblical apocrypha of which James was such a keen scholar.

Because it strikes me that an unexpected toothed mouth appearing beneath a pillow would be equally terrifying to any sleeper, regardless of whether they were a man or a woman, gay or straight.

Gordon Carey, a former King's chorister and Cambridge student who was one of James's closest later friends, told his son long after James's death that he supposed Monty was 'what would now be called a non-practising homosexual'.* However, a definitive answer to the question of the writer's sexuality – something that is ultimately irrelevant in relation to our enjoyment of his stories – seems likely to remain unknowable.

The reticence about 'Lost Hearts' that MRJ voiced to James McBryde perhaps hints at the atypical nature of the tale. In some ways it's grubbier and nastier than most of his

---

* It must be remembered that the Labouchere Amendment of 1885 had added a new layer of homophobic persecution to British society, criminalising 'gross indecency' between men, as Oscar Wilde would discover to his cost; it was not until 1967 that these laws were partially repealed, and only in 2004 (in England and Wales) that they were fully abolished.

stories – which might explain James's apparent disdain for it.* One of its main characters is a child – and children rarely feature in his work. Before the action begins, the real devil of the piece, Mr Abney, has already lured two adolescents to his grand house, removing their still-beating hearts with a knife while they lie drugged before him, then eating the organs accompanied by a glass of fine port. He plans to confer the same grim fate upon his young orphaned cousin Stephen Elliott in a ritual attempt to attain special powers for himself: invisibility, the ability to take on other forms, and the capacity for flight.

I disagree with James's own lukewarm opinion of 'Lost Hearts'. The story is viscerally effective in exploring the loss of childhood innocence (and of the boundaries people will cross to achieve their aims), though I think the adaptation I happened upon on that distant Christmas Eve is in some ways the more frightening of the two versions: certainly the gypsy girl Phoebe and the Italian boy Giovanni make petrifying on-screen apparitions with their greyish-blue skin, yellowed teeth, weirdly hypnotic swaying, and those extraordinary claw-like fingers. The maniacal movement of Mr Abney – he's usually filmed with the camera tracking him, or circling Stephen in the way a big cat circles its prey – was inspired by Robert Wiener's fêted work of German Expressionism, *The Cabinet of Dr Caligari*. And, in the appearance of the two ghost children, I see

---

* In his 1929 essay 'Some Remarks on Ghost Stories' James comments: 'Reticence conduces to effect, blatancy ruins it, and there is much blatancy in a lot of recent stories.'

echoes of another silent German classic, F. W. Murnau's *Nosferatu*, in which Max Schreck's depiction of the spindly-fingered vampire, Count Orlok, remains one of the most iconic images of the supernatural committed to celluloid.

Yet, above all in the small-screen version, it was the ghost-boy's hurdy-gurdy music that I found most unsettling. The film had no budget for an orchestral score, with scratchy vinyl 78s from the BBC archives providing the unforgettable aural chills; the adaptation makes no attempt, however, to replicate the 'hungry and desolate cries' of the dreadful pair of ghosts, a savage detail in James's original.

'Lost Hearts' has its setting at Aswarby Hall in Lincolnshire – when James was writing still a real, extant country pile just south of Sleaford, twenty miles to the north-west of the Fenland market town of Spalding where

I grew up (and where I first came across the story in the early hours of that Christmas morning). I cannot visit the hall, as it was demolished in 1951, the result of damage and neglect while under requisition during the Second World War; the parkland that is described so beautifully in the story, however, remains. The adaptation was filmed in twelve days, with Harrington Hall in the Lincolnshire Wolds taking the place of Aswarby. Another location in the

far north of the county, the Pelham Mausoleum at Brocklesby Park, was used for one of its most atmospheric scenes – when Stephen visits the temple in the grounds with its haunting, painted glass ceiling of cherubs. The mausoleum, based on that of the Temples of Vesta at Rome and Tivoli, was built between 1786 and 1794 by the First Baron Yarborough as a memorial to his late 33-year-old wife Sophia.

The TV production of *Lost Hearts* ranged widely over my home county, moving south to shoot the unvarying agricultural vistas I was so familiar with; I would have recognised the landscape of the ominous opening scene, as Stephen's carriage emerges from the morning haze of a long Fenland drove, passing vast fields where the ghost children wait.* This premature appearance of the two grey-skinned horrors is one of the film's weaknesses, for it raises too many questions about their motivation, and their foreshadowed knowledge of future events; in this way, at least, I think James's original, where the spirits are portrayed as forces of vengeful hunger, works better. But the hurdy-gurdy music of the film, the wonderful visuals of its ghosts, coupled with Joseph O'Conor's predatory Mr

---

* Although he spent so many of his seventy-three years on the fringe of the Fens, James's stories, with the exception of the 'The Fenstanton Witch' (which was unpublished in his lifetime), are not explicitly set in this flat farmland world. For an excellent example of a truly Fens-located tale, R. H. Malden's 'Between Sunset and Moonrise' is difficult to top. Malden was a fellow Kingsman and an acquaintance of James; his single collection of supernatural stories, *Nine Ghosts*, was brought out by MRJ's publisher Edward Arnold during the Second World War. Its dustjacket made the grand claim: 'Dr James has found his successor.'

Abney – and of course the circumstances in which I first encountered it – means that the adaptation retains pre-eminence for me.

It has an added layer of poignancy, I now discover: the child actor Simon Gipps-Kent, who conveys Stephen's likeability and wide-eyed terror with such effectiveness, died fourteen years after the film was made from a morphine overdose, aged twenty-eight.

From the dreaming spires, I head north-west through the drizzle and darkness, edging my way the last few miles along puddle-filled minor roads. Then, through an attractive village, an open gate and a gravel driveway, until the sturdy walls of one of the oldest continually inhabited houses in the country loom above me. It's not quite the opening of Lucy M. Boston's *The Children of Green Knowe*, in which the main character comes to his great-grandmother's – a place modelled on this building, Hemingford Grey Manor – in the middle of a flood of near-biblical proportions. But in terms of atmosphere it comes close, evoking the scene where Toseland reaches the house by boat – one of the most magical arrivals in children's literature:

> They rowed round two corners in the road and then in at a big white gate. Toseland waved the lantern about and saw trees and bushes standing in the water, and presently the boat was rocked by quite a strong current and the reflection of the lantern streamed away in elastic jigsaw shapes and made gold rings round the tree trunks. At last they came to a still pool reaching to

the steps of the house, and the keel of the boat grated
on gravel.

Published in 1954, *The Children of Green Knowe* is another
book I encountered through its BBC adaptation, which
aired in four half-hour teatime episodes from late
November 1986. As it was my second year at grammar
school I was perhaps a little too old to be watching it –
certainly the cooler boys in my class wouldn't have admitted to doing so. However, I definitely wasn't the only one,

with my friend James gaining the nickname Tolly due to his perceived likeness to the central character (Tolly is the familiar form of Toseland). The name stuck for a while, and as I view the series again now the face of the young actor, Alec Christie, who played the main role, has become insep-arable in my memory from that of my classmate.

The Children of Green Knowe is the first of six children's novels set around the eponymous twelfth-century house of its title. Born in 1892, Lucy Boston did not start writing the series until she was in her sixties; by then she had been living in Hemingford Grey, twelve miles from Cambridge, since 1937, having purchased the riverside manor after the failure of her marriage. The house (and its topiary-strewn garden) features at the heart of all of the books, with the spirits of its former inhabitants offering a usually reassuring presence.*

The Children of Green Knowe commences with seven-year-old Tolly travelling, like so many characters in bygone children's fiction, alone by train. (John Masefield's *The Box of Delights*, filmed two years before by the BBC – and also avidly watched by my younger self – is another.) Tolly, however, breaks one of the apparent rules of this kind of story by not being an orphan – his parents are in Burma and he's been summoned from boarding school for Christmas by his great-grandmother, Mrs Oldknow, whom he has never met. The wise, elderly lady seems a version of

---

* Except in the fifth of the series, *An Enemy at Green Knowe*, which gives us the malingering trace of Dr Vogel, an ominous seventeenth-century alchemist not unlike Mr Abney from 'Lost Hearts'.

what Lucy Boston herself was to become – she spent the rest of her days in the manor, where she passed away, aged ninety-seven, in 1990.

Tolly is entranced by the house and his ancient relative's tales of the past, which seem to come alive in the manifestations of the three benign ancestral Oldknow children, Toby, Linnet and Alexander. Victims of the Great Plague of 1665, they appear to him, alongside various tamed spectral animals and birds, when the whim suits, and Tolly pieces together their lost existences from the fragments they reveal about themselves. More prosaically, the young Toseland might be reconstructing the children's lives in his head from the stories his great-grandmother tells him and the family artefacts she shows him. In any case, *The Children of Green Knowe* is a magical piece of writing about imagination and what it is to be a child.

It's also a book that captures the weather in an almost touchable way – from its opening flood to the dramatic later blizzard, both of which were drawn from Lucy Boston's memories of the devastating winter of 1947. Harsh heavy snowfalls were followed, that March, by the worst flooding ever recorded along Britain's east coast, affecting a hundred thousand homes and turning the Fens into an inland sea. It was a transformation which Boston describes in her recollections of Hemingford, *Memory in a House*:

> It was like trying to shovel away the sky. The flakes
> were huge, purposeful and giddy, fantastic to watch
> when we sat inside. They descended on the garden, and

through their rising and falling play one could glimpse
the steady disappearance of all known features. The
frozen moat was filled up level with its banks, the big
yews were glittering pyramids rising from the ground;
drifts changed all contours.

I'm shown around the manor by Diana Boston – the wife
of Lucy's late son Peter, who etched the *Green Knowe*
books' striking white-on-black scraperboard illustrations
and line drawings. The atmosphere of the place hits me the
instant I enter. Diana's enthusiasm for the house and its
story is palpable. She gets me to don a pair of linen gloves,
so I can handle the numerous intricate, but now fragile,
quilts that Lucy Boston also worked on; these home-made
treasures feature at the core of the second novel in the
series, *The Chimneys of Green Knowe*. I have to admit my
ignorance at this point, as Diana has assumed my fandom
extends to every detail of the stories. At the time of my
visit I have read only the opening title and have somewhat
vague, thirty-year-old memories of its action.

She seems a little disappointed in me.

I do, however, vividly remember Toby's carved wooden
mouse, which Diana takes down from a high shelf and
places in my hands – I run my thumb over the comforting
smoothness of its dark wood, surprised by its weight. It is
exactly like its illustration in the book (executed more
than sixty years ago by Diana's husband), and happens to
be the very artefact used in the television adaptation.

We head to the first floor's imposing music room. Here,
during the Second World War, Lucy held evening recitals

for airmen from the nearby base – but because she was an eccentric outsider and fluent in German, many of the locals had suspicions that she was spying for the enemy, rather than doing her morale-boosting bit for the war effort. The men sat on cushions in the church-like alcoves as the industrial-sized trumpet of the gramophone crackled out its sound. Diana puts a record beneath its needle now, to demonstrate: the effect on the room is transformative, almost placing me among the milling throng of blue-suited young men to whom this steadfast, ancient house must have seemed such a place of sanctuary compared to the uncertainty of their own impermanent prospects.

We climb the narrow staircase that leads to the attic. The room at the top is dominated by a black-maned

wooden rocking horse, conjuring for me the opening credits of the television series in which the camera circles the
horse in close-up while the woodwinds, violins and harp of
the main theme swirl in accompaniment.* This is the
bedroom in which Tolly sleeps, and is a near facsimile of
the one described in the text. As the two of us stand there
and Diana recounts details of the furniture, something odd
happens. A hardback novel with no dust jacket seems to
propel itself, with considerable energy, onto the floorboards
from the low, built-in bookcase on the wall behind the

---

* The adaptation of *The Children of Green Knowe* wasn't actually
shot at Hemingford Grey Manor, but at the moated Crow's Hall,
near Debenham in Suffolk. Although the production team
borrowed Hemingford's rocking horse, they ended up using a near-
identical one with a blonde, not dark, mane.

horse. Her little brown terrier, who has been following us
on the tour, saunters across and sniffs it.

'What was that?' I ask.

'These sorts of thing happen here sometimes,' Diana
says, picking up the book and replacing it.*

I'm not someone who claims to have any predisposition
to such things, and I have little experience of similar incidents, but the happening is not a frightening one and seems
in keeping with the location. I suppose my rational explanation would be that our footfalls caused a vibration that
dislodged the already unbalanced book, but even so the
force of its flight was unsettling. The cynic in me wonders
for a moment whether Diana has an elaborate mechanism
to activate such a trick that she uses on all wide-eyed visitors – but I know this isn't actually the case. Indeed, Lucy
Boston comments in her memoir:

> Meanwhile the house continued its own mysterious
> life and from time to time sent feelers out from its
> darker corners, such as slight poltergeistic
> displacements, footsteps up the wooden stairs,
> wandering lights, voices, etc., but so much immediate
> and dramatic human life filled the place that irrational
> trifles did not get much attention.

---

* When I later examine the solid-feeling shelves, I find they
contain first editions of Alan Garner's *Red Shift* and *The Owl
Service* – two more important books from my childhood in which
the past parallels the present. Neither, however, was the volume
that flew out into the room; its identity must remain a mystery, as
in the excitement I forgot to check.

Later, in the music room, we sit as Robert Lloyd Parry, a Cambridge actor and M. R. James devotee with a more than slight resemblance to Monty, reads two of the scholar's ghostly tales by candlelight to a now-assembled audience.* I am transfixed by MRJ's words (and Lloyd Parry's performance), though a growing sense of weariness seems to have taken hold of me for some reason – the effect of all the Manor's encroaching history, perhaps? I feel a little like Tolly midway through *The Children of Green Knowe*, after his great-grandmother reveals to him that the house's three elusive young visitors are long dead:

---

* Lloyd Parry provides the introduction to Lucy Boston's posthumously published collection of stories written in the 1930s, *Curfew & Other Eerie Tales*; the title piece is particularly effective, along with the menacing water tower of 'Pollution'.

He must have known of course that the children could
not have lived so many centuries without growing old,
but he had never thought about it. To him they were
so real, so near, they were his own family that he
needed more than anything on earth. He felt the world
had come to an end.

Afterwards, I traverse the monotony of the moon-risen
Fens in near silence, not wanting the radio to interrupt the
drumming of the rain and the hypnotic drone of my car's
engine. As I pass a stand of willows that lines a deep dyke,
a winter moth – the hardiest of our *lepidoptera* – flutters
skywards, luminous in my headlights.

Another lost heart.

Chapter 2

DARK WATERS

Something of a dread feeling starts to rise inside me as I cross the Great Ouse, a mud-edged monument to river engineering that in 1981 became home for a few days to a disorientated immature walrus that was eventually repatriated by air to Greenland. At the roundabout a few hundred yards past the bridge, close to where King's Lynn's now-demolished sugar beet and Campbell's Soup factories once formed distinctive waymarkers, I turn my car onto the A17. I'm slipping back in time, back to my childhood, though time itself has seemed to slow as the traffic is moving at a slug's pace, the line of cars in front of me having their progress curtailed by an inevitable tractor. Elsewhere, such hold-ups at least allow drivers space to

appreciate their surroundings, but here, on a soot-grey day, there's little to savour, just endless brown fields that merge into the horizon, broken up by occasional mean stands of poplars or ugly, asbestos-roofed agricultural buildings.

It's an artificial, man-made landscape, reclaimed in part from the sea. We learnt about it at school, about Cornelius Vermuyden and the Dutch-led drainage of the seventeenth century, and of the earlier history of this ague-ridden back-water: the watery world where in 1216 King John is said to have lost his royal treasure on an ill-fated crossing of one of the estuaries of the Wash, having a few days before in King's Lynn contracted the dysentery that would shortly kill him; or of the Anglo-Saxon rebel Hereward the Wake who led Fenland resistance to the newly arrived Normans, but was more familiar through having lent his name to the Peterborough-based radio station my classmates and I would listen to – in particular hoping they'd read out the name of our school on a snowbound day and that it wouldn't be opening, a rare mythic event that actually came to pass on two occasions. Mostly though, the story of the area's past is vague in my mind, like the inconstant lie of the land in the days prior to pumping stations. Even my own connections with the region seem increasingly tenuous, liable to be leached away by one of the local rivers: the Great Ouse, the Nene, the Welland. Or the River Glen, which my grandfather – a real-life incarnation of a character from Graham Swift's *Waterland* – lived alongside.

Waterland was published in 1983 and was shortlisted for the Booker Prize in the same year. It is a novel about the forces inherent in human nature that tear people and families apart, how past events haunt the present. But, above all, for me it's a book about the unnerving flat landscape of my youth. Though I must qualify this, because it would be wrong to regard the Fens as forming a solid, distinctive whole; the country of my childhood had its own boundaries based upon the places we'd visit regularly as a family, stretching a varying number of miles in each direction from our house, but outside of which the more removed outposts of flatness seemed alien and otherworldly. One such locality that we occasionally passed through was the tiny cluster of residences that formed the village of Twenty. In 1982 it acquired a new black-lettered sign that sat below its official name – 'Twinned with the Moon' it read; soon afterwards some local joker spray-painted the retort 'No Atmosphere' beneath.

In my reading of the novel, *Waterland* has its setting among the 'Black Fens' beyond Wisbech, a town which is itself reworked by Swift into Gildsey, with the real Elgood's brewery standing in for the book's fictional Atkinson's. Despite being only a forty-minute drive from my home,

Wisbech was an unacquainted place, less familiar to me than the geographically more distant London, which most years we would make a pilgrimage to on the train. Wisbech was merely somewhere we skirted on visits to Welney, where my mother took us to watch the winter gatherings of wild swans that sought refuge on the dark fields – terrain only slightly more hospitable than their native Iceland and Siberia.

Thomas Bewick, the eighteenth-century illustrator and author of the landmark *History of British Birds*, whose surname is commemorated by those squat-necked Arctic swans we would watch feeding on potatoes on the floodlit washes, also features tangentially in M. R. James's story 'Casting the Runes'. A victim of the story's black-magic curse is sent in the post one of Bewick's woodcuts that 'shows a moonlit road and a man walking along it, followed by an awful demon creature'. If he has not concocted his own work by Bewick, James is most likely referring to the same tailpiece vignette that so disturbs the young Jane Eyre in Charlotte Brontë's novel – a tiny extraneous illus-tration tucked into the blank space at the end of the 1804 ornithological tome's chapter on the black-throated diver.* According to Brontë's heroine, Bewick's terrifying etching depicts a 'fiend pinning down the thief's pack'. And though

---

* Bewick's ornithological masterpiece does include a lengthy description of the other 'Wild Swan' – the whooper swan – that we also came to see, but its eponymous smaller Siberian relative, the Bewick's swan (*Cygnus columbianus bewickii*) was not described and named for the illustrator until 1830, two years after his death.

there's nothing that necessarily identifies the man as a law-breaker, the act of carting a heavy bag down a dark country lane does seem suspicious; the attached medieval-looking winged devil that's doing its best to pry open the contents of the sack does little to assuage our suspicions that the bearer has been up to no good and is getting his hellish comeuppance.

The narrator of *Waterland*, Tom Crick, is a history teacher who is being encouraged to take early retirement due to budgetary restraints at his school. 'We're cutting back on history,' his headmaster drily informs him, though ultimately it's the mental breakdown of his wife that speeds the process along. A precocious boy in his class questions the point of learning about what has gone before: 'What matters,' Price declares, 'is the here and now. Not the past.' So, in order to demonstrate how history does still result in consequences for the here and now, Tom Crick begins to tell them of his own eddying past, the history of the watery landscape of the 'fairy-tale place' of his youth.

Waterland swirls between earlier days and the present, between the personal family dramas of the Crick and Atkinson families, and of the shifting silts of greater events such as the Napoleonic or First World Wars, whose eventual settling has a future effect on the imprecise borderlands of the far-off Fens. And, in a nod to Melville's *Moby-Dick*, there is even an eight-page digression into the slippery natural history of the European eel, a species my grandfather, a keen angler, was well acquainted with.

I read the novel aged sixteen, a year or two after my brother had first turned its pages. It's testament to the book's power that my father, who usually distracted himself with the crime novels of Ed McBain or the thrillers of Frederick Forsyth (who he recalled meeting when they both worked in King's Lynn at the end of the 1950s), and my grandfather – more comfortable with the westerns of Louis L'Amour – both seemed to take to it. For me, I think (and probably for them too), *Waterland*'s initial magic came from its setting; although its events largely occurred in a time well before I was born and in a skewed version of a place some twenty miles distant, it was still a landscape I felt I knew – and a landscape I'd never seen depicted in fiction before.

The key attraction, however, was that the Cricks were lock-keepers. Because Grandad had been one too, looking after the antiquated sluices at the confluence of the Welland and the Glen, and at the terminus of the Vernatt's Drain. In common with the Cricks of the novel, Nan and Grandad lived in a riverside cottage that came with the job. It too was a fairy-tale dwelling of sorts, located in a place whose own name was something of a misnomer: Surfleet Reservoir (though Seas End on maps), the latter word referring to the ultimately failed eighteenth-century plan to divert river water into an artificial lake to aid the drainage of local farmland. My grandparents' post-war brick bungalow, a veritable palace among the nearby wooden holiday chalets and ramshackle fishermen's huts that lined the Glen, was where my mother spent her teenage years before she left to marry my father beneath the leaning steeple of the main village's church, moving six miles upriver to the house where I grew up. 'The Res' (as locals still refer to it) was an odd enclave populated by weekenders who moored their boats on the seaward side of the sluice – a deep tidal channel fringed by tall reeds – from .where they would head out for a spot of sea fishing, or others who preferred to spend the summer sitting outside their chalets chatting to their neighbours while their children played in the river. By all accounts the place had a distinct sense of community back then, and even today has a different feel to the rest of the uniform, arable-dominated area – bringing to mind some timeless Dutch canalside idyll.

My grandparents departed this watery haven on Grandad's retirement, moving to a ground-floor 1970s council flat in nearby Spalding fitted with wide doorways, a high-seated toilet, and red pull-cords that would summon the local old people's warden in an emergency. The freedom of the lock-side home I cannot remember the inside of (I would have been two when they left it) was exchanged for more practical – but more humdrum – disabled-friendly

accommodation that could better cope with Nan's ongoing, crippling physical deterioration from rheumatoid
arthritis.* As her condition worsened she developed a
complete reliance on my grandfather who, in a strange role
reversal for a man born in 1909, became her chief carer
and cook, lugging her into her wheelchair to transport her

---

* Despite losing the toes of one foot and being bent virtually
perpendicular by her condition, Nan was full of kindness and good
humour. At Christmas she invariably got the role of quizmaster for
family games of Trivial Pursuit, putting the questions to the rest of
us with a Mrs Malaprop-esque disregard for pronunciation. 'Who
played Dr Strangle-glove?' she asked. 'Who wrote Don Quicks
Oat?'

to the bathroom and bedroom. Occasionally, the pair of them would argue with a causticity that now, I think, was borne out of Grandad's frustrated inability to improve the situation. But, at other times, there was a tenderness in the way he gently pipetted artificial tears into her desert-dry eyes.

I follow the familiar route that hugs the river and leads away from my home town – I can still recall every curve even after all this time. This was the way I would ask my parents to come if we were returning from Peterborough of an evening, in the hope I'd spot an owl sitting on one of the fence posts strung along the bottom of Deeping High Bank. Sometimes Mum would pick me up from school and drive Grandad and me at dusk over the undulating road, while we watched through the windows for the

silent-winged birds. In my formative years I claimed a kind of ownership of the place, mistakenly believing it was named 'Deeping Our Bank' – for the hours we spent here, it might as well have been.

On the face of it there's not much to get excited about: the first stretch skirts a grass-covered strip to the left and wide fields of crops to the right, while a barbed-wire fence borders the roadside ditch. Today it's empty, but over the years various birds of interest alighted here before us: a pair of stonechats, neat little passerines, usually took up winter residence; once, a russet-barred sparrowhawk gripped a bloodied linnet in his talons; and in spring, Pinocchio-billed snipe crouched on the wooden posts in full view, their cryptic brown plumage offering no camouflage against the green of the backdrop. But the highlight was the ghost-lit barn owls that fluttered ethereally in our headlights, or materialised, seemingly from nowhere, in the late afternoon sunshine.

Always you wanted owls.

Past where the road jinks to the left and twists up the bank, bringing the river into view, is a pale-bricked barn that looked out of place, like some Spanish mission picked up and transposed to the middle of this flatness. Just beyond, tucked behind the bank, is a pond. We rarely saw anything on it – except once, when Mum braved treacherous snow on one of the fabled occasions when school was closed to drive the two of us along the track. The river was frozen solid, but not the pit: a redhead female smew, a small, toothed diving duck from the continent, had found the last ice-free stretch in the vicinity.

That day sits in my memory like one of my favourite childhood books, Susan Cooper's *The Dark is Rising* – the second (and arguably best) in the five-title series of the same name. The 1973 children's novel followed eight years after the Cornwall-set *Over Sea, Under Stone* and, in truth, feels very different and aimed at an older audience (Cooper had not originally planned on it being part of a series). It dispenses with the child leads from the opening book (though they feature again later), retaining only the wizard Merriman – King Arthur's Merlin. What we do get in *The Dark is Rising*, however, is the arrival of eleven-year-old Will Stanton, soon to discover that he's the last of the Old Ones, on the side of the Light and tasked with keeping the forces of Dark at bay in a Manichaean struggle. It is a book I loved when I first read it (I would have been a similar age to its central character), especially its depiction of the longed-for snowy Christmas that renders its time-shifting Thames Valley setting into a magical, albeit malevolent, wilderness. It's a remarkable evocation of the wintry English countryside (reminiscent of the snow in *The Children of Green Knowe*), particularly when you learn that Cooper left England for Massachusetts in 1963 with her American husband, writing all but the first of the sequence in either New England or the couple's house in the British Virgin Islands:

The strange white world lay stroked by silence. No birds sang. The garden was no longer there, in this forested land. Nor were the outbuildings nor the old crumbling walls. There lay only a narrow clearing round the house now, hummocked with unbroken snowdrifts, before the trees began, with a narrow path leading away.

The scene reminds me of an earlier remembrance – the first time I saw proper deep snow, which had fallen on our garden overnight, anaesthetising the land and deadening all sound. Dad and I placed sticks in the snow-hills that the wind had sculpted, marking each one with a makeshift wooden trig point that reminded me of the mountains I longed to climb on the holidays we took, far removed from those flatlands.

The river is choppy, its banks a dirty green – there's not a hint of snow in the sky – but I'm surprised by the new areas of wildlife habitat that have been cut alongside the water since the last time I was here: miniature inlets and scrapes, and a fledgling reedbed that would have been perfect back then for me to scan. In this same spot we watched transfixed on a correspondingly biting afternoon as a bare-chested man bobbed beside the river's metal-re-inforced far bank, a few strokes behind a paddling cow that he was trying to coax back onto dry land. My father knew him, he was a local farmer.

At the aptly named Crowland, a parliament of rooks is feeding amid a ploughed beet crop. I slow as I pass the town's Civil War-ruined abbey, commemorated in a gothic sonnet by the 'peasant poet' John Clare, whose village of Helpston is only nine miles away, and whose wife spent her dying days in my home town:

We gaze on wrecks of ornamented stones,
   On tombs whose sculptures half erased appear,
On rank weeds, battening over human bones,
   Till even one's very shadow seems to fear.

I stop in the heart of the nothingness, pulling onto the head of a dirt drove that branches off at a right angle to the main route's undulating, cracked tarmac. It's a bleak place, the very same stretch of road where, as teenagers, my friends and I would switch off our headlights while motoring at speed, briefly plunging ourselves into blindness. We were young and rash, fortunate not to suffer the classic Fenlander's end and find ourselves drowning in two foolish feet of lonely water at the bottom of one of the ubiquitous steep-sided dykes that line those routes. A patch of ice at the wrong moment could have created a local tragedy and transformed us into a carload of ghouls.

If we had perished that way, perhaps one of us might have been fated to a curious, brief half-life like the main character Mary Henry, a church organist, in *Carnival of Souls*. At the start of the dreamlike, low-budget black-and-white 1962 movie she washes up on a sand bar more than three hours after the car she was a passenger in has plunged into the Kansas River, killing her two companions. She moves from the scene of the tragedy to Utah, where she finds herself stalked by a mysterious figure – 'the Man', played by the film's director Herk Harvey – and a cast of undead dancers at the abandoned Saltair bathing pavilion that looms out of the Great Salt Lake's fluctuating dried-out flatness, a landscape not unlike the Fens. The film's

eerie discordant organ music has a similarly hypnotic effect on Mary as the hurdy-gurdy of *Lost Hearts* does on Stephen. And, indeed, as both soundtracks seem to have on me.

'It was though – as though for a time I didn't exist. No place in the world,' Mary says, after a fugue-like episode where she cannot hear external sounds or interact with her fellow townsfolk, before the song of a bird brings her back into the now. The young drowned organist, cast in the role of an awkward outsider, has been allowed to live out a brief window of her lost youth: events not actualised that should never have come to pass. Her limbo is a fleeting foretaste of what could have been.

Like my family's own future among these formless fields.

*

Fear and paranoia were staples of growing up during the late 1970s and early 1980s. Made in 1973, the year I was born, *Lonely Water* is a public information film I vividly remember seeing at the cinema as a boy, before whatever main feature I'd been brought to see.* In recent years it has acquired a deserved cult reputation for its dark, warning content. Watching it now you'd think there was little danger that any child who saw *Lonely Water* would set foot on a riverbank or the shoreline of a reservoir ever again. Yet I did still go fishing with only a friend for company, and we often did end up messing about near the water, which makes we wonder whether the film's message was lost on their target audience. Perhaps the known risk added an illicit thrill we found impossible to resist?

Just a minute and a half long, the film opens with a panning shot across a black, twig-strewn pond, accompanied by Donald Pleasance's chilling voiceover – 'I am The Spirit of Dark and Lonely Water, ready to trap the show-off, the unwary, the fool' – before the camera lingers on a hooded Grim Reaper standing in the shallows. We cut to another hooded figure, a blue-coated boy, who is playing with his friends on the muddy bank of a gravel pit. One of his companions, a lank-haired urchin, is poking a stick at a football that's fallen into the water. We look up at them

---

* I was born as Edward Heath was announcing the Three-Day Week. Towards the end of the decade – in 1977 or 1978, I think, during a power cut that was a precursor to the Winter of Discontent – I remember playing a *Space 1999* card game by torchlight on the living-room floor with my mum and brother. Thrills didn't only have to come from the supernatural; outer space and sci-fi also had its attractions.

from the position of the ball, towards the down-jabbing twig and the four shouting children; the Spirit looms behind them, unbeknown, as the boy slips on the bank. Without learning the fate of the show-off (though the implication is obvious), we switch to a bucolic scene – a tranquil duck-filled millpond. This time a lone older lad is leaning forwards, supporting his weight on the bough of an overhanging tree, again to stab at some untouchable object. Donald Pleasance's narrator informs us with great delight: 'This branch is weak. Rotten. It'll never take *his* weight.' We hear the snap as it falls, the cloaked voyeur observing the unfolding tragedy through the nearby reeds.

The final scene jumps to a close-up of a 'Danger No Swimming' sign, spelled out in large red letters. 'Only a fool would ignore this … But there's one born every minute.' A pile of clothes and a pair of shoes have been left

among a mountain of detritus as the camera pans to the pit
where a boy is struggling and shouting for help. 'Under the
water there are traps: old cars, bedsteads, weeds, hidden
depths. It's the perfect place. For an accident.'

Watching *Lonely Water* again, the grisly relish Donald
Pleasance's Spirit takes in his description of these lurking
dangers is one of the most unnerving elements about it –
this brief voiceover role might well be the most frightening
of his long career. The lad, fortuitously, is rescued from the
water by two sensible passing children who chide him in
thick cockney accents – 'Oi mate, that's a stupid place to
swim' – and the Spirit is exorcised, leaving just a discarded
robe on the muddy ground that is thrown into the water
by his rescuers. But Pleasance is determined to have the
last word, the Spirit's voice reverberating as the camera
lingers on the cape that is by now sinking beneath the
brown waves:

'I'll be back. Back. Back ...'

In works of unsettling fiction, Britain's inland waterways
are not commonly a haunted geographical feature, though
we have a vengeful spirit born of water in M. R. James's
Dartmoor-set 'Martin Close', and a canal trip looms large
in Elizabeth Jane Howard's 'Three Miles Up'. There is also
a story that I cannot seem to shake by an unfairly neglected
author of the second half of the twentieth century: A. L.
Barker's 'Submerged'.

Audrey Lilian Barker was born in Beckenham, Kent, in
1918, and died in a nursing home in Surrey in 2002. She
wrote eleven novels and numerous collections of stories

(which include several supernatural tales); her novel *John Brown's Body* was shortlisted for the Booker Prize in 1970, and her debut collection of short works, *Innocents*, won the inaugural Somerset Maugham Award in 1947. 'Submerged' is part of that collection and a powerful piece. It opens with a vivid description of a rural English river and its pastoral surrounds – of the purple loosestrife, yellow ragwort and red campion that cover its banks. Yet in this mild, sun-dappled scene we are soon reminded of the menace that lurks beneath the water's gentle eddies.

> He wasn't supposed to swim in the river anyway, there was some talk about its being dangerous because of the submerged roots of trees. Peter knew all about those, they added the essential risk which made the river perfect.

In the striking mid-century artwork of the first edition's cover, the story's adolescent protagonist is depicted as a stylised green figure part-way through a plunging dive. As the boy Peter engages in his lone swims he delights in exploring the tangled willow roots and branches that form his new benthic world; as readers we delight too, initially at least, as Barker paints an intoxicating picture of wild swimming that would make Roger Deakin proud. Having discovered a sort of tree-formed underwater tunnel, Peter has the realisation that he must explore its hidden folds, an epiphany made concrete by the sudden ethereal apparition beside him of a fleeting kingfisher, 'a flicker of cobalt, bronze and scarlet'.

I too remember my first proper view of a kingfisher, a squat-tailed sprite on the railing beneath the dilapidated railway bridge at the back of my aunt's house. It was Christmas Day 1987 and Dad and I had gone for a walk to try out my new big joint birthday and Christmas present – a telescope, so that now on trips with my brother I would have my own optics to look through at all those distant waders and wildfowl. The kingfisher perched below us for two, perhaps three, seconds before propelling itself like a tightly wound clockwork toy down the right-hand bank of the Vernatt's Drain, the uniformly straight channel that ran all the way to my grandparents' former home.* Finally the bird came into focus, on a wooden jetty that protruded through the reeds, the middle of its back illuminated electric-blue through my scope despite the dullness of the day. I was elated. Even my father, who though mildly interested in wildlife was no wide-eyed naturalist, knew we'd been honoured with a glimpse of the fantastic.

After Peter witnesses his kingfisher in the story, he dives back down to his tunnel, conquering its dark secrets, before coming to rest on the water's sunlit surface in an afternoon reverie. This heady state is ruined by the appearance of a stranger: 'It was a woman in a red mackintosh. No longer very young, and so plump that the mackintosh sleeves stretched over her arms like the skin of scarlet saveloys.' The woman orders the half-concealed boy out of the water,

---

* The waterway was named after Philibert Vernatti, one of the Dutch 'Adventurers' behind the financing of the early seventeenth-century drainage of the Fens.

in anticipation of the imminent arrival of her presumed partner, an oafish brute who, she tells Peter, wants to murder her. 'He won't lay a finger on me if there's a witness and a chance he'd swing for it …' Peter emerges reluctantly, remaining close to the thick cover of the bank's vegetation. The man arrives and the pair argue, but the expected violence does not come. The boy's sacred bathing place has, none the less, been sullied by their presence, its rhythms punctured by the intrusion of this odd, aggressive couple, with their air of illicit adult sexuality.

As the woman leaves, she steps on a weak spot on the bank and falls into the water directly above the tunnel. She doesn't surface and the man stands half-heartedly poking a stick into the depths below – like one of the lads in *Lonely Water* – before fleeing across a neighbouring field. Peter concludes that the woman must have swum further along the river and emerged while he was watching the man's cursory search. Pleased the equilibrium of his exclusive waterway has been restored, Peter makes a final dive. Reaching the entrance to the cave-like feature he finds it blocked: 'His fingers slid on something soft; his dive carried him violently against a heavy mass. The impact swung it a little away, but then, as he crumpled on the bottom, it bore down on him from above with dreadful, leisurely motion.' Kicking hard he manages to free himself: 'The mystery of how the woman left the river without a trace was solved. She had never left it, she was down at the bottom, out of sight.'

Peter returns home and mentions nothing about the incident to his parents or friends, even when weeks later it's revealed that a blacksmith from a nearby village has been found in connection with the woman's murder and is likely to hang. He realises a miscarriage of justice is about to occur but still doesn't say anything. We are left with the chilling image of his corrupted waterway: 'Those two had done something to the river. He couldn't swim there any more, his skin crept at the thought of the brown water, the soft, pulpy mud. And the underwater tunnel – it belonged to the fat woman now.'

Peter abandons his former haunt, in future joining the other boys who swim in the nearby quarry. He has developed a vital childhood coping mechanism, one that most of us, at some point I think, have employed: 'He had the weapon of youth, the power to bury deep that which was more profitably forgotten.'

Certainly, I have.

I follow the Welland the few miles to where it runs into the bird-rich basin of the Wash. Today there are well-appointed nature reserves nearby at Frampton and Freiston, complete with proper hides and even a visitor centre. However, when I was growing up 'the Marsh' meant the esoterically named Shep Whites – the lonesome southern stretch of shore that stretches from the mouth of the river to just north of the village of Holbeach St Matthew. (Rather mundanely, 'Shep' White was a local shepherd who ended up making his home beside the sea wall.) Occasionally, we used to go to the marsh at weekends when I was small, though I could never memorise the labyrinthine set of narrow single-track roads that Dad plotted a course through to get us there – they seemed to change each time we visited.

Locating a route remains as difficult but, fittingly, for the final winding stretch Lou Reed's 'Halloween Parade' shuffles into play on my phone through the speakers of my radio – my brother's cassette tape of the 1989 album *New York* on which the song appears was an ever-present fixture in the car we shared at the start of the 1990s. This track, with its elegiac roll-call of those lost to Aids, seems particularly poignant today, putting me in mind of earlier visits and faces I too will never see again. Finally, assisted by the sight of a particular Second World War pillbox, and finding the familiar crucial left turn, I arrive at the makeshift parking area behind the sea wall. It's tattier than I remember, a fly-tipper's paradise with a broken-open piano littering the scrub, its redundant loose keys strewn among the long grass.

I used to love the anticipation before you ran up the grassy bank: would the tide be in so that you'd feel yourself standing at the seaside, or would you be confronted with a green-and-brown expanse of mud and saltmarsh, the distant water barely visible at the edge of your vision? In the summer the landscape seemed kinder, its harsh edges softened by the pale blooms of cow parsley that grew rampantly along the dykes. My grandad called it 'kek', and one of his sluice-keeping tasks would be to burn off it and the other weeds that would clog the drainage ditches later in the season; in his eighties and early nineties, when I drove him around his old stamping ground, he would wistfully point out tinder-dry stands of dyke-side grasses he'd like to put a match to.

Peering into the distance you could see the shimmer – a sort of *Fata Morgana* – of ghostly half-real structures further round the coast. Like the ugly squat slab of the Pilgrim Hospital, the name honouring the group of Christian separatists who, in 1607, attempted to sail from the port of Boston to find religious freedom in the Netherlands (and later the New World), only to be betrayed by their skipper and end up imprisoned in the town's guildhall. Or the 272 foot 'Stump' of Boston's towering church, where in September 1860 an ominous-seeming cormorant alighted, its arrival presaging the simultaneous sinking a continent away in Lake Michigan of the *Lady Elgin* and the loss of 279 souls, including the town's MP, Herbert Ingram (who also happened to be the founder of *The Illustrated London News*), and his fifteen-year-old son.*

The unfortunate, portentous bird was shot the next morning, the badly stuffed specimen spending the following forty years on display in a local pub before being mislaid and vanishing from view.

One time, as a teenager, I came here late at night with my friend Piete – the spelling of his name reflecting the area's Dutch history – after we'd liberated ourselves from the constraints of small-town existence by passing our driving tests. The parking area was empty, illuminated by

---

* Despite his outward respectability, Herbert Ingram MP had a reputation as a womaniser; there were allegations that he'd sexually assaulted the sister-in-law of his business partner. His ill-fated trip to America may in part have been a means to gain respite from his troubles back home.

the full moon, but we didn't linger long after stepping
from the car because the cacophony coming over the sea
wall from the roosting curlews and oystercatchers seemed
amplified to an unnatural degree, like the 'strange cries as
of lost and despairing wanderers' that M. R. James describes
in 'Lost Hearts'. Later, while at university, I visited with my
girlfriend at dusk and we became spooked by the weird
greenish tone that the sky over the Wash had taken on: the
vista lends itself to such fancies. Now I think it must have
been the northern lights pushed far to the south due to an
unusually high level of solar activity.

Today, as on most of my impromptu visits, the water is
way out. The sky is ashen, the panorama drab. A few brent
geese, small dark-bellied wildfowl that winter in East
Anglia and breed in western Siberia, are flying over the far

mudflats; their name is thought to be derived from the Old Norse word *brandgas*, denoting 'burnt' – a reference to the species' dusky colouring. I follow the sweep of the sea bank around to my left. On the inland side the amorphousness of the marsh gives way to an artificial angularity: vast arable fields punctuated by ragged hedges and occasional coverts, bisected by wide drainage ditches. It's quiet, the only sound the familiar piping whistle of a lone redshank that flicks up from a creek.

As well as being a childhood Sunday afternoon ride out, this place was later to become a regular hangout for my brother and me, though by then we'd learnt to try and time our visits to coincide with the rising waters, arriving an hour or so before the waves were at their height, when the birds would be pushed up onto the small artificial spit of

land that extends out from the pumping house. Once a tame common seal lolled in the water a few feet away, eyeing us curiously, while on other fortunate occasions we sat entranced as whirlwinds of waders newly arrived from their Scandinavian and Arctic breeding grounds, settled close by in the late-summer sunshine.

Surprisingly, this very spot was also chosen as a location for the somewhat underwhelming 1992 adaptation of *Waterland*. The nondescript brick pumping station was temporarily transformed into a Victorian two-storey, tile-roofed sluice-keeper's cottage. Chris and I pushed Mum, now in a wheelchair like her mother before her, along this same stretch of bank soon after filming had finished in the autumn of 1991, the three of us impressed by the sham house in our midst; on the way back to the car, we paused to look at a fresh-in fieldfare – a wintering migrant thrush from northern Europe, its name literally meaning 'the traveller over the field' – that landed, cackling, on the barren ploughed ground across the dyke. Watching the film at the cinema the following year – though Mum was not with us to see it – it was hard to suspend disbelief at the Cricks in their illusory cottage, or when Jeremy Irons ascended in a few steps from what was obviously the inland Cambridgeshire Fens to these desolate coastal saltmarshes.

I stand on the bank contemplating my own history, studying the curve of two parallel creeks that meander towards the promise of the sea. I came here with my cousin a day after my dad died, to try to kill some of the empty, dragging time before the funeral. In the edgeland adjacent to the car park, a migrant grasshopper warbler – for once not skulking at the back of some reedbed – was balanced on top of a bramble, from where it delivered its song with gusto: a high-frequency staccato my ears would now strain to hear, the sound like a fishing line being reeled in. Across the mud shimmered the brooding, blocky mirage of the Pilgrim Hospital, which my father had entered a few weeks before and never left.

For me this is a melancholy place, haunted by the ebbs and flows of its past associations.

In the final paragraph of *Waterland*, as Tom Crick scans the surface of the Great Ouse for his lost brother, Swift surely alludes – 'We row back against the current ...' – to one of the great last lines of literature, and a book, *The Great Gatsby*, I was to study a few months after wheeling my mother in her chair along the bank, all those memories ago: 'So we beat on, boats against the current, borne back ceaselessly into the past.'

Out on the Wash a group of shrimp trawlers cluster together in what is left of the dying daylight.

I shall not rush to return.

Seven miles as the brent goose flies, though a winding eighteen by car, and I am between a white lighthouse and the canal-straight channel of the Nene. 'Down here the river has a surging life of its own, compensating (for those attuned) for the flatness of the surrounding country,' states Robert Aickman, author of forty-eight hard-to-classify 'strange tales' and also, perhaps somewhat incongruously, the co-founder of the Inland Waterways Association.* The building before me is Sutton Bridge's East Lighthouse; its near-identical twin is located on the opposite bank. Built

---

* Aickman's fellow founder Tom Rolt was another writer of the supernatural. L. T. C. Rolt is noted for his solitary collection *Sleep No More* (1948), a number of whose excellent stories use an industrial British setting of railways, mines and canals.

between 1829 and 1833 and designed by John Rennie, the architect of Waterloo Bridge, to delineate the river's mouth, the East Lighthouse was an early home of the conservationist Peter Scott, son of the ill-fated Antarctic explorer Captain Robert Falcon Scott. Aged twenty-four, Scott arrived at this secluded stretch of river in 1933 to find a purpose for himself; he was to live here, on and off, for the next six years. It was the place where he honed his wildlife painting and wrote his first two books, and where he kept his original collection of wildfowl on the expansive pools that used to be found on the saltings between the lighthouse and the Wash.

Those tidal lagoons have long gone, reclaimed in the 1960s and 70s into arable fields that stretch as far as you can see. My father brought me here one Sunday afternoon to an open day being held by the local farmer, and often we would detour along the top of the Nene's east bank on the way back from visiting my grandmother in Norfolk. Later

Dad got me a summer job alongside my brother at a nearby, dusty vegetable-canning factory; we looked out over the wavering wheat towards Scott's erstwhile home as we stacked boxes of tinned baked beans bound for Saddam Hussein's Iraq, while the shed's sole soft-rock cassette compilation, *Leather and Lace*, played in a never-ending loop. That summer was among my best times, I sometimes think, even though the work was tedious and physically challenging – I was sixteen and my world was awash with possibilities, had yet to start coming apart.

Despite the transformation of Scott's marshland, there are still a couple of ponds behind the lighthouse that hold a remnant selection of exotic waterbirds, including a pair of beautiful red-breasted geese and a sextet of sneering snow geese (a line of black that contrasts with the pink of the rest of the bill – the so-called 'grinning patch' – really does give the snow goose a contemptuous expression). This latter North American species gave the title to the bestselling novel by Paul Gallico, who loosely based his story of a reclusive lighthouse-dwelling painter on Scott and a wild pink-footed goose that, in 1936, took up resi- dence among the lighthouse's fledgling bird collection, returning again in following winters.*

Robert Aickman's guide to boating holidays, *Know Your Waterways*, also namechecks Scott's lighthouse as a nota- ble landmark. Aickman knew Scott – who happened, in

---

* In another coincidence the Hawaiian goose, a species that Scott's Wildfowl and Wetlands Trust was instrumental in preventing from becoming extinct, shares its Hawaiian name – the Nene – with the river where Scott spent those formative years.

addition, to write the introduction to Aickman's barge book – and the two men, surprisingly, remained friends after Scott's first wife, the writer Elizabeth Jane Howard, left the conservationist in August 1947 for the thickly bespectacled and besotted Aickman. The couple's relationship itself ended a little over four years later (in Howard's memoir Aickman comes across as a rather jealous and controlling figure), though not before the couple had collaborated on a debut 1951 collection of supernatural stories, *We Are for the Dark*. Each of them contributed three tales, including Howard's supremely ominous 'Three Miles Up', my favourite in the slim volume, which displays the enigmatic qualities we now regard as key characteristics of an 'Aickman-esque' story – pointing perhaps to the uncredited influence that Howard's writing was to have on her lover as, mainly during the 1960s and 70s, he wrote the majority of his critically lauded work. 'Three Miles Up' seems autobiographical in its depiction of a narrowboat journey gone awry, and possibly prefigures the rivalries and eventual falling out between Aickman and Tom Rolt, as well as Howard and Aickman's own parting soon after the publication of their joint collection. The story's ending offers a purgatorial, nightmare-inducing vision that's hard to beat:

> The canal immediately broadened, until no longer a canal but a sheet, an infinity, of water stretched ahead; oily, silent, and still, as far as the eye could see, with no country edging it, nothing but water to the low grey sky above it.

The unspecified inland English canal setting of 'Three Miles Up' was relocated to the Fens in an effective, though loose BBC adaptation of Howard's story, with the transformation of the central male characters into a pair of estranged brothers, and the addition of a supernatural whistle that could be straight out of M. R. James's 'Oh, Whistle, and I'll Come to You, My Lad'. The drama's final scenes were shot at the mouth of my own River Welland, the waterway that flowed along the top of my street and which I crossed each day on my walk to school. The crew had only a risky two-hour window, the director Lesley Manning tells me, filming where the river enters the Wash downstream of my grandfather's Seas End bungalow and adjacent to the marshes of Shep Whites. Those inundated mudflats make a good match for the 'infinity' of water that opens out before the reader at the story's grim conclusion.*

The Nene flowing hurriedly before me now, which has dropped precipitously on the retreating deluge to reveal sludgy cliff-like banks, has its source in Northamptonshire, and runs through an artificially straightened channel past Peterborough, where it becomes tidal. The river's outfall was completed around 1830, with 900 men and 250 horses labouring to dig out the last seven-mile stretch that replaced the meandering former route. And although in *Waterland's* final act Graham Swift has Tom Crick and his father scanning the waters of the Great Ouse – located a

---

* Parts of the 1995 television version of *Three Miles Up* also happened to be filmed on the Great Ouse at Hemingford Grey.

few miles away at King's Lynn – for a sign of his drowned brother Dick, the adaptation of Swift's novel shot the scene here on the Nene, with Scott's old lighthouse appearing briefly in frame. The mud of the river and the marshes around Sutton Bridge is often also cited as a possible resting place of King John's fabled lost treasure. The story finds its way into a book partly set around these same creeks and channels that is regarded by many M. R. James devotees as one of the few great novels in his tradition: *The House on the Brink*.

In November 2017 I noticed an obituary in my local paper, the *Eastern Daily Press*, announcing the death of John Gordon – a 92-year-old Norfolk-based children's author of whom I was unaware. Jack Gordon, as he was known to his friends and family, was born in Jarrow, Tyne and Wear, in the industrial heartland of England's north-east, before moving in 1937 as a twelve-year-old outsider to Wisbech, with its antithetical landscape of apple orchards and its boundless fields of sugar beet and potatoes. In his memoir he recalled his Tolly-esque arrival in the Fenland town: 'A full tide from the Wash had lifted the river's face to within a foot or two of the roadway and we seemed to be riding through a flood.' In many regards the place seemed magical to the young Jack, far removed from the abject poverty of post-Depression Jarrow. Later, after a stint in the navy at the end of the Second World War, he returned and became a newspaper reporter for the *Isle of Ely and Wisbech Advertiser*, where he furthered his knowledge of the town and its surroundings. This familiarity shows in his fiction, in which the unsettling flatness of the landscape is virtually omnipresent. 'It's the loneliness and absolute clarity of the line between the land and the sky where you can see for miles that always strikes me with a feeling of magic and mystery,' he said in a 2009 interview about his last novel, *Fen Runners*.

The House on the Brink was his second work of fiction, following on two years after 1968's *The Giant Under the Snow*, a highly regarded children's fantasy that centres on the legend of the Green Man. Both were written in Norwich, where Jack had moved in 1962. He wrote his early novels while working on the *Evening News*, having made the same journalistic journey – junior reporter to sub-editor – that my brother would also go on to make.

I ordered a copy of the out-of-print *The House on the Brink* from Norwich Library – except for one loan in 2003, its previous excursions from the reserve stores had been in the late seventies and early eighties. This isn't, it seems, a title in high demand, which strikes me as a real injustice, because Gordon's second book is a wonderful novel. It does indeed contain strong M. R. James-esque elements within its chapters, drawing most notably on 'A Warning to the Curious'. But, away from its cautions not to meddle with old secrets – and the arcane forces tasked with making sure any such foolish meddlers are punished – the novel is a world apart from James's comfort zones. At its core stands a burgeoning first romance between its two protagonists, Dick and Helen, aged sixteen and living in Wisbech (and a nearby marshland village, modelled on Upwell), with a supporting affair between a fragile young widow – the mysterious Mrs Knowles – and her new lover Tom Miller.

M. R. James may well not have found the focus of Gordon's novel on the emotional interaction of these characters – and the deliberate psychological ambiguity of the uncanny events – to his taste. In 'Some Remarks on Ghost Stories' he pointed out what he saw as one of the cardinal errors ruining some modern examples of the genre: 'They drag in sex too, which is a fatal mistake; sex is tiresome enough in the novels; in a ghost story, or as the backbone of a ghost story, I have no patience with it.'*

Given that *The House on the Brink* was published in 1970 and aimed at teenagers there isn't any sex involved, just a few stolen kisses. But there is a tenderness between the young lovers unlike anything we see in James's stories. The novel reminds me more of the work of Alan Garner and, in particular, *The Owl Service*, which has similarly snappy dialogue and a clever, working-class teenage protagonist feeling his way towards a different life. (Indeed, on its release Garner wrote warmly of Gordon's first book.)

I wish I'd read *The House on the Brink* as a teenager, as it would have appealed to my then whimsical romanticism and I would've identified with the brooding writer-to-be Dick as he biked around the vividly rendered, scorched summer Fens: 'They went out over the flat land, knowing

---

* James was in his late sixties when he wrote this. Taking into account the properness of his personality and the mores of the time, I think there's every chance he intended the word 'sex' in this context to have a wider meaning encompassing romance and relationships, rather than referring to the physical act.

they dwindled until they were unseen, but still he saw the haze of soft hair on her arms.' But beyond *The House on the Brink*'s appreciation of my native landscape and its timeless portrayal of adolescent angst, the novel would have thrilled me with its sense of dread, which threatens at times to overcome its characters. This fixes on a rotting ancient log (which at the story's denouement reveals its true identity) unearthed from the saltmarsh: 'The stump was almost black. It lay at an angle, only partly above the mud, and dark weed clung to it like sparse hair. Like hair.'

The teenagers and Mrs Knowles, encouraged by a local wise woman who possesses a feeling for such things (and an ability to divine water that's shared by Dick and Helen), come to believe that this figure-like fragment of wood is the guardian of King John's treasure, and has crawled out of the ooze of the marshes to protect its master's hoard from Tom Miller's over-curious pursuit. The wooden relic also seems to pre-empt the discovery in late 1998, just around the north-eastern corner of the Wash at Holme-next-the-Sea, of the so-called Seahenge, a Bronze Age circle of timber trunks uncovered beneath the transient sands by the vagaries of the tide.

Jack Gordon infuses an unhinging sense of horror into this stump, on the face of it an unlikely object of terror that seems to offer little threat. Yet the blackened wood's menace is real, as shown in one of the book's key scenes where Helen and Dick happen upon it along an overgrown marshland drove: 'And then, where the hedge clutched the gate-post, half-obscuring it, a round head was leaning from the leaves looking at them.' What is striking is how much of the action takes place during daylight hours and, given that, how effectively the reader, too, is frightened. Terror does not have to be restricted to the darkness: 'He let the yell of his lungs hit the black head. Black. Wet. It shone in the sun. And he knew what he should have known before. It had come from the mud.'

Although Wisbech itself, where most of the novel's action takes place, remains unfamiliar to me, some of its present landmarks are easily recognisable in *The House on the Brink*. They include the Institute Clock Tower and the Georgian residence of the book's title, a thinly disguised version of Peckover House, now a National Trust property sited, appropriately enough, on a real (and not just metaphorical) road called North Brink, which runs above the dirty, tidal Nene. The young Jack used to walk for miles along its banks, his younger brother Frank later tells me.

The old lighthouse that's mentioned early on in the book as guarding the saltmarshes at the confluence of the river and the Wash must refer to Peter Scott's former home – perhaps Jack ended up there on one of his long rambles.

It's a location that can't stop itself from appearing in different stories and adaptations, and which, now I think about it, has acted throughout my own life as a strangely unblinking marker that stands on the brink of my vision.

Chapter 3

WALKING IN THE WOOD

Growing up surrounded by the sterile farmland of the Fens I was starved of trees, a feeling that made me appreciate their pathless pleasures all the more whenever the chance came.

The woods enthralled me.

Our nearest woodland of note required a half-hour drive to the edge of the neighbouring town of Bourne, where the hills begin to rise from the flatness – to get there on one of our infrequent sylvan family outings we had to pass through Twenty, the village with the idiosyncratic sign. The woods I became most familiar with, however, were not on the far side of that Moon-twinned place, though they seemed a world away. In the opposite direction, across the River Nene and its nearby Norfolk border – the same stretch of monotonous mud and water where the moribund King John may have lost his treasure some seven hundred years before – were the meadows and woods that encircled my grandmother's house. Those fields and trees, which seemed so full of stories, shadows and secrets, scorched themselves into my memory and into the pages of my first novel.

I loved to explore the woods in the company of Uncle Gordon and Great-Uncle Billy. The countryside was dense and wild, and formed part of a large estate. Both uncles worked on the local farm and lived with Nan in a tied cottage. There were crystalline streams forded by narrow planks we would cross on our hikes over the rippled land-scape, watercress beds we would wade through in our wellies ('waterboots' to Uncle Billy), and numerous birds and other signs of wildlife all around. Bill, a kindly giant of a man who had barely left Norfolk apart from brief twice-yearly visits to us in neighbouring Lincolnshire, would impart rural lore and show me how to find the best branches to carve into walking sticks, or how to make a bow and shoot elder-tipped arrows.

Sometimes all of us would go on a ramble together after dinner, Mum and Nan taking delight in picking the pale-yellow primroses that emerged through the damp leaf-litter of early spring while Dad and Uncle Gordon reminisced about sport or bickered about politics. I spent several summer holidays there too, loving the freedom of being able to explore the woods every day on my own.

One time Billy pointed out the enticing, but potentially fatal, deadly nightshade berries that swathed the crumbling flintwork of an old barn. Much later, when I read L. P. Hartley's most famous novel, 1953's *The Go-Between* – set at Brandham Hall, a fictionalised version of West Bradenham Hall, a few miles across the fields from Nan's house – I was reminded of that plant, which is imbued with layers of symbolism in the book: 'It looked the picture of evil and also the picture of health, it was so glossy and strong and juicy-looking.'*

Leslie Poles Hartley was born at the end of 1895 in the Fens at Whittlesey, not far from our home. One of his earliest pieces of writing was a schoolboy essay about nearby Crowland Abbey, the partial ruin for which John Clare had composed his sonnet; the Abbey reappears as a key

---

* Deadly nightshade's Latin name *belladonna* is thought to have derived from one of the plant's medicinal properties extracts employed in eye-drops were historically used by women to dilate their pupils and enhance the attractiveness of their eyes.

location in Hartley's 1964 novel *The Brickfield*, in which its central character Richard declares: 'we were Fenlanders, as accustomed to the horizontal view as clothes-moths on a billiard table'. As fellow flatlanders, Hartley and I were bewitched by the otherness of the wooded Norfolk countryside after being raised among the empty expanse of all those breeze-stripped washes and ruler-straight droves; the same River Nene of John Gordon's *The House by the Brink* and Peter Scott's lighthouse flowed less than half a mile from the gothic Fletton Tower where the young Leslie grew up, and which Hartley's solicitor father had overstretched himself to buy in 1900.

Aged twelve, Hartley was packed off to prep school in Kent in the autumn of 1908, but was invited to Bradenham in the following August by a rather grander classmate, Moxey (his surname an approximation of *The Go-Between*'s Maudsley). The hall – the ancestral home of Henry Rider Haggard – had been rented by the Moxeys, and it was at Bradenham where Hartley found the inspiration for his book's class-warfare cricket match, its grand dances, its late dinners, and one of the most memorable opening lines in literature: 'The past is a foreign country: they do things differently there.'

The novel's thermostat-breaking weather, however, did not occur in the course of Hartley's stay at Bradenham, but was based on his earlier recollections of the burning first Fenland summer of the nascent century. I originally read *The Go-Between* in a similar heatwave, when I was travelling across the Australian outback on a Greyhound bus – the landscape of the familiar never seems so appealing as when

you are adrift in an utterly foreign one. I was captivated by
the book, which was set in the Edwardian era – though
Edwardian isn't quite accurate as its action mostly takes
place during August 1900, five months before Queen
Victoria's death and the end of what Hartley himself
would come to see as a lost 'Golden Age'.

The Go-Between isn't a disquieting novel in an M. R. James
sense – although the childish spells and curses that Leo
casts unwittingly possess more efficacy than the conjurings
of Mr Abney in 'Lost Hearts' – but L. P. Hartley did also
happen to be a solid teller of macabre tales. A number of
these were assembled in *The Killing Bottle* (1931) and *The
Travelling Grave* (1948); the latter collection was brought
into print by the American publishers Arkham House, set
up a decade before by August Derleth and Donald Wandrei
to preserve the 'weird fiction' of the early twentieth-century New England writer Howard Phillips Lovecraft.*
Lovecraft himself praised Hartley's 'A Visitor from Down
Under' as an 'incisive and extremely ghastly tale' – its title
is a play on words, as the visitor in question happens to be
the revenant of an Australian who is coming to enact icy
revenge on his murderer (newly arrived in the comfort of
a London hotel), and to 'fetch him away'.

  The Go-Between is a different kind of work, far subtler and
more refined. And yet, I find its pervasive atmosphere of
regret (an emotion the repressed Hartley had strong personal

---

* Arkham is a fictional Massachusetts university town that
features in a number of H. P. Lovecraft's tales.

experience of) and its dissection of the difficulties of trying
to make sense of what has gone before more unsettling than
his ghost stories. Re-reading *The Go-Between* it resonates
even more strongly with me now than on my first encounter,
as I, like the aged Leo Colston, attempt to exhume my past.

Unlike Leo – and possibly Hartley himself, who later
hinted that he had experienced a similarly character-
forming event during his stay at Bradenham – I did not see
something nasty in the woodshed during those Norfolk
summers. Hartley's book, with its naïve narrator – the
embodiment of 'greenness' in his newly gifted Lincoln
Green suit – who is privy to an adult world beyond his
comprehension, certainly fed into my novel *The Listeners*.
However, the most outwardly apparent influence was
Walter de la Mare's enigmatic thirty-six-line poem which
gave me the title, as well as a template for my novel's
mood, and its key location: a tumbledown cottage among
the trees being subsumed by the unrelenting forces of
nature. There was no such 'ghost house' in the woods
around my grandmother's house – at least not one I ever
came across – something I should probably be grateful for.
Spooky cottages in the heart of the forest are not safe
retreats for youthful visitors in ghost stories and fairy tales.

Take, for instance, another notable ethereal woodland
dwelling, one that exists in the hugely atmospheric 'Brickett
Bottom' by Amyas Northcote, son of the noted politician
Sir Stafford Northcote.* The young Northcote attended

---

* Sir Stafford Northcote served as Chancellor of the Exchequer
under Disraeli, between 1874 and 1880.

Eton at the same time as M. R. James (though there appears to be no evidence of any connection between them while fellow pupils), before going up to Oxford and then – following the death of his father – on to a business career in Chicago. It was in the States that his talent for writing was first publicly displayed in various pieces of journalistic political commentary. He returned to England around the turn of the new century, though little is known about his subsequent activities, except that he acted as a justice of the peace in Buckinghamshire. In 1921, out of nowhere, Northcote's sole book, *In Ghostly Company*, was published. Its contents are, on the whole, subtly mysterious tales that can seem slight, but possess a lingering ability to haunt the reader. Like 'In the Woods', in which a seventeen-year-old girl becomes beguiled by the wildness, beauty and otherness of her surroundings – 'The woods enthralled her' is a repeated refrain – it is a story bathed in a dreamlike atmosphere that's reminiscent of Blackwood's 'The Man Whom the Trees Loved' or Arthur Machen's 'The White People'.

However, it is 'Brickett Bottom' that is, rightly, the most well-known of Northcote's stories. Its setting is 'a small and very remote village in one of our most lovely and rural counties', and I can easily picture its events unfolding in the birdsong-filled thickets around my grandmother's house. Separated from her more sensible sister – I can't help wondering if the innocuous ankle injury that sidelines Maggie's level-headed influence stems from some unnatural agency – Alice becomes bewitched by the red-brick building and the polite, yet slightly odd, elderly couple she encounters tending its neat garden in the gully beneath the

Downs. And then Alice is gone from that place in the woods – a kind of ominous Brigadoon that only manifests itself every so many years to lone young women traversing the little-used track through the tree-shaded glen. She has been spirited away.

'Brickett Bottom' has familiar fairy-tale overtones of children led astray by malefic faeries or witches in the woods, or, more recently, balloon-carrying clowns; I'm almost surprised we weren't read it at school alongside the disturbing never-go-with-strangers public information films we were shown. Its execution is chilling and bleak, despite being stripped of gruesome descriptions or over-elaborate explication – a characteristic of Northcote's pared-down style. The detail that stays with me is the anguishing sound of Alice's voice, which addresses her sibling and pastor father (his religious conviction seems of little use against these forces) as they realise that no brick house has stood in the wooded gully for decades, and that their sister and daughter will never be coming home:

> Before Maggie could answer a voice was heard calling 'Father! Maggie!' The sound of the voice was thin and high and, paradoxically, it sounded both very near and yet as if it came from some infinite distance. The cry was thrice repeated and then silence fell.*

*

---

* Quite probably in a deliberate nod, Northcote here employs a phrase – 'infinite distance' – that is also used memorably in M. R. James's 'Oh, Whistle, and I'll Come to You, My Lad'.

Amyas Northcote produced just a single collection of eerie stories – thirteen in all – in contrast to the fertile output of the man who imagined that other lone phantom-filled house in the woods. Today, Walter de la Mare is sometimes regarded, rather unfairly, as a writer who was old-fashioned even at the height of his interwar popularity. He was a contemporary of Ezra Pound and T. S. Eliot – both admirers of his poetry – but his work, unlike theirs, eschews the obvious trappings of modernism, instead focusing on atmosphere and the inexplicableness of life. In this sense, his poems and stories have a timeless quality, redolent with existential unease (which, it could be said, aligns them with the tenets of the new movement) – a quality also present in the best of Northcote's handful of tales.

We must have read 'The Listeners' (the title poem of de la Mare's second collection, published in 1912) at school, because I was already aware of it when it came a surprise third in the BBC's 1995 *Nation's Favourite Poems* survey – beaten by Kipling's 'If—' and Tennyson's 'The Lady of Shalott'. Later I was to learn it was a favourite of my great-aunt, who had grown up alongside my grandmother in the same cottage before emigrating to Australia as a ten-pound Pom in the early 1950s; the poem perhaps reminded her of the sleepy village's 'starred and leafy sky', 'of the forest's ferny floor', as she tried to reconcile Norfolk's ever-distant memory from the opposite side of the world, and as she contended with the oppressive heat of Adelaide's dry-hot summers, which most years left Leo's thermometer-busting August of 1900 in the shade.

I think a lot about the separation of the two sisters: I never met my great-aunt, but I have come to be close to her sons – my dad's younger cousins – on the opposite side of the globe, and their children, who are around my own age. From them I've learned that my great-aunt missed her native Norfolk and her sister (my grandmother) immensely – despite the possibilities her new life afforded her. The pair wrote to each other with metronomic regularity: I remember staying at Nan's during the summer when the postman delivered the latest weekly missive from South Australia, sending her into a kind of reverie. Yet, even after a telephone finally arrived in Nan's cottage at some point in the 1980s, the two sisters still never spoke, let alone considered the possibility of meeting up in the flesh and of my great-aunt returning as a visitor from down under.* If they had seen each other, or heard each other's voices, I think the pain of that infinite distance would have been brought home and become a heart-breaking, unsolvable conundrum; certainly, it breaks mine now to think of it, bringing to mind Maggie and Alice's forced displacement in 'Brickett Bottom'.

In any case, my grandmother always had a sadness about her. Not only did she miss her sister terribly, her husband – my mysterious grandfather, an officer in the air force – abandoned her before the war's end for another woman, leaving her to bring up three sons. She got on with things, supported by her mother and her younger brother, but her opportunities were limited and her circumstances – and perhaps her own pride – closed her off from experiences and happiness that, in a later generation, she could have had. Yet I am making these assumptions through the filter of so much dead time, more than seventy-five years after whatever took place between her and my grandfather – so what, really, do I know? The unfortunate Seaton, the protagonist of one of de la Mare's finest and most-anthologised supernatural stories. 'Seaton's Aunt', expresses this perfectly: 'Why, after all, how much do we really understand of anything? We don't even know our own histories, and not a tenth, not a tenth of the reasons.'

*

---

* You had to press a button on the top of the phone before making a call, and check that the house across the lane wasn't on the line at the same time. To me as a sophisticated town-dweller this 'party line' seemed hilariously primitive.

Walter de la Mare was born with the rather more prosaic surname Delamare in 1873, adding the Gallic twist when he started to pursue his poetry in earnest. His father, who worked at the Bank of England, died when Walter was four years old; one of six children raised by his mother, Walter could not afford a university education, so he took employment as a bookkeeper, aged seventeen, at the Anglo American Oil Company in London. He was to work there for the next eighteen years, marrying Elfie Ingpen – a name that could be straight out of one of his poems for the young – and raising four children of his own, before a life of office drudgery was cut short with, in 1908, a welcome award from the government of the sum of £200 (equivalent to around £23,000 today). By this point he had already brought out the poetry collection *Songs of Childhood* and the gothic novel *Henry Brocken*, both under the pseudonym Walter Ramal; the former was well received, but his first work of fiction sold only 250 copies. After his Civil List award, however (and the granting of an annual pension of £100 a year from 1915), he devoted himself full time to writing.

De la Mare died in 1956 and is buried in St Paul's Cathedral. He was a prolific poet with almost fifty collections published during his lifetime – his posthumous *Complete Poems* stretches to nearly a thousand pages. His verses have a tendency towards the dreamlike and the gothic, full of powerful pastoral allusions to the natural world. But, as in his most famous work, 'The Listeners', the supernatural is never very far away, and it is this atmosphere of disquiet – of moonlit phantoms and mysterious promises – that has given the poem its popularity and longevity.

Never confining himself to poetry, de la Mare went on to write two further novels including *The Return*, which deals with supernatural possession, as well as critical works about Lewis Carroll and the dashing nearly-poet of the Great War, Rupert Brooke. De la Mare and Brooke had met in 1912 when they both contributed to an important anthology of 'Georgian' poetry (the grouping's name referred to King George V, who came to the throne after Edward VII, in 1910). Following Brooke's death on the Aegean island of Skyros – fittingly, perhaps, on St George's Day 1915 – de la Mare was surprised to find himself named as a beneficiary in the younger man's will, sharing future royalties with two other Georgians, Wilfrid Wilson Gibson and Lascelles Abercrombie.*

Walter de la Mare wrote a large body of short fiction, both for children and adults, among which are a sizeable number of exquisitely crafted and highly atmospheric stories of the uncanny. Interestingly, M. R. James was an acquaintance and fan of de la Mare, whose tales certainly do not suffer from the 'blatancy' of which the elder man

---

* Brooke won a scholarship to study at King's College, Cambridge in 1906, a year after M. R. James became its provost. Brooke's death in 1915 was not the result of a bullet fired by a German sniper, but from sepsis caused by an infected mosquito bite while the naively patriotic twenty-seven-year-old waited to see action with the Royal Navy. James spoke warmly about Brooke in that year's Vice-Chancellor's oration, his words echoing those he had earlier written about James McBryde. 'No one, I think, must call that short life a tragedy which was so fully lived, and spent itself so generously upon all who came in contact with it.'

disapproved. They are largely subtle works, their horrors
elusive – illusive even: often, the reader is unsure if there
are any actual horrors. In, for instance, 'Missing' – a tale of
1920s London (published in 1926) that captures the
oppressiveness of the ensuing heatwave as vividly as L. P.
Hartley does the scorched summer of *The Go-Between* – we
are left little the wiser as to what the mysterious Bleet, up
for the day from the country to escape the boiling temperatures, is bleating on about to the unwittingly accosted
first-person narrator. There might have been a murder –
there has, at least, been an inquiry into the disappearance
of Miss Dutton, a lodger at the house of Bleet and his sister
– but beyond that little is clear; De la Mare, it could be said,
deliberately makes sure that much is 'missing'. There are
no obvious manifestations of the supernatural, but the
story's atmosphere is disconcerting, with the odious Bleet
talking at the narrator as if he might as well not be there.

In 'Crewe', another stranger accosts a presumably different narrator – on this occasion in the first-class waiting
room at Crewe railway station. Here, the interloper, an old
man in an oversized coat – a country-house servant going
by the name of Blake – proceeds to deliver a narrative full
of gossip, rumour and betrayal, which sets off a chain of
events involving a vengeful, animated object from beyond
the grave. No less an authority than the Welsh writer
Arthur Machen was impressed by the story, commenting
in his review for the *New Statesman* that 'in that tale there
is a scarecrow which is luminous, but not in the light of the
sun – a hideous terror.'

*

There were scarecrows in the fields around my grandmother's house too. And straw bales that I would haul about and arrange into forts with the handful of other local children. But it was always the beguiling woods that held the greatest appeal, where I wanted most to walk. Sometimes we would, the whole extended family, go together, Uncle Gordon and me pressing ahead. He still lives in that same cottage, and laughed when I saw him last a couple of years ago, recalling how I always led us along the most tricky paths; I was able to duck beneath the branches of blackthorns while he would be skewered on their spines. The swathes of stinging nettles were far easier for our sticks to deal with – we could bash them down, uncovering half-forgotten tracks that reached in front of us like the ghost road in Rudyard Kipling's 'The Way through the Woods':

> You will hear the beat of a horse's feet
>   And the swish of a skirt in the dew,
>   Steadily cantering through
> The misty solitudes,
>   As though they perfectly knew
> The old lost road through the woods …
> But there is no road through the woods.

The eerily atmospheric poem prefaces the short story 'Marklake Witches' in Kipling's 1910 *Rewards and Fairies*, a collection of stories grouped together like those in its predecessor *Puck of Pook's Hill*, with each tale fronted by a related verse. In the books, the eponymous sprite from Shakespeare's *A Midsummer Night's Dream* is roused to spin yarns, with the help of characters summoned from the past, to bring alive a history of England – or at least a version of it that Kipling has fashioned – to two Sussex children, Una and Dan. 'I belong here, you see, and I have been mixed up with people all my days,' says the now aged Puck as he introduces himself.*

'Marklake Witches' is itself a story of no little poignancy, in which Una meets Philadelphia Bucksteed, the high-spirited, sixteen-year-old daughter of a Napoleonic-era squire. We learn of the girl's irritating cough, and the illicit efforts her nurse makes to enlist the local 'witch-mater' to cure her, aided by an affable French prisoner of war who is something of a medical innovator and turns out to be René Laennec, the inventor of the stethoscope. As adult readers (I'm not sure the subtext would be obvious to a child), the tragedy is that we know the vibrant, thankfully unaware, Philadelphia is dying from consumption – which is why her after-dinner rendition of 'I have given my heart to a flower' so overwhelms her father and a visiting general. On being introduced to her new Napoleonic friend, the Edwardian Una comments about Marklake: 'I like all those funny little roads that don't lead anywhere.' Given that the poem informs us in its opening line that the woodland way was shut 'seventy years ago', we can deduce that the estate of Philadelphia's father has long gone, like the teenage girl whose tale is being told by her swish-skirted shade.

---

* *Rewards and Fairies* is also notable for containing the first appearance of Kipling's most famous and popular poem 'If—', which topped the survey of Britain's favourites; 'The Way through the Woods' came forty-eighth.

H.R.MILLAR (1906)

Rudyard Kipling was born in Bombay (today Mumbai) in 1862, yet educated back in England, to which he was shipped, at the age of five, by his parents. He spent the next six unhappy years being boarded with a bullying foster family in Southsea, before going on to a military school in Devon, and then returning to India where he

worked as a journalist and where his first successes as a
writer were to come. This was followed by further spells in
London and Vermont where, by this time married, he
wrote *The Jungle Book*. Now famous, he returned once
more to Britain, settling in Torquay, and then in Sussex;
these wanderings, and his troubled childhood, perhaps go
some way to explaining his desire to construct his own
mythic version of a history of England, the country in
which he was thereafter to remain.

While on a winter visit back to the States in 1899,
Kipling, along with his six-year-old daughter, Josephine,
contracted pneumonia. Kipling recovered from the illness,
though it took him months; his daughter – for whom he
had earlier written *The Jungle Book* and the *Just So Stories*
– was not so lucky. A charming gold-framed pastel drawing
of young Josephine hangs in one of the bedrooms of his
Jacobean Sussex house, Bateman's – she looks out of the
frame, intent on something unseen – alongside a monochrome photograph that shows the pretty, smiling little
girl, then aged three, being held by her doting father.

A hint of this personal tragedy is present, I think, in
Kipling's depiction of the life-affirming Philadelphia in
'Marklake Witches'. His younger daughter Elsie, the only
one of Kipling's three children to survive him, recalled in
her memoir:

> There is no doubt the little Josephine had been the
> greatest joy during her short life. He always adored
> children, and she was endowed with a charm and
> personality (as well as an enchanting prettiness) that

those who knew her still remember. She belonged to his early, happy days, and his life was never the same after her death; a light had gone out that could never be rekindled.

In common with many other Victorian and Edwardian writers of note, Kipling occasionally turned his hand to supernatural tales, a good number of which reflected the mysticism of India. A few though take place in Kipling's adopted Sussex, the land of Puck – among them a work of utmost poignancy that reveals the depth of his sorrow following his daughter's death.

Kipling's 'They' first appeared in the August 1904 edition of *Scribner's Magazine*, and was anthologised later the same year in *Traffics and Discoveries*. An illustrated standalone version was published by Macmillan in 1905, which indicates the story's popular appeal – George Bernard Shaw, for example, sent a copy of *Scribner's* to the leading actress of the age, Ellen Terry, wondering whether she would consider playing the part of its main female character if Shaw could persuade Kipling to adapt the story into a play; she declined, stating that it was 'wondrously lovely', but that the 'stage would be too rough for it I fear'.*

In 'They', Kipling writes beautifully about the wooded enclaves of the Sussex countryside. Clues in the text point

---

* Terry's last theatre role – in 1925, a little less than three years before her death at the age of eighty-one – happened to be a non-speaking performance as the ghost of Miss Susan Wildersham in Walter de la Mare's now-obscure 'fairy play' *Crossings*.

to the story being set somewhere around the hinterland of the village of Washington, a few miles north of Worthing and forty miles west of Bateman's. When we are first introduced to the narrator it is very late spring, for – despite the brightness of the sun, at least where it's able to puncture through the tunnels of hazel, oak and beech – there are reminders of the fleetingness of the seasons and the implacability of time in the already gone-over spring flowers: 'Here the road changed frankly into a carpeted ride on whose brown velvet spent primrose-clumps showed like jade, and a few sickly, white-stalked bluebells nodded together.'

The narrator freewheels his vehicle along a leaf-strewn track, descending into sunshine and a vision of an archaic house set among a great lawn populated by topiary horsemen and their steeds. Stopping his car in the grounds of this idyll of Old Albion, the protagonist spies two children watching him from one of the house's upper-floor windows, and hears juvenile laughter coming from behind a nearby yew peacock. The owner of the Tudor mansion appears, a redoubtable blind woman (we learn in passing that she is Miss Florence) who we half-expect to berate the motorist for his noisy intrusion. The narrator expects to be scolded too and begins his excuses about taking a wrong turn, though the lady isn't at all bothered, and instead hopes an automobile demonstration can be put on for the elusive children.

'Then you won't think it foolish if I ask you to take
your car through the gardens, once or twice – quite
slowly. I'm sure they'd like to see it. They see so little,
poor things. One tries to make their life pleasant, but –'
she threw out her hands towards the woods. 'We're so
out of the world here.'

After driving his host around the grounds the visitor
departs. When he returns again a month later, by which
time the trees are in verdant full leaf, his car develops a
fault in the woodland not far from the house, and he makes
a noisy show of repairs, hoping it might entice in and
amuse the shy youngsters. The blind proprietress instead
appears and the two chat good-naturedly, though the
narrator thinks he is being left out of some enormous secret
by the lady and the little ones, who have by now gathered
stealthily behind a bramble bush with their fingers held to
their lips. Any revelation is halted by the arrival of a lady
from the village, Mrs Madehurst, the owner of the shop; it
transpires her infant grandson is seriously ill, and so the
motorist volunteers to use his vehicle to fetch a doctor,
before being enlisted on an extended expedition to taxi in
a nurse.

When the narrator returns for a third and final time,
autumn is beginning to set in on the hills and woods, with
a chill fog permeating well inland. Kipling writes of the
change that has come upon the natural world: 'Yet the late
flowers – mallow of the wayside, scabious of the field, and
dahlia of the garden – showed gay in the mist, and beyond
the sea's breath there was little sign of decay in the leaf.'

En route he calls in to the shop, where he is met with Mrs Madehurst's tears: young Arthur died two days after the nurse was brought. His mother Jenny, the shopkeeper's daughter, is out now walking in the wood.

'Walking in the wood' – it's an expression repeated by various locals throughout the story, and whose meaning will soon become clear.

Pressing on, the visitor reaches the house, proceeding within for the first time. There are signs of the recently present children everywhere in their hurriedly discarded toys.* His hostess takes him on a tour of the place, which is every bit as beautiful inside as out. The pair of them pass through the attic rooms set aside for the children, who remain out of vision. Finally, he spies them in the hall, hiding behind an old leather screen, and wonders whether today he will be introduced. While he sits in front of the grand, comforting fire (kept always lit for the little ones), there is a diversion as the lady of the house deals with one of her tenant farmers, Mr Turpin – a latter-day highway robber of sorts – who is trying to take advantage of his landlady by getting her to fund him a new cattle shed. In business though she's far from unsighted, and Turpin, who throughout appears in a state of unbridled anxiety at being in the house, is sent off with nothing. While this is going on the narrator continues to try to attract the attention of the skulking infants:

---

* The youngsters have, I think, something about them of the playful shyness of Tolly's elusive Restoration ancestors in *The Children of Green Knowe*.

I ceased to tap the leather – was, indeed, calculating
the cost of the shed – when I felt my relaxed hand
taken and turned softly between the soft hands of a
child. So at last I had triumphed. In a moment I would
turn and acquaint myself with those quick-footed
wanderers …

The narrator's patience has been rewarded, though the gift is a dubious one. His utter despair conveys an authenticity that reflects Kipling's personal and recent familiarity with bereavement. Of the loss of his Josephine.* 'Then I knew. And it was as though I had known from the first day when I looked across the lawn at the high window.'

For this, and its studied, unsentimental build-up and beautifully constructed setting, there are few short stories (ghost or otherwise) that come close to so perfectly expressing the kind of sadness and grief that is on display in 'They'. The visitor 'from the other side of the county' finally accepts why the children are there, and what they are – all that has gone before was wilful self-delusion on his part. Yet even though by this point we too have surely worked out their nature, the story's denouement is still devastatingly sad: our narrator is hit with the certainty that the hand which grasps his own belongs to his late daughter, and that he must never return to this shade-filled house again.

He has learned what the villager meant when she spoke of 'walking in the wood'. It is what the bereaved do to commune with their departed.

---

* Kipling would also go on to lose his son prematurely. Eighteen-year-old John was shot in the head at the end of September 1915, while serving in France; the boy's poor eyesight would have rendered him ineligible for active service, but he persuaded his father to pull strings to get him enlisted in the Irish Guards. Two days before his death, knowing he was about to be sent to the front, John wrote home: 'This will be my last letter most likely for some time.'

Chapter 4

THE ROARING OF
THE FOREST

A coil of movement down by the path. It's not easy to pick out, as the leaf-heavy branches of an ancient oak cast the forest floor in shadow, but something is there. Something flesh and blood.

'A snake,' whispers my brother to my dad.

'Don't get too near, just in case.'

And now it becomes apparent not merely that this is a solitary two-and-a-half-foot grass snake, but that its mouth is crudely clamped around a shape – the back of a still-moving frog – which is gulping and blinking with a resigned calmness as the reptile stretches its jaw the final inch and envelops the amphibian's head. Saliva bubbles from the taut corners of the snake's mouth, and the frog lets out a high-pitched squeak.

I imagine this is roughly how it happened, because I was not a first-hand witness to this demonstration of nature's brutality, but was playing a few hundred yards away with Mum in a New Forest car park as my dad and brother made their discovery. On their return, though, my jealousy was palpable – I'd never even seen a live snake in the English countryside before, let alone one performing a gruesome act resembling something from *Life on Earth*. We all set back out together into the hazy greenness of the late-summer woods, only to find the Eden beneath the oak empty, the unseen serpent watching us through the undergrowth.

The day before, we'd arrived at the end of a narrow track where our bed-and-breakfast was located – a two-storey cottage hung with weather-bleached deer skulls – just as an enormous pig was ambling around the dusty yard. In my memory, the setting came to resemble something out of an American horror film like *The Evil Dead*, though I supposed I'd accorded it a far more backwoods-gothic atmosphere than the reality until years later when my brother and I stumbled upon the place, its brickwork unchanged and still antler-ridden, as we searched for rare honey buzzards in the forest's depths. I've been obsessed with these wasp-eating raptors – special feathering on their head helps safeguard them from stings – from the moment a pair I never managed to witness was rumoured to be nesting in a wood close to Nan's house in Norfolk. At the time it was a species I had yet to see anywhere, but the birds – if they ever existed at all – eluded me for the fortnight I was there, despite a handful of spurious half-sightings that I tried to convince myself might be the real thing.

If the exterior of this lonely farm cottage was somewhat off-putting, then the inside was worse: ramshackle and dirty, so that Dad took the anarchic step of piling us straight back into the car and doing a flit, driving to the tourist office in Lyndhurst where alternative accommodation was found. The new guest house was better in the eyes of my parents – no dead trophy animals at least – but in my opinion (with which my brother agreed) it was spookier. The out-of-time bedroom the two of us shared was inhabited by three antique china dolls; Chris had to get up and twist them towards the wall, because we both found them menacing. It didn't help that our bedtime reading included Chris's newly purchased copy of Raymond Briggs' nuclear Armageddon parable *When the Wind Blows*, or that it was stiflingly hot – the whole 1983 holiday, which had encompassed a grand tour of England's south-west, was sun-baked, everywhere the grass dying and brown, like Leo's fateful summer in *The Go-Between*. At regular intervals my brother called out 'cold pillow', an instruction to turn over our head supports in an attempt to claim temporary relief from the oppressiveness, and an opportunity to check that the staring dolls were still facing the other way. The landlady was frightening too, an old woman with bleached hair and excessive make-up – she had something of the artificial appearance of a porcelain figurine herself – who, my parents joked, looked like Bette Davis in *What Ever Happened to Baby Jane?*

I had no idea who they were talking about, though I would have if they'd namechecked *The Watcher in the Woods*. I'd seen this Disney children's horror film – set in England, it was filmed largely at Pinewood Studios and in the surrounding Buckinghamshire countryside – the previous year with two of my classmates. To my shame, that night after the cinema I'd had trouble sleeping. My companions felt the same, I was relieved to learn, as we joked with daylight bravado about the movie at school the following Monday, having had the whole weekend to muse over it. The main source of our thankfully short-lived terror did not stem from Bette Davis's creepy performance, but from the film's copious use of tracking shots through the branches, captured from the voyeuristic perspective of the watcher and accompanied by a dramatic, jarring orchestral score. As my friends and I watched the film in our local Odeon – a building that was to close soon after, looming empty and abandoned for the next four years like the ominous pavilion in *Carnival of Souls* – we were left with a genuine fear that something malevolent was in the trees, unobserved yet observing us.

Like that frog-swallowing snake I would later fail to find.

The name 'New Forest' is something of a misnomer, as it is clearly anything but new, and large swathes of it consist of wide-open gorse- and heather-filled heathland, rather than the dense fairy-tale forest that is my landscape of memory from that family holiday. The region's poor soils have supported this mixture of lowland heath and woodland since well before 1079, when William the Conqueror declared the area to be his *Nova Foresta*, a stretch of land reserved for the pursuit of deer and wild boar by the monarch (the original meaning of the word 'forest' is hunting ground, and maiming physical punishments were meted out to commoners caught breaking the rules).

The first Norman king's successor, his ruddy-faced son William Rufus, was killed in the forest in August 1100, shot through the breast by a rogue arrow supposedly aimed at a stag by one of his companions (though assassination is not out of the question). William Rufus's older brother Richard had also died some years previously in a hunting accident in his father's preserve. And three months before, in May 1100, the king's illegitimate nephew had likewise been slain hereabouts by another arrow gone awry. These two earlier incidents should perhaps have served as a warning to the country's new ruler about the hazards, if not of the forest itself, then of his chosen pastime. But, even if the memory of how his relatives had met their end no longer weighed upon William II, various contemporary warnings and omens do appear to have had an effect and led the king to postpone the departure of his ill-starred stag hunt. However, this was to delay his doom for just a few short hours.

We visited the Rufus Stone, which marks the spot of the regicide, during that same sunburnt summer: the original stone, according to the 1841-erected replacement, was 'much mutilated, and the inscriptions on each of its three sides defaced'. Among my box of old family photos and

slides I can find only a solitary picture of the marker post
– an image of my father engaged in the act of capturing the
monument on film; the photo possesses a grainy, otherworldly hue that now would have to be digitally fabricated
by some Instagram or iPhone filter. In more recent years
the unobtrusive turnoff on the A31 has beckoned me to
the place every time I've passed it on my way to see my
brother at his nearby Dorset home.

Today is different – I'm heading in the opposite direction and there is no prospect of the two of us meeting later
and searching the skies for twist-tailed honey buzzards.
Before, though, I have often given in and broken my long
journey, turning across the busy dual carriageway to absorb
the atmosphere of the forest around the monument,
wondering if this was also where Dad and Chris happened

upon their infamous serpent. If so, perhaps another less grand marker would now be appropriate?

That the spot where an event so memorable might not hereafter be forgotten – close to here a man and his son watched a grass snake devour a fully grown frog.

Philip Hoare's book *England's Lost Eden* relates the strange events and portents surrounding the death of William Rufus in wonderful detail, before going on to catalogue the hypnotic attraction that the mysterious, superstition-filled Arcadia offered towards the end of the Victorian age to those who came here seeking a higher plane. He tells of how the forest became host to Mary Ann Girling, a farm labourer's daughter from Suffolk who claimed to be the stigmata-scarred Messiah, but ended up encamped in increasing squalor with her rag-tag band of followers outside the village of Hordle; their Rapture never did arrive, just starvation and disappointment and, for Mary Ann, the cancer of the womb that would kill her.

At the same time as Mary Ann's New Forest Shakers were attracting day-tripping tourists to gawk at their sorry spectacle, an eccentric Spiritualist barrister, Andrew Peterson, channelled the ghost of Sir Christopher Wren at séances and built a monument to the lure of the esoteric at nearby Sway. Today, as I walk along the narrow lane at its base, the 218ft folly – believed still to be the tallest non-reinforced concrete structure in the world – seems somewhat forlorn, squeezed in among houses and bungalows and crying out for a grander backdrop. Glimpsed, however, from a distance, jutting above the breeze-blown trees, its incantatory effect remains undiminished.

A mile and a half south-east of the Rufus Stone is Minstead. At the back of the village's delightfully ramshackle, red-brick All Saints' Church lies the grave of Sir Arthur Conan Doyle, another who found comfort in the forest, drawn to Spiritualism after the death of his eldest son Kingsley, who was wounded at the Somme and died in 1918 from the resulting complications. The originator of Sherlock Holmes had famously been taken in by the fairies photographed by two girls, sixteen-year-old Elsie Wright and her nine-year-old cousin Frances Griffiths, at Cottingley near Bradford. The images came to Doyle's attention via the Theosophical Society, and he broke the sensational story in a December 1920 article in *The Strand*

magazine; the women finally confessed to the fakery more than sixty years later, long after Doyle had printed his full investigation of the pictures in his book *The Coming of the Fairies*. Doyle maintained that 'there is enough already available to convince any reasonable man that the matter is not one which can be readily dismissed', albeit adding that: 'I do not myself contend that the proof is as over-whelming as in the case of spiritualistic phenomena.'

By this late point in his life Doyle's faith in Spiritualism was seemingly without scepticism. He was by no means alone in his beliefs, as the unprecedented slaughter of European youth that had taken place during the First World War had led to an upsurge of interest from those of the bereaved who wished to attempt communication with their dead loved ones. In 1927 Doyle published *Pheneas Speaks*, a catalogue of comforting messages received from

the other realm at private family séances by his second wife Jean, who acted as medium. Pheneas was their third-century BC Mesopotamian spirit guide, who directed first Jean's automatic writing (referred to as 'inspired writing' by Doyle) and later 'semi-trance inspirational talking'. Many of these séances were held at their mock-Tudor New Forest retreat, Bignell House, a couple of miles east of the Rufus Stone; Pheneas even requested a room of his own in the cottage, decorated in mauve, which would psychically lend itself to 'clearer vibrations'. The family conferred with departed relatives including their late, war-wounded son Kingsley, and Doyle's brother-in-law – the novelist E. W. Hornung (husband of Doyle's sister Connie), author of the Raffles 'gentleman thief' stories and a renowned non-believer in Spiritualism while alive. John Thadeus Delane, a former editor of *The Times* who had died in 1879 – a person and name, according to Doyle, apparently 'quite unknown to my wife' – also appeared in the ether for a chat. When asked whether he still edited a paper in the next world, Delane replied: 'There is no need here. We know everything. It is like wireless in the air, and all so much bigger and larger and so splendid. It is great, this life.'

Later, at the same June 1922 séance, Doyle's thirteen-year-old son Denis, 'a great lover of snakes', asked Kingsley: 'Where are the snakes with you?' To which his ghost brother replied: 'In their own place, old chap. We are so proud of you, Denis, and the way you are developing in every way.' Reading these transcripts now it's difficult to imagine how the man responsible for the creation of the arch-rationalist Sherlock Holmes could accept these banal

messages so unquestioningly as solid evidence of an afterlife, and not as the understandable attempts (either
consciously or subconsciously) of his wife – who had also
lost her brother during the Great War – to bring comfort
to a grieving old man and his family.

At the beginning of the 1920s Doyle struck up an
unlikely rapport with Harry Houdini, the American magician and escapologist who was starting to engage in a
mission to expose fraudulent mediums, hoping in the
process to find a genuine means of communicating with his
dead mother.* In the same month that Denis asked his
vanished brother about the snakes, Jean engaged in automatic writing in the presence of Houdini, producing seven
paragraphs purporting to be from the showman's mother.
Houdini was unimpressed – the deceased woman's English
was poor for one thing, and Jean's transcript failed to
capture her way of talking. The two men's friendship began
to fracture thereafter, their disagreement later magnifying
into a high-profile spat. Reading them now, the words
alleged to have come through to Jean from the late Mrs
Houdini bear a striking resemblance to those received
from John Thadeus Delane: 'It is so different over here, so
much larger and bigger and more beautiful ...'

In a 1927 magazine article Doyle argued the case that
various Victorian writers – notably Oscar Wilde and Jack
London – continued to produce works from the other side.
Doyle also conducted a conversation himself, through

---

* Born Erik Weisz, Houdini had arrived in the United States in
1878 as a four-year-old emigrant from Hungary.

another medium, Florizel von Reuter, with a figure he reckoned could well have been Charles Dickens, and who went
on to provide him with the solution to the mystery of
Edwin Drood: 'Edwin is alive and Chris is hiding him'
('Chris', according to Doyle, being the Reverend Crisparkle).

'Every year spring throws her green veil over the world
and anon the red autumn glory comes to mock the yellow
moon.' Purported communications from Wilde like the
preceding sentence (part of a larger tranche of writing said
to emanate from the dead aesthete) were, however, Doyle's
favoured evidence of posthumous literary work. They were
transmitted to the hand of a medium, Mrs Dowden, which
was in turn laid upon their transcriber, a Mr Soal. Doyle
seizes on their florid language and use of colourful adjec-
tives as proof of their famous sender's identity: 'This is not
merely adequate Wilde. It is exquisite Wilde. It is so beautiful that it might be chosen for special inclusion in any
anthology of his writings.' Doyle does not seem able to
countenance the possibility that he is being duped:

> What then is the alternative explanation? I confess
> that I can see none. Can anyone contend that both Mr
> Soal and Mrs Dowden have a hidden strand in their
> own personality which enables them on occasion to
> write like a great deceased writer, and at the same time
> a want of conscience which permits that subconscious
> strand to actually claim that it *is* the deceased author?
> Such an explanation would seem infinitely more
> unlikely than any transcendental one can do.

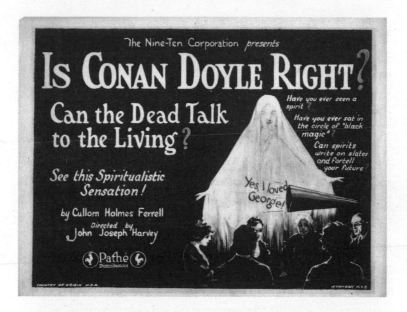

It would not be long before the 71-year-old author joined his fellow literary giants London, Wilde and Dickens, as well as his eldest son, Kingsley, and his former friend Harry Houdini.* At eight thirty on the morning of 7 July 1930 – seated in a basket chair in his bedroom, looking towards the window – Sir Arthur Conan Doyle passed peacefully at his main residence, Windlesham Manor in East Sussex. He was buried in the gardens of the house, surrounded by a sea of well-wishers' flowers, next to his writing hut. In the immediate aftermath of his death – on occasions including the memorial service held at the Royal Albert Hall six days later, at which a vacant chair was left for him

---

* On Halloween 1926 Houdini failed to escape death, following a ruptured appendix probably caused by unexpected and over-zealous blows to the stomach given nine days before by a student admirer wanting to test the performer's physical prowess.

on the stage beside his wife – numerous mediums asserted that they had received beyond-the-grave communiqués from Spiritualism's grand flag-bearer. With reports of these alleged messages threatening to become overwhelming, his widow pushed back, stating: 'When he has got anything for the world he will communicate with us first.' And it was not long before the family resumed their contact. Jean continued to hear Arthur's voice at the sittings she conducted right up to her own passing in 1940, even claiming that her husband's spirit had diagnosed her own cancer before her doctors; whether Pheneas was at this point still her otherworldly guide, I could not say.

We do, however, have irrefutable proof of at least one last earthly trip Doyle was to make, a quarter of a century after his body had departed this life: a hundred-mile hearse ride. In 1955, after the Windlesham estate had been sold, his remains were exhumed, moved and reinterred, along with those of his spouse, beneath a mature oak in the southern corner of Minstead churchyard, close to their beloved New Forest retreat. It is a pleasant, peaceful final spot of rest; when I visit, ponies are galloping after each other in the adjacent paddock. Someone has placed a bent smoking pipe on top of his headstone too, which seems an appropriate touch.

Since the Doyles' purchase of nearby Bignell House in 1925 it had acquired a reputation for being haunted – locals knew the family held their séances there, with the 1929 fire that gutted the property adding to its aura. Doyle put the blaze down to psychic forces, though sparks from the kitchen that ignited the thatched roof are the rational

explanation. And, although he brought in builders to restore his house in the woods (today a private home set back from the busy main road), Doyle did not live to see the work completed. In 1961 Bignell's new owners – both doctors trained at the University of Edinburgh, the same institution at which Doyle had also studied medicine – had the place exorcised. No more unexplainable noises were reported, and there were no further sightings of the tall, moustachioed, slipper-wearing figure of Conan Doyle's ghost, said to search the attic for a missing red leather diary the late author required for his spectral memoirs.

Something of the new beginning that the Girlingites hoped for, as well as hints towards the answers to the existential questions that those others drawn to the forest longed to find, are also present in the work of Algernon Blackwood, a prolific Edwardian writer of ghost stories and what is often classified as 'weird fiction'. (H. P. Lovecraft defined the 'true weird tale' as one that possesses a 'certain atmosphere of breathless and unexplainable dread of outer, unknown forces'.)

On the suggestion of his publisher, Blackwood also penned a number of crossover tales intended to cash in on the success of Doyle's Sherlock Holmes, successfully introducing, in 1908, the psychic investigator John Silence, who used his detective skills and other more esoteric abilities to bring about a resolution to various occult mysteries. The brilliantly named Silence is a figure similar to Sheridan Le Fanu's Dr Hesselius (from the tale 'Green Tea' some forty years earlier) and was followed two years later by William Hope Hodgson's Carnacki 'the Ghost Finder', and several lesser imitators right up to *The X-Files*' Fox Mulder.*

Blackwood's apparent belief in the numinous power of the woods is shown in a story set within the New Forest. 'The Man Whom the Trees Loved' was written in 1911 and first appeared in the March 1912 issue of the *London Magazine*. The monthly literary periodical paid £60 (*c.* £6,500 today) for the 26,000-word, 70-page piece before it became the opening work of Blackwood's nature-themed fiction collection *Pan's Garden*. The story centres on David Bittacy – his pre-retirement career is not explicitly defined, though he previously worked in India as some sort of forest

---

* The Irishman Joseph Sheridan Le Fanu (1814–73) was M. R. James's favourite writer of ghost stories – the boy in 'A Vignette' that we take for the young James happens to be reading Le Fanu's *The House by the Churchyard* at the time he glimpses the malign face in the garden of Livermere's rectory.

official – and his wife Sophia, daughter of an evangelical clergyman (the kind of man, perhaps, who would have been mesmerised by Mary Ann Girling's Christ-like wounds). The couple live in an idyllic Hampshire house at the edge of the forest – I picture it as somewhere not dissimilar to Conan Doyle's Bignell – its garden dominated by an enormous cedar tree, while the woods themselves border the property: 'He saw the great encircling mass of gloom that was the Forest, fringing their little lawn. It pressed up closer in the darkness.'

Into this seemingly happy union comes, at the invitation of Bittacy, the artist Arthur Sanderson, a young man with a creative gift: 'He painted trees as by some special divining instinct of their essential qualities. He understood them.' According to Blackwood's biographer Mike Ashley, Sanderson is loosely based on his dandyish friend and mentor, the painter, illustrator, theatre designer and art collector Walford Graham Robertson. Robertson's large circle of celebrity acquaintances included Oscar Wilde, Henry James and Ellen Terry (whose portrait he painted). And he himself featured as the subject of a well-known canvas by John Singer Sargent, now in the collection of the Tate. In the portrait, Robertson's thin boyish frame (he was twenty-eight when he posed for it) sports a full-length, fur-collared black coat, his left hand clasping an elegant jade-handled cane and his right resting on his waist; by his feet lies his oversize poodle Mouton. Robertson was to illustrate *Pan's Garden*, and his striking frontispiece for 'The Man Whom the Trees Loved' has an appropriately decadent, almost Aubrey Beardsley-esque feel – though to

my mind there's also something of Marvel Comics' Silver
Surfer about the figure that dominates the foreground of
the composition.

THE MAN WHOM
THE TREES LOVED

The quiet retirement of David Bittacy changes with the arrival of Sanderson. The artist, thanks to his profound empathy with the forest, manages to unlock a latent fellow-feeling in his older friend, who for the first time realises that the trees he has always loved possess, in isolation, a cognisance approaching that of a person, and together a swarming collective consciousness capable of influencing their surroundings, including the very air itself. Indeed, the wind is another natural force imbued in the story with a strange power, a power that Sophia fears because of its ability to 'blow something from the trees – into the mind – into the house'. Though this is the very reason David is so ecstatic when the breezes build: 'They blow the souls of the trees about the sky like clouds.'

The exotic introduced cedar on the lawn – standing apart from the massed, native woodland trees – acts as a guardian of David Bittacy's human existence, keeping the encroaching forest from enveloping the old man.* Damage to the tree by a storm, however, starts to strip this protection, and the rapturous connection that David has with the woods – walking for hours through them on his own, during both the day and the darkness – appears to be changing him, certainly in the eyes of his increasingly estranged wife. She fears he is becoming a shell of a person, presenting only a trace of the man he once was, while his true being is close to fusing with the forest. She tries to

---

* Three cedars flanked Blackwood's childhood home Shortlands, near Bromley in south-east London; their night-time mystery and grandeur impressed him from a young age.

save him, but the forces are too powerful for her and the God of her oversized Baxter Bible. When the sinuous physical manifestations of the trees crowd around the bed of her sleeping husband she knows he is lost:

> She saw their outline underneath the ceiling, the green, spread bulk of them, their vague extension over walls and furniture. They shifted to and fro, massed yet translucent, mild yet thick, moving and tuning within themselves to a hushed noise of multitudinous soft rustling.

At the end of the story, catching sight of the cedar of Lebanon now finally felled on the grass outside their bedroom window, Sophia gets confirmation of the thing she most dreads: 'And in the distance she heard the roaring of the Forest further out. Her husband's voice was in it.'

'The Man Whom the Trees Loved' is an atmosphere-laden story that offers a vision not unlike that of the early English Romantics – a feeling that the forces of nature and the universe are greater than man and possess a timeless, unknowable power. Blackwood was influenced by the nineteenth-century Theosophical writings of Franz Hartmann, particularly his *Magic: White and Black*, and the work and animistic outlook of the psychologist and philosopher Gustav Fechner. The 1911 edition of the *Encyclopaedia Britannica* – the same year Blackwood's New Forest-set story was written – had the following to say about Fechner, a sentiment equally applicable to Blackwood:

He feels the thrill of life everywhere, in plants, earth, stars, the total universe. Man stands midway between the souls of plants and the souls of stars, who are angels. God, the soul of the universe, must be conceived as having an existence analogous to men.

Algernon Blackwood achieved popular fame in his last few years through his appearances on Saturday night BBC television, where, working without a script, he delivered his

ghost stories straight to camera. He had a splendid voice and looked the part: avuncular, with a wizened face etched with age and tanned by a life spent outdoors. From photographs, Blackwood bears a passing resemblance to my lock-keeper grandfather – as well as their sun-cooked features, both possessed impressively aquiline noses and an infectious impishness about their expressions.* Blackwood's peak-time live broadcasts began at the end of 1947, when he was seventy-eight, and led to him being awarded the Television Society Medal the following year – marking him out as 1948's outstanding, albeit unlikely, TV personality.

In truth, the later stories of Blackwood's prolific career don't come close to his formative works, the best of which were based on his own experiences. He spent large early chunks of his rich and varied life living among or near to wild places, and he draws strongly on these memories in the settings of his stories. For instance, for a little over a year of his education, Blackwood was schooled in Germany's Black Forest at a strict institution run by the Moravian Brotherhood, where long hikes into the woods were one of the few available pastimes; the school and its surroundings forms the basis for his John Silence story 'Secret Worship', which is tinged with obvious autobiographical detail – though whether his own teachers resembled the story's devil-worshipping acolytes is another matter.

---

* The Cornwall-based writer of the fantastic, Frank Baker, neatly summed up the elderly author's appearance when he recalled meeting 'the wrinkled mummified visage of old Algernon Blackwood' at the eightieth birthday party of Arthur Machen.

Aged twenty, Blackwood undertook a three-hundred-mile trek across the Alps, before a later failed dairy-farming venture outside Toronto and a moose-hunting expedition to the wilds of Quebec. The latter inspired one of his most highly rated short stories, 'The Wendigo', written a decade after the trip, in 1908. In the story, the vast 'bleak splendours of these remote and lonely forests' are haunted by the *wendigo*, a shifting, ventriloquial entity that shares the name of a spirit creature from Algonquian legend; Blackwood, however, subsumes the original First Nation myth into his own distinct creation, which is memorable for its indescribable call and fetid, rotten, but strangely sweet scent, carried on the breeze like the stench of the slaughterhouse. It's a good story, but not to me quite among his best – though Robert Aickman regarded it as 'one of the (possibly) six great masterpieces in the field' – as I find the undoubted horror of the monster and the claustrophobic atmosphere of the endless northern woods diluted by distracting lines of dialogue ('Oh, oh! This fiery height! Oh, oh! My feet of fire! My burning feet of fire …!').

The wendigo also features notably in Stephen King's novel *Pet Sematary*, the first of the American author's books that I read, though I'd previously been terrified after being allowed to remain up to watch the TV mini-series of *Salem's Lot* while staying at my grandmother's.* The jagged-toothed, blue-skinned vampire Barlow is still, I

---

* 'Wendigoes' are also mentioned briefly in Henry Wadsworth Longfellow's epic 1855 poem *The Song of Hiawatha*.

think, one of the scariest screen images of the undead, right
up there with Max Schreck's cadaverous Count Orlok; I
had to knock on Nan's door in the middle of the night
because foxes were barking in the blackness of the fields
and I could hear tapping from behind my curtains. In the
scene from the 1979 television adaptation that most frightened me, a grinning pyjama-clad Ralphie Glick floats
outside the bedroom window of his soon-to-be victim (his
older brother), scratching his nails down the glass pane;
viewed again now the young vampire happens to bear a
more than passing resemblance to the razor-clawed hurdy-
gurdy boy Giovanni in M. R. James's 'Lost Hearts'. My
grandmother emerged in her white nightgown, suitably
spectral herself, but we went down the twisting staircase
together and she made hot chocolate to take my mind off
the imagined tapping.

To me, 'The Man Whom the Trees Loved' surpasses the
'The Wendigo'. Blackwood places the events in a landscape
that would have been more recognisable to his British
readership – though at the time he penned the story the
New Forest would have been quieter than the tourist-
thronged destination it's become. He manages to infuse the
familiar with an aura of dreamlike otherness, of the
Romantics' sense of the 'sublime' – although these age-old
English woodlands exist on nothing like the insanity-
inducing scale of the Canadian wilderness. Yet even now, a
century on, there remain silent corners of the Hampshire
countryside where you feel you're the only person ever to
have set foot, where the trees and topography mask the
sound of traffic; there are still secret heathland glades

where spindle-tailed Dartford warblers skulk among the gorse, or blocks of impenetrable conifers above which goshawks might deign to display to a fortunate few on bright spring mornings. There can be surprises and strangers too – odd gale-borne waifs such as the chaffinch-sized dark-eyed junco from North America that my brother and I watched feeding beneath a fallen New Forest pine in late January 2012, a lost slate-and-white songbird destined never to find its way home.

I am close to that spot today, having pulled my car down a narrow track that skirts one of the forest's clearings. A swift spears silently through the wind-wasted sky beyond the space in which I am paused, twisting its wings to navigate the ebbs and flows of the fast-moving air. In a month or so – as July drifts towards August – I shall watch them gather high over my house in excited shrieking groups. A few days later they will begin to make their way south of the Sahara, where they will spend their perpetual summer skimming the vast rainforests of Conrad's *Heart of Darkness*. This lone bird above me – above this infinitely smaller, drizzle-dampened forest – will have been back in English skies since the beginning of May, among the latest of our migrants to return. I always think it noteworthy to see the species in April, and can recall exactly the last time I saw one in that cruellest of months: I know the date because I have found a forgotten fragment of text conversation on my phone. It was only ten miles from here – a short flight for a swift. My eyes followed its movement as it scythed above the massed buildings beside the multi-storey car park of Southampton's General Hospital. Chris replied, joking, to the message I sent him that I was a 'stringer', that I had made the swift up.

It was real though, Chris. Like your frog and the snake. Are they in their own place now too?

Afterwards I headed across the dusk-washed forest, back towards his house, where I was staying. 'The Night trans-figures all things in a way,' says the artist Sanderson in Blackwood's story. And perhaps he is right, because I had the urge to traverse the darkness of the woods, rather than the emptier predictability of the quicker road. Somewhere, before the light was lost entirely, a woodcock beat heavily above the tops of the trees in front of me.

That was real too.

All of it was real, I think.

They are mesmeric in the way that they move. On calmer days these sixty-five-foot giants that shield my garden sway like wave-washed sea urchins, but whip to and fro with an unpredictability bordering on violence as the wind strengthens. In a gale their smaller twigs are shed like confetti and the precarious angled boughs make strange high-pitched squeals that have me puzzling momentarily what species of bird they might be – before I realise that the sounds originate from the trees themselves.

From the willows.

Not that they aren't home to a good variety of birds – wood pigeons gorge themselves on the berries of the ivy that stifles the leaning trunks, while cryptic treecreepers pick delicately beneath their skin of flayed bark, and, in most summers, the half-hearted midnight begging whistles of young tawny owls can be heard as they wait behind the screen of narrow leaves to be brought their next feed. The willows are a haven for other, largely unseen, wildlife too, with a legion of insects, including ephemeral day-flying red-tipped clearwings and pale, nocturnal furry puss moths and sallow kittens, regarding these trees as the entirety of their world. Indeed, the time towards dusk when the light starts to die is when I find the willows at their strangest, their most beguiling. In the greyness their bowed branches take on different forms, like the appearance of large nodding beasts – perhaps an elephant or mastodon swaying its trunk, or a herd of antediluvian aurochs shuffling through the air – or, as Algernon Blackwood would put it, 'a host of beings from another plane of life, another evolution altogether'.

After his travels in Canada and a poverty-stricken stint among the riotous hustle of 1890s New York, where he got his first proper writing job as a junior reporter on the *Sun*, Blackwood, now aged thirty-one, undertook an ambitious dawn-of-the-century canoe adventure from the head-waters of the Danube in the Black Forest. He and his companion planned to navigate the entire course of the great river, but the impracticability of this soon became apparent. The curtailed trip, however, proved to be the initial inspiration for what is widely considered to be the greatest of Blackwood's supernatural stories, 'The Willows'. H. P. Lovecraft rated it as one of his favourite works of weird fiction, stating that 'an impression of lasting poign-ancy is produced without a single strained passage or a single false note'. I would agree.

'The Willows' was published in 1907, in Blackwood's second supernatural collection *The Listener and Other Stories*. It is another of his tales, like 'The Man Whom the Trees Loved', in which the foreboding power of nature features at the forefront, though here the overall impres-sion is more unsettling still. The action of Blackwood's masterpiece takes place in a lonely stretch of the Danube downstream from Pressburg (now Bratislava, the capital of Slovakia) – 'the wilderness of islands, sand-banks, and swampland beyond – the land of the willows'.

The story's willows are quite unlike the tall, branch-shed-ding crack willows (*Salix fragilis*) that line my garden. And they're nothing like Old Man Willow, the demonic tree at the heart of the Old Forest in J. R. R. Tolkien's *The Fellowship of the Ring*, or Green Noah, the shambling weeping willow that pursues Tolly at the climax of *The Children of Green Knowe*. Blackwood describes his Danube trees as 'willow bushes', and it is their sheer unending multitude that seems to give them their dominion over the human world, rather than some individual, animated Ent-like majesty:

> Their serried ranks, growing everywhere darker
> about me as the shadows deepened, moving furiously
> yet softly in the wind, woke in me the curious and
> unwelcome suggestion that we had trespassed here
> upon the borders of an alien world, a world where
> we were intruders, a world where we were not
> wanted or invited to remain – where we ran grave
> risks perhaps!

Adrift from the world of men in the water- and tree-filled vistas of the roaring Danube, the narrator and his companion, a laconic Swede, make camp on a sandbar and are doing their best to enjoy the sublime spectacle. They have already fulfilled the first rule of the horror story by ignoring earlier cautions, from a Hungarian officer they encountered in Pressburg, not to carry on with their expedition: 'There are no people, no farms, no fishermen. I warn you not to continue. The river, too, is still rising, and this wind will increase.'

Blackwood's descriptions of the two explorers' temporary island home, constantly under assault from the angry waters, and of the primordial willows that crowd the horizon, are vivid. From the beginning of their mid-stream encampment the narrator is aware, of a sense of pervading unease, of terror-tinged awe:

> Altogether it was an impressive scene, with its utter
> loneliness, its bizarre suggestion; and as I gazed, long
> and curiously, a singular emotion began to stir
> somewhere in the depths of me. Midway in my delight
> of the wild beauty, there crept, unbidden and
> unexplained, a curious feeling of disquietude, almost of
> alarm.

Two incidents occur as the men gather driftwood for their fire in preparation for their first night on the islet. The Swede notices what he believes is a dead human body washing past in the current – 'A black thing, turning over and over in the foaming waves' – but as it twists in the water they see its eye gleaming yellow before the shape plunges below the waters: a hunting otter, they decide. Soon after they think they really are witnessing another person – this time alive – in an incident which, for me, ranks as the most troubling of the story's events:

> It seemed, however, to be a man standing upright in a
> sort of flat-bottomed boat, steering with a long oar, and
> being carried down the opposite shore at a tremendous
> pace. He apparently was looking across in our
> direction, but the distance was too great and the light
> too uncertain for us to make out very plainly what he
> was about.

The narrator and his companion believe that the gesticulating figure, who they assume to be a superstitious local, is crossing himself as his strange craft floats – almost seeming to fly – through the miasma of mist and sunset. He is too far away, however, for them to catch his attention.

'There was something curious about the whole appearance – man, boat, signs, voice – that made an impression on me out of all proportion to its cause.' After this, things rapidly move out of control – and out of reason – as other-dimensional forces intersect with the willow-infested wilderness. The narrator witnesses monstrous shapes, or figures, above the willows in the night sky (a vision reminiscent of 'The Man Whom the Trees Loved', as is the story's preternatural driving wind), and strange pattering sounds outside the tent that seem to be the unrooted trees themselves drawing closer. The following morning the Swede reveals that their canoe has somehow acquired a deep gouge in its hull, and their paddle has been ground down to an unusable thinness. Thousands of small hollows pocket the surface of the ever-diminishing island. Stranded while they make repairs, their conversation turns to the previous day's otter sighting. The narrator laughs off the Swede's doubts as to whether it was such a creature (though it is noted that otters do not have yellow eyes) by joking that next he'll be querying the identity of the local they glimpsed in the hazy craft.

'I *did* rather wonder, if you want to know,' he said
slowly, 'what the thing in the boat was. I remember
thinking at the time it was not a man. The whole
business seemed to rise quite suddenly out of the
water.'

The gale drops, but the situation is not improved, for now
the two men are able to hear the sounds of the willows –
'something like the humming of a distant gong'. Events
cascade and the pair become convinced that they are on a
frontier that straddles the human world and some other,
unaccountable one. As readers, we too are drawn into this
vortex of wind-funnelled terror, increasingly certain things
will not end well. When the end does come it is not,
perhaps, quite as we might expect, though no less effective
for it.

'The Willows' is another of Blackwood's stories in which
his own experience is writ large. During his own first expedition along the Danube in June 1900, he and his companion (an English friend named Wilfrid Wilson, not a terse
Swede) followed a comparable route downriver and
camped on a similarly ephemeral islet. In the introduction
to his 1938 anthology *The Tales of Algernon Blackwood*, he
recalls how 'a year or two later, making the same trip in a
barge, we found a dead body caught by a root, its decayed
mass dangling against the sandy shoreline of the very same
island my story describes'. This second trip actually took
place in August 1905 – Blackwood's biographer notes the
inaccuracy of his subject's recall of dates – so the strange
coincidence of finding the corpse on the island he had

earlier camped on would have been fresh in his memory when he came to write the story.

'The Willows' features a landscape that does not really resemble anywhere in Britain – the Flow Country of Scotland might possess the right scale of loneliness and a hotchpotch of disorienting watery channels, but the willows themselves are absent. And those trees, while a common enough sight in isolated clumps along my own familiar East Anglian waterways, or mixed in alongside other trees in damp carr woodlands, are not found growing naturally anywhere I've visited in Britain in the correct, unceasing concentration. The nearest vistas I can equate to those of the story are the now-diminishing poplar planta-tions of the Fens. I always felt a certain otherworldliness in their angular, light-stealing uniformity when my brother and I used to visit them that puts me in mind of Blackwood's story – despite the difference in the trees themselves.

We were searching for golden orioles, a spectacular thrush-sized songbird that, between the 1960s and the end of the first decade of the new millennium, was confined in the UK to a small population numbering just tens of pairs in those waterside woodlands along the border between Norfolk and Suffolk. The bright-yellow males were, for such a gaudy bird, surprisingly elusive – the best chance of locating them was to listen for their flute-like piping song, delivered most frequently at a premature hour on late spring and early summer mornings. These sounds are hard to describe (the second word of their English common name is supposedly onomatopoeic), but I'm always tempted to transcribe it as 'Poo-tee-weet?'

– the repeated refrain that the birds sing after the destruction of Dresden in Kurt Vonnegut's time-flitting anti-war novel *Slaughterhouse-Five*, one of my favourite books and one which Chris gave me for my eighteenth birthday. It was an apt present, I think, since like Vonnegut – and the biblical Lot's wife who's described so memorably in the book's opening chapter – I seem unable to stop myself from gazing backwards into the ruins of my own past.

The orioles were dreamlike, as were the woods they inhabited. The first one I ever saw flickered through the mist that clung above the surface of the Ouse's undeviating cut-off channel, moving swiftly from the left bank of poplars to the right, a three-second flare of gold before it was gone. Its periodic song serenaded and tricked us for the next few hours, the mellifluous, questioning melody mingling with the babble of blackbirds, blackcaps and garden warblers that seemingly sang from every other low branch and bush, and transformed the early morning into a cacophonic approximation of the last verse of Edward Thomas's poem 'Adlestrop' – only with Suffolk and Norfolk now taking the place of Oxfordshire and Gloucestershire.

The hybrid poplars at Lakenheath Fen, the orioles' stronghold, had been planted by the Bryant & May match company to fuel smokers' pre-lighter and pre-vaping demands, their repetitious shade-filled stands forming an unwitting place of refuge for these rare avian visitors from the continent. Bryant & May's distinctive yellow-and-black matchboxes – a fitting *Oriolus oriolus* colour scheme

– which depicted, oddly, an animal-free Noah's Ark emblazoned with the word 'SECURITY', were another integral
part of my childhood. My grandfather, an inveterate pipe
smoker, had a collection of over thirty thousand match-
books and matchboxes, including hundreds of variants of
the iconic Ark safety matches, all of which now lie mould-
ering in my brother's garage. As a boy I would greedily
snatch a discarded box off the street to present to Grandad,
who would claim to know instantly whether it was one he
already possessed – a sizeable proportion of our holidays
seemed to be spent searching for souvenir boxes to take
back to Lincolnshire for him.

Today, Lakenheath's poplar plantations offer only a trace
of their former glory, like the now-defunct UK match
industry itself.* However, the reedbeds of the reserve that

---

* The UK's last factory producing standard household matches,
located in Liverpool, closed in 1994.

occupies the site are in fine health, having been encouraged
and expanded with two decades of careful conservation
management. Magnificent common cranes that stand four
feet tall have colonised in recent years – Chris and I waited
hours for them to show soon after they first arrived –
alongside cryptic, grunting bitterns: strange squat herons
which haunt these yellowed acres (the esoteric Norwich-
based seventeenth-century writer and philosopher Sir
Thomas Browne is said to have kept a live one). Nature is
being given the opportunity to make up for the broken
biodiversity of the neighbouring over-farmed Fens by
reverting to a fowl-laden waterland in which Hereward the
Wake would feel at home – a growing wilderness that
offers a suitably inspiring Blackwood-esque backdrop in
which to contemplate the sublime. Members of the genus
Salix will themselves feature more prominently at the
reserve in future too, as its poplar plantations are being
diversified to include a greater proportion of native trees,
including alders and willows, among its wet woodland.

As to the orioles, their final confirmed nesting at
Lakenheath was in 2009, with the site's last definite singing summer male ghosting through the dark canopy in
2013. The species did not return to the Fen the following
year – a year when, for me, so much was to become absent.

Poo-tee-weet?

Chapter 5

MEMENTO MORI

I arrived with the dusk on a biting, slate-skied afternoon, a mixture of sleet and snow starting to fall as I made my way up the path that coiled around the hillside. The light, dim to begin with, grew steadily darker as I wound higher. Three redpolls – small finches I picked out from their high-pitched, questioning calls – flew over my head, looking for somewhere to roost, though they would have more luck down in the shelter of the mound than at its summit.

I was visiting Glasgow's gothic monument to death, its sprawling *memento mori* (from the Latin 'remember you must die'): the Necropolis. The site covers a hill behind St Mungo's Cathedral, giving an impressive panorama of the city. Formerly rocky parkland, in 1831 it was given over to

afford 'a much wanted accommodation to the higher classes' that would be 'respectful to the dead, safe and sanitary to the living, dedicated to the Genius of Memory and to extend religious and moral feeling'. Since then, various extensions to its original area have been made, alongside fifty thousand burials in 3,500 brick-partitioned tombs.*

No one else was about – they probably had more sense on this bitter afternoon at the back end of 2014. I'd

---

* I'm not sure anyone else does a graveyard with quite the grandeur and solemnity of the Scots. Edinburgh, too, is riddled with impressive assemblages of dark-stoned monuments to the departed, in kirkyards like St Cuthbert's and, particularly, Greyfriars. At the latter, the maudlin Skye terrier Bobby supposedly sat in mourning by his master's grave for a fourteen-year stretch in the middle of the Victorian century – the canine embodiment of the public grief of the monarch for her lost husband, with which the lone dog's vigil coincided.

gravitated here, pulled by the name, and by the pictures I'd seen of the place's impressive architecture – as well as the melancholia of my own mood – after tagging along to the city with my partner, who was here for a work conference.

In particular, I was drawn to one of the Necropolis's most imposing structures, the Aiken Mausoleum, its classical pillars and portico half-hidden by tangled ivy and creepers. Peering through the wrought-iron gates that locked across its front I could just read some of the words on the memorial plaques inside.

More disconcertingly, in the darkness I could also make out a rectangular opening that presumably marked the steps down to the graves themselves, though the paltry torchlight from my phone did not show any detail. Was it

spooky? Perhaps a little, but the lights of the city, multiplied at this time of year by those of Christmas, were close. And I was used to wandering in such places – albeit not quite as grand as this – as, for five years as a boy I had been a chorister;* for a dare we would sometimes run through the graveyard of the town's thirteenth-century church after evensong on winter Sunday evenings, pausing midway to touch the top of the coffin shaped tomb with the foreboding cleft through its lid.

In my present, too, walking back from the train station to my own house after dark I have to pass along an unlit lane that runs beside the local cemetery. Just before the darkest point, where the trees crowd in from both sides, the curve of the road and the low flint wall to the left look almost identical to the Victorian artist John Atkinson Grimshaw's *Moonlight Walk* – the self-taught Yorkshireman specialised in realistic, slightly unsettling nocturnal scenes – which features on the cover of my paperback copy of M. R. James's *Collected Ghost Stories*. Sometimes as I enter that last stretch I picture myself as the painting's lone figure, dwarfed by the darkness.

So, wandering in the Necropolis at dusk – even with the ghost of a snowstorm in the offing and ghosts in my head – I didn't find the surroundings frightening. Indeed, the stones, with their solidity and timelessness, seemed to extend a kind of comfort to me. I felt worn out and undone

---

* I was lured into joining my local church choir through the promise of its midweek games club and various exciting-sounding day trips out – not because of any religious devotion on my part (or of that of my parents).

and, at that moment, if I had been offered the chance to step inside the bars of the mausoleum and to take an unending sleep within its walls, I might well have chosen the memory-wiped relief of that option. But the stinging wind had gathered pace and was pushing me onwards, along with a darkling winter thrush – a redwing that skittered up in front of me from a leafless tree.

Towards the lights of the city, towards the lights of the living.

*

Below Glasgow, just inland from Ayrshire's coast, stands the roofless ruin of Alloway Auld Kirk – situated in the centre of another of Scotland's most atmospheric graveyards. Its hallowed ground is filled with headstones that seem to have been dipped in ochreous lichen, while impenetrable-looking iron grilles guard a number of the graves: *mortsafes* like those in Edinburgh's Greyfriars, placed to prevent grave robbers. Though it would be a brave man who would have dared come here on a stormy night to dig up the kirkyard's dead, given that the location was the inspiration and setting for the 'Ploughman Poet' Robert Burns's mock-epic supernatural poem 'Tam o' Shanter'.

A church has stood on the site since probably the thirteenth century, with the present roofless outer walls dating from the early sixteenth. By 1791, when Burns's famous

poem was published, the church had long been a ruin, and the poet's father William, who had earlier tended these very graves, had lain here for seven years in his own. Robert was born in 1759, just up the street in a simple thatched cottage (now part of the excellent museum complex that marks his birthplace) on, of course, 25 January, the night honoured with his name. The derelict church was associated with various local superstitions that held it to be a favoured haunt of the devil, tales that Robert would have been familiar with from a young age – his mother's widowed cousin Betty Davidson, a lodger in their cramped cottage, was a repository of spook stories. Robert lived in Alloway for his first seven years (he was the oldest child, over time acquiring six siblings), before the family moved the short distance to nearby Mount Oliphant, where his father took the lease of an unproductive seventy acres of land in an attempt to better their prospects. Prior to that William had worked a smallholding and been engaged as head gardener for the local estate.*

Alloway Auld Kirk is today managed by the National Trust for Scotland. It's tucked between affluent-looking houses, opposite the new parish church on a busy tree-lined road. Perhaps my timing is fortunate, because it is midweek and the only other visitors are leaving as I arrive

---

* The name Oliphant is shared by the excellent Scottish Victorian ghost story writer, Margaret Oliphant, whose much-anthologised 'The Open Door' – set on the outskirts of Edinburgh – is, according to M. R. James, one of only two ghostly tales known to him 'wherein the elements of beauty and pity dominate terror'; it too features a haunted, roofless ruin with a discomfiting 'door that led to nothing'.

– yet once through its gates suburbia slips away. An ancient, gnarled sycamore has grown up the outside wall of the ruin, its bark near-identical in colour to the stone of the building. Many of the graves are graced with elaborate carvings including the usual skeletons and cherubs, but also featuring pictorial representations of the trade of the deceased: a miller, a farmer, a blacksmith. I soon locate the grave of William Burns. Inscribed on the rear of his much plainer memorial are eight lines of verse composed by the poet in honour of 'The tender father, and the generous friend'. The headstone is not the original from the end of the eighteenth century, but the third to have been erected at this spot: the previous two were vandalised by souvenir hunters wanting a morbid Burns keepsake, a *memento mori* worthy of the name.

Burns's epic is written in a mixture of Scots and English, composed to add folkloric colour to his friend Francis Grose's inclusion of Kirk Alloway in *The Antiquities of Scotland*. It begins with the eponymous, probably alcoholic, Tam drinking and sharing stories by the fireplace in an Ayr public house with his pal Souter Johnny (a *souter* being a cobbler), the pair of them putting away 'reaming swats [creamy ales], that drank divinely'. Outside it's a foul night, a night on which the Devil himself has 'business on his hand'. The time eventually arrives for the bonhomie of the pub to come to an end, and Tam bids farewell to the evening's passing pleasures. He heads towards home and his long-suffering wife, riding his grey mare Meg. His pace understandably quickens as he approaches the ruined Kirk Alloway – a spot where ghosts and owls cry, and where various unfortunates have met sticky ends: drunken Charlie broke his neck, Mungo's mother hanged herself, and the body of a murdered child was found there.

It doesn't seem like a good place to linger.

Tam presses forward, emboldened by the earlier beer and whisky. Before him he sees an incredible sight among the ruins of the church, a dancing mass of warlocks and witches. There in the upper window of the ruin 'sat auld Nick, in shape o' beast', taking the form of an oversized, shaggy black hound – the whole thing certainly has the ring of a shaggy dog story – who is playing unearthly music on the bagpipes. The scene is scattered with open coffins that 'shaw'd the dead in their last dresses' – perhaps those mortsafes were added later to prevent the corpses from rising, rather than robbers from digging down? Tam is

spellbound by the leaping, withered hags who dance wildly in their underskirts. In particular, there is one attractive younger witch in her short skirt – her 'Cutty-sark' – who causes him to cry out in praise of her efforts, breaking the reverie and alerting the 'hellish legion' to his presence.

Tam flees on his dependable steed, the witches, warlocks and other ungodly creatures in close pursuit, praying he can make it the few hundred yards to the keystone of the old bridge: 'A running stream they dare na cross'. His horse moves swiftly, but the young Nannie, the short-skirted witch, is not far behind. Flying at Tam, she grabs Meg's tail, ripping it clean off just as the mare jumps to safety. The bridge today, in the wan spring light, offers a more serene vista: a couple are posing for their wedding photographs while a piper regales them on the cobbles; later, I suspect, some reaming swats may be sunk at the reception in tribute to Tam.

Nearby, in the extensive gardens of the museum, stands the Burns Monument. A small building at its base hosts two full-scale sandstone statues of Tam and Souter Johnny, sculpted in 1828 by a local, self-taught stonemason, James Thom. I find the seated figures, which are arranged so that both stare blankly past me into the distance, rather disconcerting. I'm not sure why – I think they remind me of the clay Golem from the silent German expressionist film by Paul Wegener of the same name, a rampaging statue animated by a sixteenth-century Prague rabbi in order to save the Jewish population from the tyranny of Rudolf II (*golem* means 'unformed matter' in Hebrew); I half expect the pair to come to life of an evening when all the visitors have left.

In the 1830s Thom's Tam and Souter Johnny were perhaps the closest visual equivalent to cinema, seemingly capturing the essence of Burns's characters and his poem. They were taken on a tour of Britain that called at Glasgow,

Edinburgh and London, with people paying an entrance
fee to view them. Thom even hired an agent and sent
copies of the figures around the United States, though
none of the profits found their way back to him and he
eventually was forced to take a ship across the Atlantic to
rectify the embezzlement.*

The Bard of Ayrshire was himself long gone by the time
the statues went on their travels, having died in 1796 from
a presumed heart condition. He was thirty-seven. When
his Dumfries grave was opened in 1834 to allow his wife's
body to be placed beside him, casts were made of his skull
– an attempt inspired by the new pseudo-scientific craze of
phrenology to divine the nature of genius from the shape
of a person's head. After the coffin lid was removed, Burns's
body lay, according to John McDiarmid, editor of the
Dumfries Courier, perfectly preserved, 'exhibiting the
features of one who had recently sunk into the sleep of
death'. However, the sight that transfixed all those involved
in the grave's exhumation was short-lived, 'for the instant
the workmen inserted a shell beneath the original wooden
coffin, the head separated from the trunk, and the whole
body, with the exception of the bones, crumbled into dust'.
It's a description reminiscent of the climactic scene of
Nosferatu, F. W. Murnau's 1921 unauthorised reworking of

---

* Thom ended up staying in America, producing more statues,
before carrying out decorative stonework on buildings including
the Gothic Revival Holy Trinity Church in Manhattan – the tallest
building in the country from the time of its completion in 1846
until 1869, but which today is dwarfed by the office blocks of Wall
Street.

Dracula, in which the cadaverous Count Orlok walks into a ray of dawn sunlight and fades away, leaving only a thin wisp of smoke. As has been made clear in 'Tam o' Shanter', earthly delights are transient. One minute we are here and the next we are gone:

> But pleasures are like poppies spread:
> You seize the flower, its bloom is shed …

Three months after visiting Glasgow and its Necropolis I was back in Scotland – or at least in Scottish waters. I was travelling through the Minch, the strait that separates the Highlands and Skye from the Western Isles. It was a mist-filled, mid-March day and occasional clockwork-winged seabirds – black-and-white guillemots or razorbills, it was hard to tell in the poor conditions – beat low across the water, fleeing from the bulk and noise of the cruise ship I was journeying on up to the Faroes and Norway. Now and then I caught a glimpse of land on the horizon, but, staring down into the greyness, I saw no semi-translucent movements among the waves that might have been the Blue-Green Men. These folkloric underwater mermen, fond of rhyming and wordplay, are said to accost fishermen in their boats in this stretch of the Minch; they're wonderfully described in Adam Nicolson's *Sea Room*, his memoir about the tiny Shiant Islands, which sat somewhere in that Hebridean mist.

Further out, eighteen miles into the Atlantic, beyond the obscured mass of Lewis, lay the Flannan Isles – a remote

collection of islets uninhabited since 1971, when the lighthouse was automated. The place is known chiefly for a
still-unsolved mystery that occurred there in December
1900. It was reported by a passing vessel that the light had
gone out – although its continuous warning presence was
the major task of the island's three lighthouse keepers. A
ship was sent to investigate, its crew found the building
(which had only been completed the previous year) empty,
but in good order. No trace of the men was ever discovered, nor anything to explain what had happened, and over
the following years the public developed a growing fascination for the story. Wilfrid Gibson, the Georgian poet
who, along with Walter de la Mare, would become a beneficiary of Rupert Brooke's will, commemorated the incident in his 1912 poem 'Flannan Isle', an imaginative
embellishment of the evidence that added details subsequently fixed as fact – particularly the set dinner table in

the men's living quarters.* Ominously, as the rescue party approaches the 'lonely Isle', the poem's narrator notices 'three queer, black, ugly birds – / Too big, by far, in my belief, / For guillemot or shag'. They plunge from sight as the boat nears, a portent of the scene that will shortly present itself to the searchers. The birds – if they are birds of this world – would seem most likely to be cormorants, like the ill-omened fowl that landed on Boston Stump and foretold the distant death of the town's Member of Parliament aboard the *Lady Elgin*.

A haunted lighthouse also features in the evocatively titled film *Thunder Rock*, a 1942 slice of supernatural British wartime propaganda from the Boulting brothers (who went on to make the classic, though rather different in tone, *Brighton Rock*). Set in the recent past of 1939 on a remote lighthouse in Lake Michigan, *Thunder Rock* centres on its reclusive English keeper, David Charleston, played by Michael Redgrave. Before shutting himself away, Charleston was a campaigning journalist battling to expose the rise of fascism in the Europe of the 1930s. He wrote a well-received book about the subject, *Report from Inside* (which sports a sleeping John Bull on its cover), but became disillusioned with the apathy that greeted the increasingly urgent warnings of his 'Britain Awake' speaking tour, leading him to take refuge in the solitude of

---

* The true fate of the three Flannan Isles keepers was presumably more prosaic – and more poignant – most likely involving them being washed out to sea and drowning during fierce winter storms; I picture them perishing each in turn while trying to come to the aid of their stricken colleagues.

Thunder Rock. He retreats into his imagination, conjuring up half a dozen ghosts whose names are in the log book of the *Land o' Lakes*, a sailing ship that sank – like the *Lady Elgin* – in the lake, and is commemorated with an inscription on the lighthouse's wall that details how the packet struck a nearby reef. Now the structure promises to 'Turn friendly light across these forbidding waters.'

Charleston tries to piece together what caused the various passengers to leave Europe ninety years before, though his early efforts fall short, being a reflection of his own world-weariness. 'These skimpy, bickering characters were not my passengers!' objects the ghost of Captain Joshua Stuart – a sterling performance from the Scottish actor Finlay Currie, who would go on to play Magwitch in David Lean's 1946 adaptation of *Great Expectations*, as well as the dour, but kindly, boatman in Michael Powell and Emeric Pressburger's tribute to the magic of the Hebrides, *I Know Where I'm Going!* In the latter film supernatural weather forces might just be responsible for keeping Wendy Hiller's headstrong Joan Webster and Roger Livesey's Torquil MacNeil together, while a Walter Scott-like curse and a fierce whirlpool, the dreaded Corryvreckan, try to keep them apart.

Michael Powell's first outing as director, 1937's *The Edge of the World*, was inspired by the 1930 evacuation of the last thirty-six residents of St Kilda, fifty miles to the south-west of the Flannan Isles and even further out into the rugged Atlantic. It's a beautiful film of a lost way of life – and lost existences – that early on features a moving sequence as one of the islanders, Andrew (played by Niall

MacGinnis), returns to the place a decade after leaving for what he thought was the final time: the half-faded imprints of his family and friends file past him once again, taking their laboured steps down to the quay. 'The slow shadow of death is falling on the lonely Outer Isles. This is the story of one of them – and all of them.'*

The spirits of *Thunder Rock*, of course, might exist only in Charleston's head – though towards the end of the film when he tries to banish the passengers as figments of his imagination they stubbornly refuse to leave, suggesting they have corporeal substance. The Captain takes on a role similar to Dickens', Ghost of Christmas Past, flitting back to the English Midlands of 1849 to show how one of the doomed immigrants, Briggs, has been worn down by life's hardships in the Potteries, abandoning his children to an uncertain future while he and his wife, who is pregnant again, allow themselves to be cajoled into heading to the New World. The other fellow travellers, like Charleston, have given up their efforts to educate and improve society: we have Ellen Kirby, a Mary Wollstonecraft-like campaigner for women's rights; and Dr Kurtz, whose new-fangled anaesthetics have proved too ahead of their time for Vienna's medical establishment. These phantoms drift around the lighthouse as if it's a stage, highlighting the film's origins as a play. Tragically, they have no

---

* The film wasn't shot on St Kilda, but on the most westerly of the Shetland Isles, Foula. As well as the finished print, Powell also left behind an evocative contemporary account of the filming (in which, memorably, the crew were marooned by October storms), originally published as *200,000 Feet on Foula*.

comprehension that they are dead. Only the Captain knows the truth that all sixty hands perished, and he urges Charleston to see the true meaning in the passengers' spent lives – and to recover a proper purpose for his own. Unlike the lost souls, David has the chance to stop running away, the chance to make a difference.

Later, in the waters north of the Scottish mainland, my ship was to take me in sight of Britain's most isolated, formerly manned lighthouse: Sule Skerry, some thirty-five miles west of Orkney. Barely breaking the waves, the low uninhabited islet is nowadays home only to hordes of seabirds, since the operation of the light was taken out of human hands in 1982. Around a tenth of the UK's breeding puffin population nest here, as do gannets, fulmars, kittiwakes and storm petrels. And although scientists visit the island in the summer months to monitor seabird numbers and ring the chicks, no one comes here at other times, meaning the skerry's undoubted potential as a hotspot for tired spring and autumn migrant songbirds is virtually unknown.

It is this potential for rare birds that draws the narrator of an excellent Algernon Blackwood-esque tale – just as the remote spot calls to me. The Scottish author of the story, John Buchan, is most famous for his novel of adventure and international intrigue set in the months before the First World War, *The Thirty-Nine Steps*. He also wrote a number of supernatural stories that utilised his knowledge of his native landscape and its wildlife, of which 'Skule Skerry' is one of my two favourites – along with 'No Man's

Land', written while Buchan was at university. The latter paints a vision of an ancient stunted race still holding out among the Highland hills that could pass for the work of Arthur Machen.

In Buchan's 'Skule Skerry' the narrator, Mr Anthony Hurrell, a pioneering ornithologist, has come to the fictional Norland Islands, hoping to find a place called the Isle of Birds that is mentioned in the Nordic sagas. He concludes that this must be the remote Skule Skerry, clearly modelled on its near-namesake to the west of Orkney. The local fisherman, John Ronaldson, tasked with dropping off Hurrell for a few days of birdwatching, tries to dissuade him, his warnings of doom at times beginning to sound like John Laurie's Private Frazer from *Dad's Army*. (As a young man Laurie, who was a favourite actor of Michael Powell, starred in *The Edge of the World*, and later had a minor role in *I Know Where I'm Going!*)

'Not Skule Skerry,' he cried. 'What would take ye
there, man? Ye'll get a' the birds ye want on
Halmarsness and a far better bield. Ye'll be blawn away
on the skerry, if the wind rises.'

But Hurrell's mind cannot be altered, even when Ronaldson
lets on that local superstitions lend the place an 'ill name'.
Indeed, if anything, this makes Hurrell keener to visit and
he is dropped off the next afternoon. He has his tent and
enough provisions for a few days' stay – Ronaldson will
pick him up at an arranged time; he does have an emergency flare he can use to summon help if events take a turn
for the worse. The idea of the trip is immediately justified,
because as the ornithologist sits cooking supper on his first
night, scores of migrants – fieldfares, bramblings, buntings,
and various waders – pass close to him in the gloaming.
When he awakes the following morning, however, the
scene outside the canvas is much changed: it is colder and
all the flocks of the previous evening have departed, leaving
behind only a solitary Sabine's gull, a beautiful, rare High
Arctic nester that has come to rest fleetingly on the skerry.
Then comes the arrival of winds that seem preternaturally
strong, like those in Algernon Blackwood's 'The Willows'
(of which the story reminds me); they soon build, lifting
away Hurrell's dinghy and tent, before dying down during
the ensuing, interminable hours. He is overcome by a deadening terror, exacerbated by the increasingly numbing
temperatures; filled with a certainty that 'This island was
next door to the Abyss, and the Abyss was that blanched
world of the North which was the negation of life.'

Finally, Hurrell finds strength to release his flare and muster John Ronaldson to his rescue. Yet under its strange, artificial brightness he sees the arrival of 'someone' from the sea. 'I saw a great dark head like a bull's – an old face wrinkled as if in pain – a gleam of enormous broken teeth – a dripping beard – all formed on other lines than God has made mortal creatures.' And then he passes out, only returning to proper consciousness back in the Norlands several days later, where he wonders if he has seen the legendary Black Silkie that the locals talk about.

The real Sule Skerry has its own version of this legend, 'the Great Silkie of Sule Skerrie'. Silkies (or selkies) are seal beings, not unlike the Blue-Green Men of the Minch, that can remove their outer skins to appear like people. Using this deception the Sule Skerry silkie is said to have made a woman on the coast pregnant, afterwards paying her in gold to raise the child; several archaic songs, the lyrics of which were gathered in the 1850s, retell the tale. In Buchan's story, Hurrell, recovering in bed from his delirium, overhears his rescuer talking to a local farmer about a moribund walrus that came ashore nearby – surely the awful creature he witnessed on the madness-inducing isle.

I too experienced a similar apparition coming out of the waves, as I trudged along Norfolk's Blakeney Point at the end of September 2010. I had made the arduous walk in the afternoon to watch an alder flycatcher, only the second ever to be seen in Britain – an olive-coloured American songbird that had somehow found its way to Britain's east coast in the strong westerly gales we'd been experiencing (it's the sort of vagrant Anthony Hurrell might have dreamt

about prior to visiting his far-flung skerry). The three-mile
trek is hard work at the best of times, as the shingle saps
your strength and the lack of landmarks, particularly if you
follow the beach route, is monotonous and demotivating.
But if you take the more inland path through the tangled,
scratchy *Suaeda* shrubs there is more to look at, including
the Halfway House, which offers a dispiriting indication of
the distance still to go.*

Near the end of the Point I, along with a huddle of
others, watched the flycatcher as it periodically showed

---

* The lonely waypoint, which wears 'an indefinable look of
desertion, as if man had attempted to domesticate himself here
and failed', features as a haunted dwelling in E. F. Benson's
Norfolk-set story 'A Tale of an Empty House'.

itself, taking refuge in the selection of stunted pines and sycamores that make up almost the entirety of the tree cover of this slither of land (a small fenced-off rectangle known, with some overstatement, as 'the Plantation'). The darkness descended rapidly as I made my return and I opted, perhaps in retrospect somewhat foolishly, to walk beside the breaking waves. Foam was carrying far inland – beyond even the Halfway House – but at least the going was easier with the wind behind me.

At some stage a shape drifted out of the whiteness, an immature seal driven in by the force of the storm; on surfacing in such proximity to me it hauled itself hurriedly back out. The waves were striking the shore with a relentless violence, when in front of me lay another,

much larger seal. Only this time one that did not move as I approached.

A dead adult grey, its body mottled and pristine, its skull stripped of skin – a thing like Sule Skerry's Great Silkie. With an unfilled eye that seemed to stare right through me.

As I came alongside the Halfway House – still more than a mile to go in near-darkness – I felt a similar kind of elemental dread to that which overcomes Anthony Hurrell in Buchan's story. When, finally, I reached my car and could take cover from the gale's incessant roar, I phoned my brother. Normally in such circumstances I would have regaled him – 'gripped him off', in birding parlance – about the rarity I'd seen and he 'needed'. Yet the little lost bird paled in comparison to the awesome sublimity of the crashing waves, the shore turned to snow, and the life – and death – that crawled before me from the water.

'It was biblical out there,' I said to him.

Beyond the last static caravan, I take the track to the left that skirts – a little too closely for my liking – the cliff edge.* On the guano-stained rocks below a few pairs of herring gulls are beginning to think about nesting, though no other seabirds are yet present. It's the very end of March and the evening light makes the landscape blush, but offers

---

* As I've grown older my own fear of heights has increased, a trait I share with my father. Since we lived in the flattest part of the country this was not ordinarily a concern. However, on holiday certain routes took on a foreboding mystique in his head, so that he was loath to drive along the dreaded Wrynose Pass when we visited the Lake District, or ascend Exmoor's mighty Porlock Hill.

scant comfort against the biting breeze. A male wheatear, my first of the year, flashes up in front of me from a hollow in the short, rabbit-cropped turf, showing off its rump – the 'white arse' that this long-distance migrant's Middle English name is derived from; the grey-backed songbird will have wintered somewhere south of the Sahara and is now presumably en route inland to the Highlands where it will breed. The land continues to rise before me and I realise I'm heading away from the spot I'm trying to find, so I turn back towards the sun, which is dipping below the Mull of Galloway. Two middle-aged men and a lad wearing a Rangers shirt are having a kickaround on the bleak football pitch. One of them, the boy's father, crosses the ball and the other, the uncle I presume, runs in and jumps to nod it into the netless goal, only for it to skid uncontrollably off his bald patch into the surrounding tall grass, causing them much amusement.

Burrow Head in Dumfries and Galloway. It's an unlikely, end-of-the-world location for a holiday park, anchored miles from anywhere on a treeless promontory overlooking the Irish Sea. It isn't an island, though it feels cut off enough to be, doubling for one in the climactic scene of an iconic work of Scottish cinema. *The Wicker Man* was released in the UK in December 1973, a few days before I was born, and a couple of weeks before Lawrence Gordon Clark's *Lost Hearts* was scaring Christmas television audiences, but it was not until soon after I'd started secondary school that I first watched it, on my aunt and uncle's video recorder.

The Wicker Man is a horror film – at least in a sense – yet it contains no monsters, no ghosts. I don't want to say too much about its plot because if you have seen it you'll already know, and if you haven't then I envy you watching its surprises unfurl for the first time. Essentially, it depicts a clash of beliefs between two opposing faiths that results in a vision of nihilistic, godless indifference. Until that point it doesn't seem a bleak film, but a clever, atmospheric unravelling of a mystery – the disappearance of a young girl, Rowan Morrison, on the fictional Hebridean island of Summerisle, a fecund pagan paradise that benefits from the caress of the Gulf Stream. An island remarkably self-sufficient and cut off from the mainland, until the arrival of Edward Woodward's devout Christian policeman Sergeant Howie.

Robin Redbreast, a seventy-minute TV production, pre-dates *The Wicker Man* by three years, yet shares a similar set-up and sensibilities.* It was written by John Bowen (who adapted the Christmas 1974 version of M. R. James's 'The Treasure of Abbot Thomas') and aired in December 1970 as part of the inaugural season of what would become a landmark BBC drama strand: *Play for Today* ran until 1984, and was responsible for many classics of UK television including Dennis Potter's *Blue Remembered Hills* and Mike Leigh's *Abigail's Party*. It also gave us a number of now-seminal works that explore the eerie.

---

* Although *The Wicker Man*'s scriptwriter Anthony Shaffer never mentioned having seen *Robin Redbreast*, it's tempting to imagine it had some influence – the BBC play explicitly references the Scottish anthropologist Sir James George Frazer's 1890 study of ancient pagan cults and rituals, *The Golden Bough*, which Shaffer used in his research for the film.

Notably, in addition to *Robin Redbreast* we have, from 1974, *Penda's Fen*. Set in the shadow of the Malvern Hills, the play's landscape shares little with my Lincolnshire upbringing beyond the 'Fen' of its title. It was directed by Alan Clarke, feted for gritty social realism like the borstal-based *Scum*. Scripted by David Rudkin (who went on to adapt M. R. James's 'The Ash Tree', the 1975 'Ghost Story for Christmas'), this is very different in tone – lyrical, intense and strange. At its heart is Stephen, recently turned eighteen and coming to the end of his stuffy grammar school education, who is trying to make sense of himself and the world through visions of demons, angels and the ghosts of Edward Elgar and Penda – the last pagan king of England. With its complex concerns about society and class, sexual identity, religious faith, and perhaps above all, its search for answers about what it means to be English, *Penda's Fen* carries enormous current cultural relevance.

I visit the small village where most of the play was filmed – Chaceley, part-way between Gloucester and Worcester – two weeks after coming to Scotland. When I arrive, the scene is like the beginning of *The Children of Green Knowe*, with several of the roads into the village flooded. I recognise a couple of buildings used as locations, including the Church of St John the Baptist. I unlatch its heavy, stiff door to be greeted by a circling black-winged apparition: a jackdaw that has been trapped inside for an unknowable measure of time. For the next few minutes I try to coax the bird out – fortunately it doesn't take long, unlike a marooned pigeon or sparrow, for it to spot the gap of daylight and head for freedom. Relieved, I sit down at the same organ where Stephen practises Elgar's *Dream of Gerontius*, trying to recreate one of the play's most striking sequences.

And I wait. Wait for a fissure to open up in the floor of the nave – or for the crucified Christ to speak.

At seventy minutes in length *Robin Redbreast* is only fourteen minutes shorter than the UK theatrical release of its better-known Scottish counterpart, *The Wicker Man*, though the difference in the look of the two could not be more different. *Robin Redbreast* was shot in grainy black

and white, and takes place largely in and around a single location, adding to its sense of claustrophobia.*

After the jaunty *Play for Today* credits the mood is set by the sound of the menacing, whistling wind that plays over a still photograph of a shabby cottage with boarded windows. 'That's the before picture,' says television-script editor Norah Palmer, as she chats to two of her middle-class London friends, Madge and Jake. We learn she's recently broken up with her boyfriend and is moving to a remote place in the Midlands that was meant to have been their bolthole. The same background wind is present more or less throughout, heightening our sense of unease as we try to work out what the busybody housekeeper Mrs Vigo, who's always there with a handy piece of local lore, and, in particular, the learned village elder Fisher – who manages to make the wearing of glasses the epitome of sinister – are planning. On a weekend visit Jake attempts to put Norah off the cottage and hasten her return to the city by delivering a dramatic monologue about the breeze that blows outside, a speech that holds more truth than he knows: 'Comes down the hills through the trees. Comes down that nasty little private road of yours, whipping in and out of the potholes. And you hear the voices. Drunken voices, singing. Shouting things. Frightened women. A child …'

'I don't hear any such thing,' Norah replies, unconvincingly.

---

* Even though *The Wicker Man* was made on a modest budget for a cinema feature – said to be around £335,250 – its resources still dwarfed those of a British television drama.

A supposed infestation of mice in the cottage roof leads Norah, at the insistence of Mrs Vigo, to seek the services of the handsome Rob, a young, ripped gamekeeper in his twenties ('If you've got vermin, Rob's your man'). Norah sees him practising karate outside his house in the woods – he's wearing only his underpants and attacking a bare tree trunk with comic ferocity. She has a short-lived fling with him, but realises they have little in common besides their mutual physical attraction – and the pregnancy she is left with. Events subsequently take a turn reminiscent of *Rosemary's Baby*, though not perhaps quite in the way the viewer would guess.*

The programme's enigmatic final shot, in which Norah, like Lot's wife, looks back as she is driving off, shows the four principal villagers standing in a line outside the cottage. To begin with they are wearing their normal, everyday clothes, but when she stops for a last glance they've been transformed: the two hefty labourers now in archaic overalls, Mrs Vigo a witchlike black cape, and Fisher as a kind of stag-horned Herne the Hunter. It's the perfect ending to this most sinister of dramas, which, despite its grainy footage, and being almost fifty years old, seems hardly to have dated.

Leaving aside its obvious parallels with *Robin Redbreast*, what makes *The Wicker Man* stand out from other horror films of the time? (Its high-profile contemporaries include

---

* Roman Polanski's satanic 1968 film is another I first watched at far too young an age.

The Exorcist and *Don't Look Now* – it was even shown as part of a double bill with the latter.) To begin with it's much less polished, probably a result of having a debut feature-film director, Robin Hardy (he'd previously made television commercials), at the helm; I think the resultant idiosyncrasies add to its atmosphere. Above all, *The Wicker Man* is imbued with the folklore and rituals that dominate the lives of the islanders. From the children's maypole and stone circle dances to the creepy costumes of the hobby horse procession, which culminates in a druidic vision similar to that laid down by Julius Caesar in his account of the Gauls ('Others have figures of vast size, the limbs of which formed of osiers they fill with living men'), this is a film steeped in the land and a mythic past. Which is partly why it is now regarded as one of the three cornerstones of the 'folk horror' sub-genre, along with two other movies from the era, both set in England, *The Blood on Satan's Claw* and *Witchfinder General*.*

Folk horror is a difficult term to pin down, but seems to have first been used (at least in cinematic terms, as there are a couple of earlier art-criticism references) by Piers Haggard, the director of *The Blood on Satan's Claw*, in a 2003 magazine interview. Tellingly, Haggard has also commented on how he tried to bring 'the sense of the soil' into the picture – something he manages literally in the

---

* Interestingly, in *Witchfinder General* no black magic or signs of the supernatural are on display, just the eerie East Anglian landscape and a surfeit of sadism. The horrors of *The Wicker Man* are entirely the result of human agency too, though this certainly isn't the case in *The Blood on Satan's Claw* ...

opening scene, where a seventeenth-century ploughman notices a flock of doves and a solitary carrion crow picking at an object in one of the furrows of the field; on closer inspection he sees a worm-ridden human-like eyeball in an exposed skull, along with several unidentifiable clumps of fur in the surrounding dirt. More recently, the writer and actor Mark Gatiss in his 2010 BBC documentary series *A History of Horror* gave the following definition, which would seem a good starting point:

> From the late sixties a new generation of British directors avoided the Gothic clichés by stepping even further away from the modern world. Amongst these are a loose collection of films which we might call 'folk horror'. They shared a common obsession with the British landscape, its folklore and superstitions.

Today, we seem to have reached a moment where society is increasingly attempting to find comfort in the simplicity and certainties of the past – Christopher Lee's Lord Summerisle might even say the people have been roused from their apathy and are returning to old gods. Unsettling works that hark back to or evoke an earlier pastoral era, or esoteric traditional country beliefs, are once again in vogue. It's tempting to wonder whether folk horror films awaken within us cultural memories of these imagined former times. However, I think much of their current power and relevance comes from their portrayal of the manipulative forces of authority, which use individuals (such as Howie or Norah) as unwitting participants in their schemes.

Schemes that themselves, we realise, are ultimately futile and doomed to failure.

The thing that, to me, most separates *The Wicker Man* from its contemporaries (and more recent admirers) is its soundtrack.* It's practically a musical in the way that key scenes involve songs, though that's not to say other films in the genre don't also use their scores to great effect. In particular, *The Blood on Satan's Claw* has a sometimes beautiful, sometimes sinister Vaughan Williams-like orchestral accompaniment by the composer Marc Wilkinson, which utilises a discordant, descending 'Devil's interval' (or 'tritone') refrain. In *The Wicker Man*, however, the song interludes are a deliberate part of the script, a quick means of avoiding long blocks of exposition about the unconventional lifestyle of the islanders. They could be considered a little jarring – they're certainly not for every-one – yet are probably my favourite ingredient. Interestingly, the man behind these traditional-sounding tunes was a young American, Paul Giovanni, with no experience of having scored a film before; in an odd coincidence, he met with and was advised by Marc Wilkinson on how to go about the task. The musicians, who are billed as 'Magnet', were also not an actual, established folk group, but six youthful session players, recent graduates from London music schools.

---

* Recent examples of films often bracketed as 'folk horror' include the New England-set *The Witch* (2015), and Ben Wheatley's disconcerting *A Field in England* (2013), which features an alchemist and dark magic at the heart of its psychedelic portrayal of a fractured land haunted by the spectre of the Civil War.

'The Landlord's Daughter' is a bawdy number based on an authentic eighteenth-century ballad that is performed in the aptly named Green Man inn shortly after Sergeant Howie turns up for the first time – the overdubbed Swedish actress Britt Ekland is the song's object of desire. 'Cornrigs and Barleyrigs', which appears over the end of the opening titles, has an original tune but takes the words to a song, 'The Rigs o' Barley', which Robert Burns himself had adapted from a ballad at least a century old at the time ('It was upon a Lammas night, / When corn rigs are bonie ...'). Likewise, the lyrics of three traditional pieces were melded together into 'Gently Johnny', a song about desire used to show the sergeant's inner conflict as he prays to God while trying to rise above Summerisle's worldly temptations (the scene was cut from the theatrical release but restored to the later 'Final' and 'Director's' cuts).* Similar in spirit is 'Willow's Song', in which the naked Britt Ekland (and her body double) ratchets up the virginal Howie's torment as she sensually knocks on the wall of his bedroom – this must be one of the few horror films where a character is punished for not acquiescing to their sexual desires.

The one jarring musical note (apart perhaps from Diane

---

* The butchering and reordering of the original script has generated much debate, including Allan Brown's book *Inside The Wicker Man*, which tells in detail the convoluted story of the film's genesis, production, and fitful forays into cinema theatres on the way to achieving cult-classic status. Despite enjoying the individual scenes subsequently restored to these longer edits, I still find that on balance – though Christopher Lee would not agree – I prefer the more enigmatic tone of the shorter version.

Cilento's vocals on her duet with Christopher Lee) is an ill-judged piece of seventies funk that sounds more like something off the soundtrack of *Get Carter* and which accompanies Howie, fittingly dressed as the Fool, as he ascends the path above the cave near the film's end. The scene was shot just a mile and a half around the coast from Burrow Head, at St Ninian's Cave – tradition has it that the recess in the cliffs was used by the saint as a place of personal prayer. Ninian is the first recognised Christian missionary to Scotland, though little is known about the life of the man said to have built, *c.* AD 397, in the vicinity of nearby Whithorn, perhaps the earliest church in Scotland. (Whithorn was also a location for several scenes from *The Wicker Man*, including Howie's visit to the library, where his comprehension of the islanders' pagan beliefs and rites becomes solidified.)

Little appears to have changed at the cave in the four and a half decades since filming took place – the scene looks barely different to that in the movie where the islanders pour ale into the sea as an offering, and where the sergeant breaks his cover to rescue Rowan Morrison. I approach via the inland route, which takes me through a tree-lined valley more akin to Cornwall's Land's End peninsula than somewhere I'd expect to find in Scotland; halfway along, a hare streaks up the bank on the opposite side of the swift-moving stream, which seems fitting given the abundance of hare imagery and motifs that occur throughout the film. Emerging abruptly onto the beach it's a long walk across flattened over-sized stones before I reach the sheltered, half-hidden hole. If I were from Summerisle I might well see the cave – with its vagina-like cleft recessed into the rocks of its back wall – as some sort of monument to fertility. In fact, here on the real mainland, paganism

doesn't seem to be obviously on display; this is still an active site of Christian pilgrimage, a shrine to the enigmatic St Ninian. Crossed pieces of driftwood tied together with washed-up lengths of blue binding twine are stacked inside – some with accompanying messages ('May there always be an angel by your side') – or placed prominently on the cliffs above.

They remind me of the makeshift symbols a vampire-hunter in a horror film might employ as an ineffective last-ditch measure.

Beyond the football pitch at Burrow Head the land slides towards the sea. The cliffs at this point are more stunted, and at my feet I find what I've been searching for – the final visible remnant of the film's production. Two tree trunks protrude above a rough base of weathered concrete that bubbles over the grass like cooled lava. Almost illegible is the date, 1972, drawn in with a stick at the time the concrete was poured. These sorry-looking stubs were once the supports of the secondary wicker man statue that was built here, using woven hurdles like those you can buy in any garden centre, for close-up cutaways – and the film's fortuitously captured end sequence where the figure's head drops off to reveal the flaming, setting sun behind. The primary structure, thirty-six feet high, was constructed further back on higher ground (I later think I have located the flattened area on which it was situated, though cannot be entirely sure I'm in the exact spot).

The mess before me now is not much of a monument – the two wooden stumps previously rose to around four feet in height, before, in 2006, souvenir hunters chain-sawed them away as illicit keepsakes. But these rotten remains do at least provide a tangible memento of the long-ago production.

Driving back, I pass through Wigtown, designated in 1998 as Scotland's official 'National Book Town', home to an annual literary festival and a variety of second-hand bookshops strung along its grey-stoned high street. At the edge of the town lies its wide bay. A couple of white-faced barnacle geese are feeding out on the saltings, a tiny fraction of the entire 35,000-strong population that breeds in the Arctic archipelago of Svalbard and winters around the Solway Firth. The twelfth-century *Topographica Hibernica*, written by the Welsh cleric Giraldus Cambrensis,

maintains that these geese, which he had observed on a visit to Ireland, grew out of some kind of seashell (hence their name). It's a belief that persisted widely until the seventeenth century, and even later in some parts of County Kerry – though there it was likely a knowing way of continuing to eat meat during Lent, by taking advantage of the birds' supposed maritime origins.

A boardwalk leads across the *merse* – the grass and marshland – of the bay. The tide's out, but I can see that at high water it would inundate the surrounding vegetation. In times past the River Bladnoch scored a deep channel through the marsh. It was into this mud, in May 1685, that two local women, sixty-three-year-old Margaret McLachlan and eighteen-year-old Margaret Wilson – painted two centuries later as a beautiful Pre-Raphaelite redhead by John Everett Millais – were tied to stakes and left to drown.

Their 'crime' was that they were so-called Covenanters – a movement engaged in a nearly fifty-year struggle to maintain Presbyterianism as Scotland's sole form of religion. The consequences for those caught up in the Galloway protests had a brutal conclusion: you know that events will not end well in a period (which finally concluded in 1688) labelled 'the Killing Time'. A granite stake by the narrow dyke of the channel roughly marks the spot where the two women – the 'Wigtown Martyrs' – were executed, an event that's every bit the equal of the pointless cruelty carried out in *The Wicker Man* or *Robin Redbreast* in order to appease a god of the harvest, or enacted in *Witchfinder General* by Vincent Price's archly misogynistic hammer of witches, Matthew Hopkins.

Set against the acts we inflict upon each other, or the things that cause us harm over which we have no control, the horrors of fiction and film feel inconsequential.

Next day I stop off at nearby Creetown. Here, the interior of the Ellangowan Hotel was used as the bar of the Green Man, though it's hard to see any vestigial resemblance on my brief visit; an unpromising sign pasted to the door warns that there's 'No food available until April 9th', making me wonder whether the harvest has finally failed.

I move on to Gatehouse of Fleet, where the white-walled estate offices doubled as the exterior of the inn. Finding locations from the production is becoming addictive. I worry that visiting these places will shatter the spell, but it doesn't seem to be the case – if anything it makes me more appreciative of how the film was put together, of how the topography of such a convincing fictional island was conjured from these disparate mainland sites. I end up further up the coast – back in Burns's Ayrshire – at the grand Culzean Castle, which functioned as the outside of Lord Summerisle's ancestral home. Then down along the deceptively distant Rhins of Galloway peninsula to Logan Botanic Gardens, whose tropical palm trees were used to illustrate the island's surprising floral bounty. At last to Anwoth, the hamlet that provided Summerisle's graveyard.

Barring Burrow Head, Anwoth's Old Kirk is, for me, the most evocative of all the locations from the film. It's reminiscent of Alloway, with a roofless ruin, and similarly grand headstones bedecked with lichen and moss. The setting

though is far lonelier, with just a scattering of nearby residences, including the old schoolhouse opposite the
entrance gate – a holiday home that reclaimed its original
role during the packed seven-week shoot. Inside, Howie
questions the children about Rowan but is met with a
unanimous denial of her existence. He's drawn to the
empty desk in the centre of the classroom and opens its lid,
hopeful perhaps of some evidence of the girl. Within, a
beetle is tethered by a piece of black thread to a nail. It
moves in a continuous anti-clockwise circle; eventually the
poor old thing will become trapped up tight to the nail, a
dark-haired girl in pigtails explains.

'Poor old thing! Then why in God's name do you do it,
girl?' is the sergeant's outraged response. And he's right –
to me this remains one of the most chilling and memorable
sequences of the film: an odd forewarning of the callous
indifference to come.

There is no maypole standing by the wall as I pass
through the kirkyard gate, no singing children. It's virtually
silent. No noise of traffic, just distant birdsong punctured
by the insistent monosyllabic call of a great spotted woodpecker that passes overhead and lands in a birch on the
gorse-covered hillside that rises from the boggy depression
away at the rear. Six sizeable yews, ambiguous symbols of
both death and resurrection (and also thought to possess
properties that ward off the Devil), tower over the graves.
I come across a table-like slab dedicated to the memory of
a murdered Covenanter:

Here lyes John Bell of Whitesyde who was
barbourously shot to death in the paroch of Tongland
at the command of Grier of Lag anno 1685. This
monument shall tell posterity that Blessed Bell of
Whytesyde here doth ly.

I enter inside the walls of the tumbledown church, where
Sergeant Howie places an improvised wooden cross, like
those I saw earlier at St Ninian's Cave, on the redundant
altar. Next to him an islander breastfeeds her baby, her
outstretched left palm balancing a bird's egg as part of an
esoteric fertility ritual. At least one of the headstones in
the film was a prop – there is no grave of Beech Buchanan
'protected by the ejaculation of serpents' – but the distinctive skull and crossbones of the *memento mori* on the large

tomb in the centre of the hollow-skied nave is present. The exhumation of Rowan was carried out in this place too. On that icy-cold October evening the stoic crew were no doubt mindful of the words carved above the locked door-way of the mausoleum beside the ruin: 'Until the day break, and the shadows flee away.'

Before I leave Galloway I call in at Kirkcudbright. With its attractive whitewashed houses and narrow passage-ways, the small town is where many of Summerisle's village scenes were filmed. (The pretty harbour where Howie lands his seaplane, however, is at Plockton – 180 miles to the north, on the west coast of the mainland across from Skye.)

Kirkcudbright was also home to Edward Atkinson Hornel, one of the 'Glasgow Boys', an impressionistic Scottish art movement at the end of the nineteenth century – albeit a loose one – that was a precursor to modernism. From the 1880s and into the twentieth century the town became something of an artists' colony in the mould of Newlyn or St Ives: its residents included E. A. Taylor and his wife, the illustrator Jessie King, while other painters such as George Henry were frequent visitors. The gaudy palette, in particular of Hornel's oils, many of which are on display in his impressive residence, Broughton House, seem in stark contrast to the muted colours of the early spring country-side I passed through on the way from Burrow Head.

In the tourist office I get into a conversation with the friendly woman who works there about why I'm in the area. 'Have you not seen him yet?' she asks. 'I've had a few visitors coming in saying he's out on the main road out past Dundrennan, past the Abbey.'

'Who do you mean?'

'The Wicker Man! We used to have the Wickerman music festival out there in the summer, you see. But it's not run now for the last few years. They've still got his statue

though. He's in a field on the left once you're out of the village. You'll not miss him.'

As it isn't much of a detour from my route home, of course I go and look. And indeed there he is, rising more than twenty feet in height, the wicker gatekeeper that greeted the visiting crowds.* It doesn't at all resemble the squared-off structure of the film, but is like some sinuous, faceless elemental guardian that might inhabit the depths of an Algernon Blackwood story.

I have come of my own free will to the appointed place. The game's over.

---

* Each year, another even larger statue was set alight on the Saturday evening of The Wickerman Festival. This one remains as a testament to the now-lost event.

Chapter 6

BORDERLAND

The shore he used to look out across, over which he would sometimes walk, shimmers through the glass. Perhaps this was even the room in which he wrote – it's said he preferred to work at night – though I'd hazard that would have been up on the third floor. The great boulders of the wall that form a defensive line before the blue would not have stood there in his time, being added in 2011. Beyond them the beach is starkly demarcated, the rounded stones of grey shingle replaced with light-brown sand that, from the photograph I have seen of him promenading, appears more in keeping with how he would have known it. In the picture he stands in the foreground, this side of his bonnet-clad favourite sister, Lissie, almost as if they are joined at the shoulder. He is looking into the distance, out to sea, his mouth slightly agape in a smirk, his hands in his pockets. He is dark haired and tanned, and at five foot four and a half is only just taller than her, but undoubtedly he is handsome; by all accounts he was a hit with the young women of the village.

Bookcases fill two walls of the room, a mixture of titles stretching from floor to ceiling. Proust's *Remembrance of Things Past* sits alongside Joyce's *Ulysses*, and in turn the pair are sited above a shelf containing the poetry of R. S. Thomas and texts on the history of art. A rugby match – I have no idea which teams are involved – is playing out

silently on the television that stands on a low occasional
table in front of the window. I had doubted whether I
would be able to find this place: the Welsh house in which
one of the greatest English writers of weird fiction wrote a
significant amount of his work, including my favourite of
his four novels, *The House on the Borderland*. Like many
details about this author's life, the exact timing of when
and where he worked on each of his books is subject to
debate, though it seems he was living here during the book's
completion and publication. This much we know, because
he signs and dates his name below the introduction to *The
House on the Borderland*'s mysterious manuscript:

> William Hope Hodgson
> 'Glaneifion,' Borth, Cardiganshire,
> December 17, 1907

I had arrived sometime after lunch in the likeable coastal
resort of Borth, a few miles north of Aberystwyth. It's
mid-April and, after a harsh winter, feels like the first
proper day of spring – the sun finally has some warmth to
share, which is an unfamiliar feeling. After squeezing my
car into one of the few available spaces, conveniently next
to a pleasant-looking café, I take advantage of the weather
and buy an ice cream: a local flavour whose unlikely name,
'Squirrel', appeals – it's actually crème brûlée and is good.
I expect the ad-hoc mission I've given myself – to see if I
can find William Hope Hodgson's house – will prove fruitless, as in the century that has passed I'm sure names are
bound to have changed. I do know, however, that the

Hodgsons' accommodation had its back to the sea, so I concentrate on that side.

I've just started into my ice cream and crossed the road and there, directly in front of me, it is – a quest that has taken less than a minute. Glaneifion. The name, I am to learn from the house's present owner, Anthony, has its own mythic connotations and loosely translates as 'Eifion's shore'. Eifion, it is said, was the grandson of Cunedda, one of the earliest founders of the Gwynedd dynasties – a great chieftain who was brought down from Scotland to North Wales to help defend the region from Irish invaders around the fifth century. It seems a suitably poetic epigraph for the place.

An attractive three-storey villa, Glaneifion has a claret-coloured door and windows. Its dark exterior has a mottled appearance, as if capillaries flow beneath its surface. There is nothing to confirm this is where Hodgson lived on and off between 1904 and the end of 1910, and where in earlier summers his family holidayed. But it feels right. I stare at the building and wonder if I should knock, though as I'm still scoffing my ice cream, which is doing its best to drip down my shirt, I figure I'll take a walk first. A passageway bisects the terrace a few doors down and I emerge from shadow onto the upper beach, which resembles the familiar shingle shorelines of my native East Anglia – only here the pebbles are much larger and flatter. I'm not sure whether I will be able to work out which is Glaneifion from this new angle, but it's instantly obvious. Four figures sit at the boundary of its garden, overlooking the glinting sea; I decide to wander to the shoreline before accosting them.

William Hope Hodgson was born in November 1877 in the Essex village of Blackmore End, a few miles north of Braintree and thirty miles south of where M. R. James grew up. Like James, Hodgson's father was a curate, though there the comparisons stop, as the Reverend Samuel Hodgson was an unorthodox character prone to disagreements with his superiors, which led to him being posted to various disparate parishes around the country. William Hope Hodgson – known to his family as Hope, to distinguish him from his well-to-do tailor grandfather – was the second of twelve children, three of whom (all of them boys) were to perish before reaching the age of two.

Unlike James, and unlike his parents, the young Hope showed an aversion to organised religion, though a spiritual element is present in his second novel *The House on the Borderland* (published in 1908), and his final full-length work *The Night Land* from four years later. The earlier book is ostensibly set around an otherworldly mansion located 'some forty miles distant' from Ardrahan on the west coast of Ireland's County Galway, the place where the Reverend Hodgson was exiled as a missionary in 1887. There he was charged with converting the local Catholics to Protestantism, an exercise doomed to failure as the resident population resented the presence of an Anglican English family in the Old Rectory, out of sight and apart from the village like the titular house of the novel, down a lengthy drive encased by vast orchards. These same expansive surroundings, in which the unruly Hope once spent several days stuck up a tree he had climbed – he was fed and sustained by the family's servants before he finally descended – were stripped of their fruit by the villagers as tensions between the two strands of Christianity came to a head, resulting in the Hodgsons' return to England.

There, in 1890, they settled in the northern industrial heartland of Blackburn. Late the following year, Hope, aged thirteen, ran away properly after a ratcheting up of the friction between father and son, signing on for a four-year apprenticeship as a cabin boy in the Mercantile Navy, which paved the way for a further stint of similar length as a seaman. By the time Hope came back from sea in 1898 – a spell that was to have a profound influence on his first works of weird fiction – his father had long departed, a victim at the age of forty-six of cancer of the neck or throat. This, it has been speculated – though the claim sounds spurious to me – resulted from the tight dog collars the Reverend Hodgson was forced to wear. His death plunged the family into several years of financial hardship alleviated only by the passing of Hope's wealthy grandfather and namesake.

After his return to Blackburn, Hope opened 'W. H. Hodgson's School of Physical Culture' during the second half of 1899. His early gymnasium apparently proved popular with the local police force, running for the next few years and perhaps right up until he moved to Borth in 1904. Hodgson also wrote various articles for national magazines on 'scientific exercises' – as a result of his short stature he had long been conscious of the importance of building his own strength, and prided himself on his physical prowess. In October 1902 he was involved in an extraordinary incident in the Lancashire town's history, when the American escapologist (and later debunker of fraudulent mediums), Harry Houdini, visited:

> Mr W. H. Hodgson, principal of the Blackburn School
> of Physical Culture, took up the challenge issued by
> Houdini, the 'Handcuff King' who engaged to forfeit
> £25 to the infirmary if he failed to free himself from
> any irons placed upon him.

Far from delivering good publicity for Hodgson's gym, the
episode proved shambolic. Houdini struggled for over
three-quarters of an hour to loosen himself from irons
supplied by Hodgson that the showman claimed had been
tampered with; over the noise of the increasingly vocal
crowd Hodgson was overheard to say: 'If Houdini is beaten
then let him give in.' Hodgson left the theatre before the
end of the performance, having being ordered home by a
police sergeant who was fearful that a dangerous public
disturbance might result. Addressing the audience when
he finally freed himself, Houdini stated that in fourteen
years he had 'never been so brutally treated'.

I perch on the seaward side of the new defences that have
allowed this fragile stretch of coastline to evade the worst
ravages of the waves for the past six years – enormous
boulders shipped in from Norway that already are dotted
with barnacles. I watch as a herring gull picks lethargically
at the gouged-out shell of a crab near the water, and can't
help wondering whether I have been here before, whether
it is possible we visited on our 1978 Snowdonia family
holiday – because I possess unlabelled photos of my
brother and me on a not dissimilar beach from that trip. I
have no way now of knowing – and there must be other

Welsh resorts that fit the bill – but still, it does not seem impossible.

Offshore, long inundated by the waves, is said to lie the lost land of Gwaelod, a kind of Welsh Atlantis that dominates the final part of Susan Cooper's *Dark is Rising* sequence – *Silver on the Tree*, to me the least satisfying of

the five fantasy books I loved so much as a boy. The
stronger, more atmospheric and landscape-rooted fourth
book in the series, *The Grey King*, is set just a few miles
away in the valleys inland from Aberdyfi, and around the
regal mountain of Cader Idris.

A light turquoise post that rises fifteen feet from the
sand is plastered up to its high-tide mark with seaweed and
a skin of encrusted shells, reminding me of Hodgson's
sea-based strange fiction. In addition to various short stories
he also wrote two novels of maritime horrors. His first
book, *The Boats of the 'Glen Carrig'*, published in 1904, is
an adventure in which the weed-choked Sargasso Sea

harbours all sorts of marine monstrosities, giant crabs, abandoned hulks, and peculiar islands; *The Ghost Pirates*, which came out five years later, features supernatural (perhaps even inter-dimensional) beings that haunt the high seas, and is to my mind the superior work as it manages to retain its ominous, claustrophobic atmosphere throughout. I first read many of these tales on that cruise through Scottish waters, periodically lifting my eyes from the pages to scan for whales, which added to the experience of reading about Hodgson's grotesque krakens – like Herman Melville and Joseph Conrad before him, he drew on his own first-hand nautical knowledge to confer authenticity upon his writing.

Hodgson's finest short sea-set tale of the fantastic, 'The Voice in the Night', was published in the November 1907 edition of the *Blue Book Magazine*. In it, the lone sailor awake on the deck of a fishing schooner 'becalmed in the Northern Pacific' – the story's narrator, George – is shocked by a voice that drifts upwards out of the blackness. The occupant of the unseen rowing boat, who claims to be an old man, insists that George and his now-alert crewman stop shining the beam of their lamp out onto the waters. He asks, in 'a voice curiously throaty and inhuman', for food to take to his starving female companion, who is waiting on a nearby island. In an act of kindness the two sailors float a box of provisions to him, which the old man gratefully receives. Later, still under the cover of darkness, the speaker returns alongside, and tells the men the story of how, some four months previous, he and his fiancée – he is not, it transpires, old – were abandoned by the crew of their doomed vessel the *Albatross*, before they managed to construct a raft and escape. Days afterwards the pair found a deceptive haven in a lagoon housing a ship shrouded in a 'grey, lichenous fungus' that also covered the entire island.

'The Voice in the Night' is an intense, powerful work about infection and altered bodily states; most certainly, the couple 'suffer a sea-change, into something rich and strange' that would make Ariel in *The Tempest* – or the film director David Cronenberg – proud. The moment the fiancée discovers the beginnings of the thing that will consume her is horrifying and resonant: 'It was on the thumb of her right hand that the growth first showed. It was only a small circular spot, much like a little grey mole. My God! how the fear leapt to my heart when she showed me the place.'

Hodgson's story spawned two of its own on-screen adaptations: an episode of the 1958 US television series *Suspicion*, and, very loosely, the 1963 Japanese horror movie *Matango*. Released in the States the following year as *Attack of the Mushroom People*, the film was nearly banned in Japan as some of the facial disfigurements it depicts – presumably the more subtle effects revealed in the film's denouement – were said to bear an unnerving resemblance to those of survivors of the atomic bombs dropped on Hiroshima and Nagasaki.

I crunch up the shingle to the back of Glaneifion, where now just three people – a middle-aged couple and a woman – are enjoying the spring sunshine at the boundary of beach and garden. 'Sorry to disturb you,' I ask, 'I was wondering if you knew whether an Edwardian writer used to live in this house ...'

'Do you mean William Hope Hodgson?' the woman replies, and I nod, surprised. 'My husband's who you want to speak with. He's watching the rugby at the minute – are you around this evening?'

'I've got to head up the coast later, but it'd be good to talk to him.'

'Hang on. I'll go see.' She heads inside and I'm left chatting to the couple who, I work out, must be friends of the owners here on a visit.

'Who's this author?' they ask me, and I reel off more detail than they require, eulogising about *The House on the Borderland* until the woman re-emerges with her husband, a man I'd guess is in his early sixties, with shoulder-length, silvery-grey hair and thick white eyebrows. He greets me with a smile and asks me to follow him inside.

'I'm Anthony,' he says, and as we climb the stairs I thank him, apologising for disturbing his rugby viewing.

'Don't worry, it isn't much of a match.'

I explain what I'm doing and Anthony wonders whether I have all of Hodgson's books – in the brief period before my entrance he's already gathered a collection of lurid 1970s and 80s paperbacks in a pile on the floor of the lounge. He gestures to the sofa and then disappears to fetch more ephemera. And I am sitting alone in this room overlooking the beach and it's so exciting and unexpected to be here that I half expect time to start cascading forwards and back as it does in *The House on the Borderland*. I realise that in just a few days it will be the centenary of when Hope was lost: 19 April 1918 (though like most things with Hodgson even this date is not clear-cut, as official contemporary reports erroneously stated the seventeenth was the day of his death).

My host returns with various items of correspondence, including from R. Alain Everts, an American who compiled one of the few biographical pieces on Hodgson. There are also the transcribed reminiscences of a neighbour of Hope's mother and sister from when they relocated a mile inland to their newly built hillside residence called Lisswood –

Hope visited the pair there when he was on leave from the war. Anthony tells me that despite being from Borth, he hadn't heard of Hodgson when he moved back to the village twenty-two years ago. But afterwards people would keep mentioning that they were in the house where William Hope Hodgson used to live, and although Anthony wasn't a particular fan of horror or science fiction he searched out and bought all of his books. Since then, a few waifs and strays like me have swept up unannounced, including, once, two Americans. Probably because of the posthumous praise accorded to Hodgson by H. P. Lovecraft, and later, August Derleth, who reissued his works under his Arkham House imprint, Hodgson enjoys a much higher profile in the States than in his native Britain.

Anthony asks if I'm familiar with the region, and I admit I'm not. Just behind the village there's a flat amphitheatre-like area of bog, not unlike the topography of 'the Plain' that features so strikingly in *The House on the Borderland*. After a pint or two in the pub, Anthony says, talk sometimes turns to whether it was Hodgson's inspiration for his novel's enigmatic arena. And in February 2014 this wild expanse at the back of Borth was temporarily transformed into a Hodgson-esque vision of hell, when a peat fire engulfed the land.*

---

* Other commentators have speculated whether the cascading waterfalls, narrow gorge and deep potholes at Devil's Bridge, sixteen miles to the south-east of the village – the 'dread chasm' commemorated by William Wordsworth in his poem 'To the Torrent at the Devil's Bridge, North Wales, 1824' – formed the blueprint for 'the Pit' that dominates the first half of the book.

The strangeness of *The House on the Borderland* has stayed with me ever since I first read it a few years ago, and I still can't quite believe I'm in the place where Hodgson signed off its introduction under his guise of editor of a mysterious handwritten journal that had come into his possession. Apart from his brief overview and a few foot-notes, we have no more interventions from Hodgson; in the atmospheric prologue, we learn of the manuscript's discovery from our initial narrator, a Victorian gentleman tourist, Berreggnog, who is on a fishing trip to the west of Ireland with his equally oddly named companion Tonnison. Having arrived the previous evening at the nearest train station of Ardrahan – the Galway village to which Hodgson and his family were sent – the two men travel all of the next day, some forty miles over rugged tracks, before they reach the fictional hamlet of Kraighten. 'Far around there spreads a waste of bleak and totally inhospitable country; where, here and there at great intervals, one may come upon the ruins of some long desolate cottage – unthatched and stark.'

Kraighten, where the locals speak only Gaelic, is not depicted on any maps, which should serve as a warning. Neither is the village's fast-flowing river, which Tonnison discovered on a walking tour the previous year, noting that it looked to offer decent fishing for a future angling holi-day. Exploring downstream, the two men find that its waters disappear abruptly into the ground, emerging more than a mile away in a spray-filled chasm concealed in a long-overgrown area of gardens and orchards. An arm of rock projects above this abyss – 'the Pit' – holding the faintest traces of an ancient house, in which Tonnison uncovers the manuscript. As the pair explore the domain they hear a foreboding wailing from among the crowded fruit trees, causing them to hurry back to their camp; they vow never to return to the malevolent vicinity. Over supper in their tent Berreggnog reads aloud from the dusty, part-illegible book, and it is this narrative that fills the remainder of the novel's pages, save for a short concluding chapter.

'I am an old man. I live here in this ancient house, surrounded by huge, unkempt gardens.' Thus begins *The House on the Borderland* proper, as the story of what befell the mysterious, nameless 'Recluse' and his sister, some seventy years or so previous, is revealed. It's a novel of two distinct halves: the first, in which the man's isolated house – said by the local country people to have been built by the Devil – is held under siege by otherworldly humanoid 'Swine-creatures'; and the second, a visionary astral journey through the outer reaches of the cosmos to a parallel dwelling on the borderland, set among a vast, alien amphitheatre-like plain overlooked by madness-inducing mountains that swarm with colossal demonic forms. During this epoch-traversing vision the hands of the clock in the Recluse's study hurry forwards until they are a blur – a scene reminiscent of H. G. Wells' *The Time Machine*, a book Hodgson himself owned.

As I glanced about, it seemed to me that I could see the very furniture of the room rotting and decaying before my eyes. Nor was this fancy, on my part; for, all

at once, the bookshelf, along the sidewall, collapsed,
with a cracking and rending of rotten wood,
precipitating its contents upon the floor, and filling the
room with a smother of dusty atoms.

We get hints too within the fragmented manuscript of the
Recluse's semi-spiritual, but all-too-abrupt reconciliation
with his dead lover in the so-called 'Sea of Sleep'. This
theme is explored further in Hodgson's final novel
The Night Land, a kind of heroic quest of redemptive love
set on a dying Earth peopled with vicious entities that
assail the last human survivors. Much as I admire the later
book I prefer *The House on the Borderland*, which I find
easier to connect with. This, I think, is largely down to the
strength and tangibility of its setting – even though I have
never visited the wild Galway landscape where its mysterious residence is located.*

In some ways *The House on the Borderland* is an unbalanced novel, an odd juxtaposition of events. And yet –
perhaps partly because of this structure – it works
wonderfully. I prefer its beguiling first half – the swine-creatures, the apocalyptic atmosphere of the house straddling
two planes, the devastatingly sad fate of the Recluse's dog

---

* In my teens, my dad regaled me with tales of his own trip taken
with two friends during the early 1960s to the west of Ireland. I
was mesmerised by the sound of its superstition-swathed scenery
and the ambrosia-like thickness of the mythic stout he
remembered drinking in welcoming village pubs; I was in love
with all things Irish at the time, half-constructing an imagined Irish
ancestry out of the pedigree of my absconded airman grandfather's
surname.

Pepper – but the uncanniness of the imagined second-act journey to the outer reaches of time and the universe, and the seeming chaos and decrepitude at the heart of existence, is the vital ingredient that elevates the work into a classic of cosmic horror.

As to what it all means, Hodgson's own introduction leaves that up to the individual reader, which is just as well, given there are so many possible interpretations, so many unanswered questions: what, for instance, is the relationship between the desolate dwelling and its twin on the plain at the periphery of the universe? Why is the Recluse's sister so apparently insensible to what's taking place around her – is there a *Cabinet of Dr Caligari*-esque explanation that all the happenings are merely the construct of an unhinged man? And if not this, then why are the Recluse and his sister impervious to the ravages of time while his dog is not? Even if Hodgson's editorial intro is something of a cop-out, it's a clever one: 'Of the simple, stiffly given account of weird and extraordinary matters, I will say little. It lies before you. The inner story must be uncovered, personally, by each reader, according to ability and desire.'

The novel's end comes with a brutal suddenness, as we read the Recluse's tailed-off final words. In a fate like that which befalls the island-marooned couple from 'The Voice in the Night' we learn that a 'foul growth' has also come to affect the Recluse, though in his case it began with a growing, other-dimensional speck of phosphorescence on his wrist, rather than rampant fungal spores. I can't help wondering whether the spreading cancer on his father's throat played into these fearful depictions of contagion.

(According to his youngest brother, Hope Hodgson was something of a hypochondriac.)

Despite the generous modern-day critical acclaim afforded *The House on the Borderland*, and the earlier praise heaped upon his work by commentators as diverse as H. P. Lovecraft, Clark Ashton Smith, George Bernard Shaw and C. S. Lewis, Hodgson's four novels did not sell well. The commercial failure of the book he considered his masterpiece, *The Night Land*, led him to abandon the genre, though not before his publisher Eveleigh Nash brought together the six John Silence-like occult detective tales he'd written for magazines in the excellent *Carnacki the Ghost-Finder*.

Hodgson turned to the ocean again for his last stories, now stripped of the supernatural. These were collected, in 1917, as *Captain Gault: being the exceedingly private log of a sea-captain*, and feature at their heart the eponymous British smuggler, as he goes about outwitting US customs officers. Hodgson also delivered lectures about the maritime life to paying audiences as a way to supplement his meagre writer's income – he was an outstanding early amateur photographer and used the images he had taken during his far-flung travels in the 1890s to illustrate his talks. Some were sold at the time to periodicals and others, after his death, to the Meteorological Office, including shots of phenomena rarely before captured at sea, such as cyclones, leviathanic waves, fork lightning and the aurora borealis.

Having relocated to London from Borth a couple of years earlier – a move he hoped would ignite his career as an author – in February 1913, aged thirty-five, Hodgson married Bessie Farnworth, a girl he'd known from school in Blackburn, and who now worked on a women's magazine in the capital. Shortly afterwards, the newlyweds settled in the south of France on the Côte d'Azur, where Hodgson continued to plug away at his writing.

When war was declared the couple returned to England. Rather than go back to sea with the navy, Hodgson was commissioned as a lieutenant in the Royal Field Artillery. As well as letters and articles about French spies, Hodgson also sent home patriotic poetry. He recovered from a serious head injury suffered after being thrown from his horse in June 1916 – though he did subsequently experience the intermittent effects of concussion – and rejoined hostilities on the Western Front. Events might have turned out differently if Hodgson had not been so stoic – indeed, just a week before his death he was briefly hospitalised once again after a heavy German attack. Instead, he volunteered as a Forward Observer (FO), the precarious role responsible for directing artillery fire onto a target; bravery was nothing new for Hodgson, as in 1898 he had been awarded a Royal Humane Society medal for diving into shark-encircled waters off New Zealand to rescue a fellow seaman.

Having managed to survive in his hazardous FO duties until April 1918, Hodgson's good fortune finally expired. A direct hit from a German shell on the nineteenth of the month, near the village of Kemmel in the borderlands of Belgium, transformed him into fragmentary pieces. His remains were said to be unidentifiable, though a helmet bearing the name Lt. W. Hope Hodgson was retrieved by French soldiers.

'If I live and come somehow out of this (and certainly, please god, I shall and hope to),' he had earlier written home, graphically describing the otherworldly desolation and destruction of Flanders, 'what a book I shall write.'

After leaving Glaneifion I climb the clifftop path that skirts the headland at the northern end of the village. The sky could hardly be bluer, with only a few wisps of white high above the sea. There, with a glorious view of the sweep of the bay, the brightly coloured houses of the resort and the hills of southern Snowdonia, stands a memorial to Borth's Great War fallen. A 'Roll of Honour', as the grey slate proclaims. Anthony told me about how the monument had been struck by lightning in 1983 and reconstructed the following year after a public subscription, with locals hauling the new stones up the steep route by hand.

And here is Hodgson's name, faint but legible, sandwiched between Desmond M. Filgate and William John Jones: I wonder about their all-too-brief lives. Later, I learn that Desmond Maurice Macartney-Filgate had originally enlisted in the Royal Inniskilling Fusiliers, but had been discharged after it was discovered he was underage. On turning eighteen he joined the Royal Flying Corps but was injured in a training flight during May 1918 when the engine of his aircraft stalled; he died at the end of the month and was buried at Wye in Kent. Before the war William John Jones worked as a bricklayer, entering frontline action on Christmas Eve 1915 with the Royal Field Artillery. It seems he also was spared from perishing in the sludge of Flanders' fields, being relieved of duty the

following December because of tuberculosis, and dying at home in Borth, aged twenty-four, in August 1917. These, though, are the barest of facts: as to who Desmond and William might have loved, who might have been left bereft by their absence – as to who they really were – I remain in the dark.

What *is* certain, however, is that at some point over the years following 1919, the next of kin of these men – along with Hope's mother and sister at Lisswood – all should have received a circular bronze plaque four and a half inches in diameter depicting Britannia holding a trident, with a lion at her feet and two dolphins at her shoulders: a so-called 'Dead Man's Penny'. Additionally, an

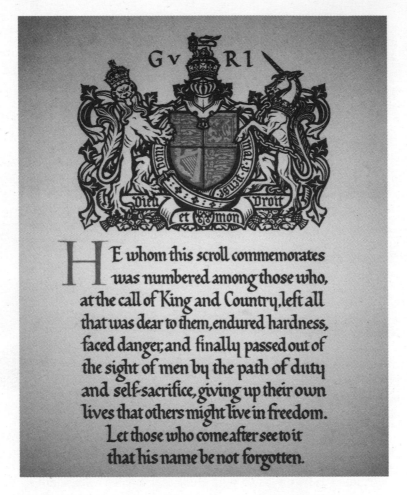

HE whom this scroll commemorates was numbered among those who, at the call of King and Country, left all that was dear to them, endured hardness, faced danger, and finally passed out of the sight of men by the path of duty and self-sacrifice, giving up their own lives that others might live in freedom. Let those who come after see to it that his name be not forgotten.

accompanying memorial scroll was sent out. The text on its fine paper was composed by M. R. James in late 1916 (earlier suggestions from others including Rudyard Kipling were not adopted), after he was asked by the Admiralty to provide suitable wording. After the conclusion of the war to end all wars, it is thought that more than a million of these plaques and scrolls were posted to the bereaved.

The left behind.

James himself, worn down by the toll the conflict had taken on Cambridge life and his former students at King's – including the loss of several to whom he was close – returned to Eton shortly before the Armistice to become the school's provost, a role he was to hold until his death on 12 June 1936. He is buried in Eton Town Cemetery.*

Unlike his two nearest neighbours on Borth's understated grey stone cross, Lieutenant William Hope Hodgson's final resting place is today indeterminable, though it is thought that whatever physical traces of him endured the fatal shell's impact were buried in situ at the foot of the eastern slope of Mont Kemmel – a glorified Belgian hill rising a little over five hundred feet in height and said to derive its name from Camulos, a Celtic god of war. Hodgson is remembered, alongside thirty-five thousand other phantoms of doomed youth whose unknown graves lie in that same night land, on the vast semi-circular arc of Passchendaele's Tyne Cot Memorial.

Dulce et decorum est pro patria mori.

---

* James had spent thirty-six years at King's when he left the college for Eton. The move could, in some sense, be viewed as an attempt to reclaim his own youthful 'Golden Age' – an unobtainable retreat to an unscarred ghost land.

Chapter 7

GOBLIN CITY

When, exactly, the word was first whispered I cannot say. It was dressed up for my benefit to begin with, I'm sure. A check-up, a procedure. A lump.

Just a pea-sized lump.

I wasn't, though, as guileless as all that and realised the gravity of what was beginning to unfold around me. The defining incident occurred when I was at my aunt and uncle's – I had been left there while my parents went to a hospital or doctor's appointment, so it would have been during the school holidays. I think I was thirteen, but it might have been a year either way: how is it that the timing of something so momentous can now prove so elusive? Mum phoned with an update and I could tell from my aunt's stilted side of the conversation – I was listening from behind the lounge door – that the news was not promising. I imagine Dad took me aside that evening – certainly that became the later pattern, signalling the start of the familiar feeling that would rise in my stomach – which must have been when the word broke cover. 'Mum's found a little lump. They've done a test and it needs to come out so she's going to have an operation. Good thing is they've got it early, so they'll be able to sort it.' Or words to that effect.

Two syllables, that's all.

Cancer. The Crab, the fourth sign of the Zodiac. And the illness my mother now had, which would not be so simply sorted.

Her own luminous speck.

The disease's name is attributed to the classical Greek scholar Hippocrates (c. 460–370 BC), the Father of Medicine, who is said to have first described the appearance of a tumour as akin to how a crab digs itself into the sand with its legs circled around its hard carapace – the ten folded limbs resembling the engorged blood vessels that nurture the destructiveness. (Though, perhaps, Hippocrates was likening the pain to the pinch of a crustacean's claw?) I could add that the progress of the illness might seem as inexorable as the processionary movement of the migrating Christmas Island red crabs I found so fascinating on natural history documentaries, or its grip as tight as those two oversized crustacean front fingers. Whatever its exact etymology, my mum now had it – this word I hated to hear spoken aloud – and life in our house would not ever be the same: the disease would not bury its way back below the sands, even if my head were to.

After the initial diagnosis comes a fog. Mum went into the same Pilgrim Hospital that shimmered, so full of malevolence, out of the flat emptiness when you gazed across the Wash from the saltmarshes of Shep Whites. There she underwent a partial mastectomy, which clearly was not a roaring success; my sister-in-law recalls her saying quite matter-of-factly as she visited her at her bedside in the immediate aftermath that the surgeon admitted they

hadn't got everything so they were going to have her back for another go. I guess I should be angry when she tells me this – it is a detail I'd wiped from my memory, or else forgotten – but I'm too resigned after all this time to feel any rage.

I do just about remember Mum returning to hospital, which was presumably when the follow-up procedure was carried out. After she came home she had to be driven each day to the outskirts of Lincoln, the nearest location in the county where she could undertake her next course of treatment. (As a young boy I had, years earlier, been excited to see the city's famous stone imp, carved into a pillar in the cathedral – though, expecting a huge statue, I was underwhelmed by its small size, more of a goblin than a devil.) While Mum underwent her punishing daily journey, a round trip of ninety miles, I was at school, so only got to keep her company once. I have a photo in which she stands grinning in front of a pointing arrow on which the words RADIOTHERAPY CENTRE RECEPTION are spelled out in capitals – she delighted in the incongruity of the ramshackle nature of the place and used to enjoy telling everyone that she was having radiotherapy in a portacabin. After a month or six weeks (I can't recall exactly how long), her visits to the borders of that goblin city were done with. There followed courses of various drugs before she was given an all-clear.

She was going to be fine, they said. She was a fighter.

The word had been defeated.

*

Coming off the M4 into the urban sprawl of Newport, the ancient Roman fortress I'm aiming for is surprisingly difficult to locate, with counterintuitive road signs seemingly sending me the wrong way before, at last, there's a gap in the incessant straggle of houses and I'm crossing a muddy-banked tidal river. Finally, I've arrived in the small town of Caerleon – still in Wales, though a little over a hundred miles to the south-east of William Hope Hodgson's Glaneifion. The location is steeped in history and archaeology with its impressive Roman ruins, and its later associations – it's the site where Geoffrey of Monmouth's twelfth-century chronicle of British monarchs, *Historia regum Britanniae*, places the court of King Arthur, and where, some 350 years on, Thomas Malory staged the legendary figure's coronation in *Le Morte D'Arthur*. Tennyson came here too, in 1856, apparently writing part of the epic *Idylls of the King* in the town's Hanbury Arms. And a nearby cave is said to harbour the sleeping monarch and his knights until the day they are needed by the nation, a local variant of the same piece of folklore that was to spawn Alan Garner's *Weirdstone of Brisingamen* trilogy.

This too is a place on the borderlands: the ancient Kingdom of Gwent (now covering Monmouthshire and Newport) once spanned the area between the Usk and Wye rivers, while the course of the latter, twelve miles to the east, still forms much of the modern-day boundary between Wales and England. Caerleon and its surrounding hills, and tracts of timeless woods, was also the childhood home of one of the most remarkable writers of the supernatural: one whose work reaches out with an inherent strangeness, straddling a landscape of the recognisable and another, concealed world of the sort of 'sequestered places' and beings that M. R. James alludes to in 'A Vignette'.

The writer is Arthur Machen (pronounced 'Macken'), born a year after James, in 1863, although he made his literary name earlier, during the decadence of fin-de-siècle London, with his novella *The Great God Pan*. Much to Machen's delight the *Manchester Guardian* described the book as 'the most acutely and intentionally disagreeable we have yet seen in English. We could say more, but refrain from doing so for fear of giving such a work advertisement.' The 1895 review's level of criticism appears harsh today, and Machen's novel, though far from his best, remains effective and atmospheric. In it he sets out many of the themes that were to become key features of his writing. Most noticeably, we are introduced to Machen's search for the meaning of life's hidden mysteries – 'the shadows that hide the real world from our eyes' – and the timeless pagan forces of (and beyond) nature, embodied as a carnal, faun-like deity, which corrupt both the flesh and the spirit of those exposed to them: those who 'see the god Pan'.

The appearance of Pan reflected the zeitgeist, as the goatish figure (depicted rather androgynously in Aubrey Beardsley's illustration for Machen's first edition) was to become prevalent in literature over the course of the next three turbulent decades, celebrated by writers as diverse as Aleister Crowley, D. H. Lawrence and E. M. Forster. Perhaps most notably (and unexpectedly), a gilded, horned Pan appears on the cover of Kenneth Grahame's 1908

children's novel of anthropomorphised badgers, moles, toads and water voles, *The Wind in the Willows*, in which he takes the form of a protective god of nature and the wild – the 'Piper at the Gates of Dawn'.*

A number of supernatural short stories of the period feature a more ominous, feral Pan, however, including two of my favourites. Henrietta Dorothy Everett's 'The Next Heir' contains an eerie vision that reminds me of the unearthly boatman glimpsed in Algernon Blackwood's 'The Willows', while Saki's (the pen name of the Edwardian English writer Hector Hugh Munro) 'The Music on the Hill' warns against treating local rural folk traditions with disdain. Jumping a century forwards, the

---

* *The Piper at the Gates of Dawn* also gave the title to Pink Floyd's psychedelic 1967 debut album, which seems rather apt given that the band's founder member Syd Barrett could himself be said to have seen Pan after excessive LSD consumption opened the singer's doors of perception.

Mexican film director Guillermo del Toro's admiration for Machen can be seen in his Spanish Civil War-set fantasy *Pan's Labyrinth*.

Arthur Machen was, like M. R. James and William Hope Hodgson, the son of an Anglican clergyman. (In an odd twist of fate, he was to share another familial tie with the Borth-based writer – Machen's only son, Hilary, was to marry Hodgson's niece.) His father John Edward Jones had adhered to the family tradition, studying Divinity at Jesus College, Oxford and thereafter becoming curate at Alfreton in Derbyshire before taking over as the interim vicar of St

Cadoc's in Caerleon on the death of Arthur's grandfather in 1857. In the following year John Jones was given his own parish, Llanddewi Fach with Llandegfedd, a sprawling rural collection of farms and cottages five miles north of the town. In March 1863 Arthur was born in his grand-mother's house on Caerleon's main street: a blue plaque marks the site, though there is little other obvious commemoration of the author elsewhere in the town today. He was christened Arthur Llewellyn Jones-Machen, as his father incorporated the surname of his Scottish wife into their name as part of a family legacy settlement; Arthur would later drop the Jones.

Contemporary Caerleon is dominated by its three grand reminders of the Roman legionary fortress of *Isca*: the amphitheatre on the edge of the town – lauded, by the reign of Elizabeth I, as the site of King Arthur's Round Table; the Fortress Baths, which remained buried in Machen's day, being painstakingly uncovered between 1964 and 1981, and now housed inside an impressive edifice; and the Roman Legionary Museum – known in Machen's time as the Museum of Antiquities – which, along with many items from its collection, features in *The Great God Pan*, and in his semi-autobiographical *The Hill of Dreams*. Here in this hard-to-classify novel we can explicitly see the influence the landscape of Machen's youth had upon his writing. I particularly love the atmos-phere of the scene in which its protagonist Lucian takes an unfamiliar route home across the Gwent fields: 'A dark wild twilight country lay before him, confused dim shapes of trees near at hand, and a hollow below his feet, and the further hills and woods were dimmer, and all the air was very still.'

The house in which Arthur Machen grew up is tricky to locate, and even more difficult to get a decent look at, perched as it is on the upslope of a hill climbed by a narrow minor road with no passing places. Eventually I manage to abandon my car in the least dangerous spot and proceed down the blind track until I am standing at the cast-iron gates of the former Llanddewi Fach Rectory. From this angle I'm looking at the side of the solid two-storey, grey-brown building designed by Machen's father. On its impressive chimney stack he inscribed the year it was built; fittingly, given the location, this was carved in Roman numerals – MDCCCLXIV – alongside his own initials.

I drive the short distance to the church of St David's where Machen's father preached – and where both he and Arthur's mother are buried – a private home since the mid 1990s. From here I can look back across undulating fields of grass and brown-wooded gullies to the rectory, whose cream-edged windows are just visible through the leafless trees. Another winding lane, down which half a stream appears to be flowing, past various cottages, and I arrive at an 'old foot bridge tremulous with age'. This is the country where Machen, an only child with an invalid mother, grew up, finding entertainment in his love of reading and explorations of impressive local landmarks such as Twyn Barlwm, his 'hill of dreams' six miles to the west.

In addition to the Gwent countryside, Machen's work is dominated by the vast mystery of London – the place where he was to spend the majority of his of adult life.* The seventeen-year-old Arthur was enchanted by the city from the off, after taking the six-hour train journey from south Wales with his father for the first time, in June 1880. On that foremost evening they walked along the Strand: 'it instantly went to my head and my heart, and I have never loved another street in quite the same way.'

Machen returned the following summer for his initial attempt to become a journalist and learn the craft of writing, a time spent living alone in Turnham Green, which he described later as 'rather a goblin's castle than a city of

---

* Further details can be found in *The London Adventure*, Machen's final autobiographical volume, published in 1924.

delights'.* Things were gradually to improve for the young
Arthur after he moved to Clarendon Road in Notting Hill
Gate and procured a job at a small publisher's. One of his
tasks was to catalogue a collection of esoteric works on the
occult, though he still occasionally terrified himself by
trudging northwards through grim suburbs to the 'goblin
city' of Kensal Green Cemetery – 'a terrible city of white
gravestones and shattered marble pillars and granite urns,
and every sort of horrid heathenry'. This was a vast
Victorian land of the dead, like Glasgow's Necropolis; its
famous under-the-earth dwellers would come to include
Wilkie Collins, author of the sensation novels *The Woman
in White* and *The Moonstone*.

In August 1887, only a few weeks after the death of his
father, Machen, who by this time had been living on and
off in London for six years, married the bohemian Amy
(Amelia) Hogg. Thirteen years his senior, and an acquaintance of Jerome K. Jerome (soon to find fame with his
comic novel *Three Men in a Boat*) and A. E. Waite, she
introduced Arthur to Waite – a folklorist and member of
the so-called Hermetic Order of the Golden Dawn, a society devoted to occult, alchemical and spiritual study –
initiating the two men's lifelong friendship. Algernon
Blackwood was also to join the Golden Dawn towards the
end of 1900, having recently returned to London from his
first trip along the Danube that would lead to 'The

---

* Machen's struggles at the time put me in mind of two unnerving
London garret-set stories that deal with the disconcerting
loneliness of the writer's existence: Oliver Onions' 'The Beckoning
Fair One' and Robert Aickman's 'Meeting Mr Millar'.

Willows'. However, the order's most notorious adherent was Aleister Crowley, 'the Beast' – later, perhaps, to inspire the demon-summoning Karswell in M. R. James's story 'Casting the Runes', and the title character of Somerset Maugham's *The Magician* – whose involvement and rivalry with fellow adherent William Butler Yeats would splinter the Golden Dawn into factions. Maugham's novel was made into a 1926 silent movie of the same name, directed by Rex Ingram and starring Paul Wegener – who had previously played The Golem – in the role of Oliver Haddo, the figure inspired by Crowley.*

The Machens were married for twelve years, for half of which Amy was engaged in a struggle against an unspecified form of cancer. This trying time happened to be a period of surprising creativity for Arthur, during which he wrote many of his best works of fiction. Yet mentions of Amy in his autobiographies, written a quarter of a century later, are notable by their absence. Just a single sentence in the second volume, *Things Near and Far*, alludes to the enormous sense of loss and grief that overwhelmed him following her death in 1899: 'Then a great sorrow which had long been threatened fell upon me: I was once more alone.'

In his own memoir, Jerome K. Jerome (who two years after penning his most famous book wrote *Told After*

---

* Perhaps the most notable thing about *The Magician* today is that it was the first film the future director Michael Powell worked on from start to finish (as a kind of production assistant): he even features in a cameo as a balloon-holding onlooker when Haddo is having his silhouette drawn by a fairground artist.

Supper, a collection of ghost stories that fuse humour and the supernatural) recalled visiting the couple at their Gray's Inn house shortly before Amy's death:

> The windows looked out onto the great garden, and the rooks were cawing in the elms. She was dying, and Machen, with two cats under his arm, was moving softly about, waiting on her. We did not talk much. I stayed there until the sunset filled the room with a strange purple light.

The Hill of Dreams was written between the autumn of 1895 and the spring of 1897, although it remained unpublished for a decade; three years before it came out in book form it was serialised in *Horlick's Magazine and Home Journal for Australia, India and the Colonies*, issued by the manufacturer of the famous malted hot drink.* Many critics regard the novel as Machen's finest literary achievement, a view Arthur himself shared. The Anglo-Irish fantasy author Lord Dunsany, who provided an introduction to a later reissue, commented how 'clearly and beautifully' Machen transferred his vision to paper. I too can appreciate its aesthetic, visionary qualities, though I will admit finding *The Hill of Dreams* a more difficult work to

---

* The debut appearance of *The Hill of Dreams* in this unlikely periodical is less surprising when you discover Machen's friend A. E. Waite was the London manager of Horlick's for most of the first decade of the new century. Waite edited and wrote for the journal, which he filled with stories featuring occult and related themes that interested him, such as mesmerism and hypnotism.

enjoy than some of his others. Perhaps its subject matter – its depiction of isolation and of artistic rejection – is too close to the bone? I suspect it's one of those books that reveals more of itself on re-reading – and on each subsequent revisit the quiet power of its cryptic pages have resonated more strongly with me. At its heart is the struggle of its central character Lucian Taylor's quest to perfect his art – and his struggle against crippling depression and self-doubt – swapping his native Caermaen (a barely disguised Caerleon) and the 'the faery dome of Twyn Barlwm' for the loneliness and brooding menace of London and the life of a writer.

It's a journey that mirrors Machen's own, though Machen avoided the doomed, opiated Dorian Gray-esque demise of his novel's alter ego and managed to emerge from the despair of Amy's death; for most of the first decade of the new century he successfully took up the less solitary career of acting (in a touring repertory theatre company), marrying his second wife, Purefoy, in 1903. The pair remained happily together for the rest of their lives, eighty-four-year-old Arthur following his beloved into the hereafter nine months after her death, in December 1947. Their shared headstone in the graveyard of St Mary's churchyard, Amersham, contains a cross bearing the Latin inscription OMNIA EXEUNT IN MYSTERIUM. *Everything ends in mystery.*

The first two words, at least, we know hold true.

*

After university I too moved to London for my own adventure, half-fancying myself as a writer, though doing little to pursue it other than enrolling on an evening scriptwriting course in Ealing, just up the road from the studios where two of my favourite films of the supernatural, *The Halfway House* and *Dead of Night*, were made. Indeed, *Dead of Night*, a portmanteau movie from 1945, features a ground-breaking (and still influential) framing device linking together its disparate strands that wouldn't be amiss in one of Machen's early books. The most remarkable episode stars Michael Redgrave in a performance which captures a similar fragility and nervousness to that of his lighthouse keeper in *Thunder Rock*. Here he plays a disturbed ventriloquist increasingly under the spell of the wooden half of his act. 'What sort of dummy do you think I am? You shot

him, didn't you?' taunts the terrifying, undersize figure of Hugo in the final scene of the segment.*

I also find the more low-key Christmas-party storyline in which a teenage Sally Ann Howes ends up consoling the ghost of a young boy particularly affecting, with its dream-like tone and setting reminiscent of the children's fancy-dress games from the aborted wedding festivities of *Le Grand Meaulnes*, Alain-Fournier's 1913 masterpiece. The French author wrote just that one solitary, magical novel – an exploration of how our adolescent dreams can never live up to their unrealistic possibilities – before, like William Hope Hodgson and countless others, his own youthful promise was extinguished in the all-consuming conflict of the Great War.

I was twenty-two when I came to the capital, a decade fresher than Machen when he began *The Hill of Dreams*. I spent those two years in west London localities frequented more than a century before – though I did not know it at the time – by the young Arthur, and not far from Chiswick where the nineteen-year-old Henri Alban Fournier (the French novelist's real name) lived during the summer of 1905, working in the unlikely setting of a large nearby factory that manufactured wallpaper. My first shared flat was located in a former council house on the seedier fringes of Ladbroke Grove, a short walk from the Clarendon Road attic that Machen moved to in 1883 and close to the

---

* The German actor Frederick Valk, who plays Redgrave's Freud-like psychiatrist Dr Van Straaten in *Dead of Night*, also appeared in *Thunder Rock* as the ghostly Austrian anaesthetist Dr Kurtz.

famous market which forms the backdrop for Muriel
Spark's terrific narrator-reversing 1958 ghost story 'The
Portobello Road'.

Machen's predilection for nocturnal rambles intensified
after his arrival in the city – 'the habits of the country,
unlike those of London, generally fail to give reason or
excuse for night wanderings' – an experience vividly
captured in *The Hill of Dreams* and in his oddly compelling
1904 novella of suburban domesticity, ennui and tran-
scendence, *A Fragment of Life*. Somewhat eerily, the name
of the main character of the story, Edward Darnell, is only
one letter different to my own. I too had taken solace in
late-night walks through the more mundane surroundings
of the Fenland town in which I grew up, as I tried to make
some sense of what was happening around me; Lincolnshire,
though, lacked the magic of the hills of Gwent, and shared
nothing of the atmosphere of the capital that so captivated
my near-namesake:

> London seemed a city of Arabian Nights, and its
> labyrinths of streets an enchanted maze; its long
> avenues of lighted lamps were as starry systems, and its
> immensity became for him an image of the endless
> universe.

On a late winter's evening, aged seventeen, when I could
no longer stand the suffocating sorrow of our family house,
I went on one of my circuits of the town, orange-washed
under sodium streetlights. I passed through the stillness of
the centre – it must have been the middle of the week as

the place appeared so empty it might as well have been deserted – along the artificial straightness of the river and over the disused railway bridge where, as a young boy, trains had still crossed before the line was closed during the early 1980s. I can recall the feeling of lying in bed searching for sleep, listening for the far-off sound of the train's horn while I waited for my father's footsteps to fall on the drive. Sometimes, when he was back very late from whatever work meeting or committee he'd been away at, snatches of muffled speech would float up from the street below my room. I loved hearing these odd splinters of conversation in the darkness, usually men walking home from the pub; there was something reassuring about their banality, something that reminded me that the world was as it should be.

My route pressed on past countless diminutive terraces and a 1960s housing estate where the identikit streets were named after royal palaces. Somewhere near the church, in which a few years before I'd wasted far too many Sundays as a choirboy, there was an old, white-haired woman standing in front of her house, staring across at me through the darkness. She was only there for a few seconds before she slipped back inside, but she had an unnaturally pale, lime-lit look, which I found unnerving.

I half-wonder now whether I imagined her. Whether she had even been there at all.

I love Machen's autobiographical writing, with its meanderings around the capital, but it's his earlier supernatural work to which I was first drawn, particularly that which relates to the 'Little People' who dwell beneath the hills of our wild, ancient places. To me, the most memorable of these dark tales is 'The Novel of the Black Seal'. Often printed as a self-contained story it originally formed part of *The Three Imposters*, a collection of linked narratives that takes its title from an apocryphal heretical work (*De Tribus Impostoribus*) mentioned by Sir Thomas Browne – a favourite of Machen, and later of W. G. Sebald – in his *Religio Medici* of 1642. The structure of Machen's book was influenced by Robert Louis Stevenson's *New Arabian Nights*, with one of its stories, 'The Novel of the White Powder', containing a sickening, chemically induced bodily transformation reminiscent of *The Strange Case of Dr Jekyll and Mr Hyde*.

I prefer 'The Novel of the Black Seal' as a standalone story, which is how I first encountered it. Despite the undoubted manic energy of *The Three Imposters*, Machen ends up undermining the power and authenticity of its various plots through the trickery of the device he employs to bring them together. Yet even here, as a separate work, 'The Novel of the Black Seal' utilises several stories-within-a-story as a way of conferring validity upon its hyperreal goings-on. After the opening framing section showing the interchange between Miss Lally (stripped here, in the standalone version, of the duplicity she is revealed to possess in *The Three Imposters*) and the amateur detective Phillips, the distressed young woman recounts her version of events before reading out an expositional account left by the now-vanished William Gregg.

A chance meeting with Gregg, a noted professor of ethnology, on a London street results in Miss Lally

becoming the governess of his children and his unofficial
secretary. She accompanies the professor on a trip to 'a
country house in the west of England, not far from
Caermaen, a quiet little town, once a city, and the
head-quarters of a Roman legion'.* There, having
completed his monumental ethnology textbook, he aims
to solve a mystery connected to the small black, rune-in-
scribed stone in his possession.

I wasn't familiar with any of Machen's work until a few
years ago. My introduction came with 'The Shining
Pyramid', another short story in which the existence of a
race of hideous fairy folk sequestered beneath our hills is
uncovered by a pair of amateur gentlemen detectives.† Its
climactic scene, in which the two men witness a writhing
mass of hidden beings upon an ancient summit, is mirrored
in a tale by L. T. C. Rolt – Robert Aickman's co-founder of
the Inland Waterways Association – set in the Welsh
borderlands. Rolt's atmospheric 'Cwm Garon', which takes
place north of Abergavenny in the Black Mountains, sings
from the same unholy hymn sheet as Machen's dark tales

_____

* It's interesting that Machen locates the house in England,
because quite clearly Caermaen represents Caerleon; a similar
coyness about its Welshness is displayed in *The Hill of Dreams*,
though by the time of *Far Off Things* – the first of his
autobiographical works from the 1920s – there's no such
ambiguity.

† Despite my earlier ignorance of Machen, I would have seen
references to him among the 'weird fiction' of H. P. Lovecraft, who
I was obsessed with during my first years at secondary school; two
of his best stories, 'The Call of Cthulhu' and 'The Whisperer in
Darkness', owe a considerable debt to, and even namecheck, the
Welsh writer.

with its midnight rites populated by squat, guttural-sounding figures that the protagonist initially confuses with children: 'Their bodies, however, belied this impression, as did
their faces, for their countenances were such that Carfax
was grateful for the smoke which prevented him from
seeing them clearly.'

I was not alone in coming late to Machen. His literary
star, which had risen fleetingly in the 1890s, was already
waning once the twentieth century got under way.
Ironically, his re-emergence into the popular consciousness
was the result of a rather slight story – Machen thought it
'an indifferent piece of work' – composed while a journalist on the *Evening News*. 'The Bowmen' first appeared in
the London newspaper at the end of September 1914 and
is Machen's own piece of unintentional Great War
myth-making, written in response to the British army's
retreat from Mons at the beginning of the war. In 'The
Bowmen', Saint George and a division of shining Agincourt
archers materialise just in time to beat back the German
onslaught; later Machen was to say he was inspired by
Kipling's Afghanistan-set 'The Lost Legion', a tale with a
similar premise.

For a period after 'The Bowmen' was printed (it was
subsequently published in a high-selling standalone
edition), events took on a life of their own, and it came to
be widely believed that supernatural forces really had
come to the aid of the embattled Tommies in the trenches,
despite Machen's insistence there was no factual basis
behind what he'd written. This didn't seem to matter
though, and in the fake news of the time the Agincourt

archers morphed into a more divine form of assistance, the so-called 'Angel of Mons' – with numerous people reporting that their soldier sons, brothers and uncles had been witness to the Heaven-sent help. Unfortunately Machen, who throughout much of his life walked a precarious financial tightrope, did not fully benefit from the story's popularity, as the copyright was held by the paper.

Machen's work draws on Celtic and northern European folklore – of changelings and of hidden fairies, of the Welsh 'Tylwyth Teg'. Less mystically, in *Dreads and Drolls*, a 1926 anthology of his writing that deals with historical mysteries, Machen entertains the euhemeristic view that his little people of the Welsh hills are subterranean-dwelling 'small, dark aborigines who hid from the invading Celt somewhere about 1500–1000 B.C.' This chimes with the major theme of Kazuo Ishiguro's surprising fantasy novel *The Buried Giant*. Set in the Dark Ages and taking place after the death of King Arthur, the book explores how we are capable of jointly forgetting – or burying – unwholesome truths about our shared past: in this case the earlier ethnic cleansing of Britons by the Anglo-Saxons that has been obscured behind a fog of enchantment emanating from the breath of a dragon. One of its most powerful scenes could be straight out of Machen's fairy stories, when a swarming mass of malevolent pixies emerges from a river to take Beatrice, the wife of the novel's central character Axl: 'He knew more and more creatures were rising from the water – how many might have boarded now? Thirty? Sixty? – and their collective voices seemed to him to resemble the sound of children playing in the distance.'

In 'The Novel of the Black Seal' we see something of the horror of these hidden creatures that have always shadowed us in the 'not too keen-witted' boy Cradock – a boy born of a human mother and fairy father, like another supernaturally conceived abomination Machen gave us in *The Great God Pan* (or like the satanic offspring of *Rosemary's Baby*). Miss Lally is shocked one afternoon to watch the boy having an apparent fit and to hear him talking in awful, guttural, half-sibilant whisper, a language the local vicar says is most definitely not Welsh: 'I should say it must be that of the fairies – the Tylwydd Têg, as we call them.'*

Machen's 'Little People' are responsible not just for scaring children, but for their disappearance: the unfortunate Annie Trevor in 'The Shining Pyramid' who vanishes on a walk over the hills to visit a relative, or the 'servant-girl at a farmhouse' who is lost without trace in 'The Novel of the Black Seal'. Machen is working, albeit more darkly, with the same strand of folklore that a few years earlier fuelled the Irish poet W. B. Yeats's 'The Stolen Child', written in 1886, when Yeats was twenty-one. The two men were acquainted with one another, as both were concurrent members of the Golden Dawn in London – Machen for a short, grief-stricken spell after the death of Amy in 1899. At least, however, in Yeats's poem the hope remains that

---

* The harsh 'hissing syllables' of Machen's fairy language are mirrored in Lovecraft's 'The Whisperer in Darkness', where we learn of 'Tales, besides, of buzzing voices in imitation of human speech which made surprising offers to lone travelers on roads and cart-paths in the deep woods …'

the beguiled boy might have a better faery future in store – in a place perhaps preferable to that of the tumultuous fin-de-siècle human world – which we can assume is not the case for the missing girls in Machen's stories.

> *Come away, O human child!*
> *To the waters and the wild*
> *With a faery, hand in hand,*
> *For the world's more full of weeping than you can*
>   *understand.*

In appearance, Machen's fairies, too, are of an altogether darker persuasion than the classical, angelic winged figures that dominated the Victorian fairy-painting craze which flourished between 1840 and 1870. The 'little stunted creatures with old men's faces, with bloated faces, with little sunken eyes' described in Machen's later story 'Out of the Earth' do, however, bear a resemblance to some of the figures depicted in Richard Dadd's *The Fairy Feller's Master Stroke*. The schizophrenic artist's tour de force was undertaken over a decade while he was incarcerated in Britain's most notorious asylum for the insane; he was to languish in Bedlam for the rest of his life after stabbing and murdering his father, who he thought had been trans-formed into a demon.

The paintings of the less well known John Anster Fitzgerald, a frequent exhibitor at the Royal Academy from 1845 to the first years of the dawning century, occa-sionally offer an even more disturbing vision of the 'fair folk', who appear as grotesque spirits and demonic

hobgoblins conjured straight out of a laudanum-induced nightmare, or borrowed from the oils of Bosch.

Both artists' work would seem a fitting match for the 'loathsome forms' that inhabit Machen's dark fairyland.

At the conclusion of 'The Novel of the Black Seal', Professor Gregg goes up from his own rented house on the borderland into the 'Grey Hills' – which appear to be a gateway into a more foreboding netherworld – to 'meet the "Little People" face to face'. And though there is no geographic range of peaks in Machen's home country that shares the name, just seven miles to the east of Llanddewi's rectory, looming above an ancient wood, stands Mynydd Llwyd – the Grey Hill. Machen's friend Fred Hando's 1944 guide *The Pleasant Land of Gwent* – in which Machen was to pen his last published piece, the book's brief but lyrical introduction – refers to the word *llwyd* (grey) as being 'associated here, in other parts of Wales, and in Brittany with elves, with ghosts, with death itself.'

Heading towards the Grey Hill's invisible peak I weave around a narrow road that rises northwards from the plain of the coast. Halfway up I pass an emptied reservoir, its gothic tower emerging forlornly from the muddy dregs of a languishing puddle. The waters were drained in 2017 so that maintenance work could be carried out on the late-Victorian structure; during the process the body of a local woman murdered twenty years previously by her husband was found.

As the road presses higher and the woodland becomes denser, the visibility drops to next to nothing: thick, low cloud has brought a shrouded, stilting opaqueness to the world. I'm in another location Machen fondly namechecks in his work: the 'green, great and exalted' Wentwood. At one point a roe deer bounds in front of me, terrified yet

drawn by the twin pinholes of my headlamps in the ghost-light. And without warning I am arrived at the site of the infamous Forester's Oaks where, in ages past, poachers were executed for daring to take a stag or steal a sheep. The vast trees, including the hollowed-out hanging-oak itself, have been gone for more than a century, but as the only living soul among the white-out I am suitably impressed by the eerie ambience. There is no spring birdsong; indeed, hardly a sound at all, except the quiet drip of precipitation onto the undergrowth. I start on the muddy track that climbs to the Grey Hill, but soon realise it's futile in the mist and that I will see little from its peak should I even find it; I return to my car, relieved when I've descended out of the whiteness.

Because in this place white is significant, I'd like to think.

En route to my night's accommodation I stop off at dusk in another nearby Roman settlement, Caerwent,

where I walk along the top of dark stone walls that date from the third century after Christ. I watch a black rabbit hopping among the ruins, which brings to my mind the film *Watership Down*. Our class crowded together into the hotel lounge to be shown it one evening on a week-long primary school trip to London and its ending caused the supposed toughest boy to cry; were I to see the death of Hazel again now I'm sure it would have the same effect on me.

The next day I try for the Grey Hill once more. This time the cloud has cleared and the woodland is transformed by birdsong, yesterday's ominous stillness replaced by the pleasant haze of a spring afternoon. Now I can ascend to the ancient rocks on its summit like Professor Gregg before me. And, perhaps, like the central character in my favourite of Machen's stories – and the reason the whiteness of the Wentwood last night struck me so vividly. Because surely Machen had this place at least a little in mind when he described his Grey Hills in 'The Novel of the Black Seal', or 'the hill of the grey rocks' above the woods in 'The White People'.

Written in 1899, 'The White People' is a masterful naïve narration by a bewitched adolescent girl (or perhaps just a girl possessing a furiously overactive imagination?) that brings its strangeness to the page in a formally surprising way. It feels ahead of its time, anticipating the modernist first-person streams of consciousness that two decades later – when employed by James Joyce, Virginia Woolf and William Faulkner – would seem so innovative. Like the stories from *The Three Imposters*, this one is bookended by

a framing device – in this case a dry scholarly discussion
about the nature of sin and evil. I find myself skimming
through this opening discourse to get to the good stuff, the
embedded 'Green Book': the journal in which we learn of
the unnamed girl's disconcerting childhood. It's a remarkable read, full of cryptic words that put me in mind of
Lewis Carroll's nonsense poem 'Jabberwocky' – the 'Aklo
letters', 'Dôls', 'Jeelo', 'voolas' – words we can only half-
guess the meaning of.* There are also references to various
arcane rites that are never explained: 'the White
Ceremonies, and the Green Ceremonies, and the Scarlet
Ceremonies'.

'The White People' is a rambling, mesmerising piece of
writing that does, I think, effectively capture the voice of a
young teenage girl of the period. It's not easy to take in,
given that it's rendered in large blocks of text with barely
the concession of a paragraph to assist the reader, but it has
a hypnotic quality that takes us deep inside the narrator's
dreamlike world:

> When I was very small, and mother was alive, I can
> remember remembering things before that, only it has
> all got confused. But I remember when I was five or six
> I heard them talking about me when they thought I
> was not noticing.

---

* This use of esoteric terminology is something Lovecraft is fond
of too – he even co-opts the 'dark Aklo language used by certain
cults of evil antiquity', mentioning it in two of his stories.

The girl recalls overhearing the adults discussing her when she was a toddler, a time when she babbled phrases no one else could understand – words in the 'Xu language' about 'the little white faces that used to look at me when I was lying in my cradle'. Later, aged about five, she remembers being taken by her nurse – who, we infer, is complicit in the events that are to come – to a deep pool in a wood. The nurse leaves her there while she goes off with a tall man who has followed them. And the little girl is alone on a patch of moss as 'out of the water and out of the wood came two wonderful white people, and they began to play and dance and sing'.

It's a haunting image of two nymph-like creatures, but the more I read it the more I wonder whether the girl has in fact witnessed her nurse and the man emerging naked from the pool, with their subsequent dancing and singing in fact being the couple engaging in sex. Because when the nurse returns 'she was looking something like the lady looked' and she is angry and upset when the girl tells her everything she has seen, making her promise not to say a word about it to anybody. If this is what has happened then, unlike Leo in *The Go-Between*, the girl seems enchanted, rather than horrified, by this window into an adult future.

After this, the girl's journal records the momentous 'White Day', just before her fourteenth birthday. Her description of her walk up through the woods and into the ominous country beyond resembles the scenery around Wentwood and the Grey Hill, and paints a powerful picture of this history-ridden landscape:

> I went up and up a long way, till at last the thicket
> stopped and I came out crying just under the top of a
> big bare place, where there were ugly grey stones lying
> all about on the grass, and here and there a little twisted,
> stunted tree came out from under a stone, like a snake.

My own ascent of the Grey Hill is less dramatic; I do not snag myself on thorns, and the path, though in places eroded by people's footfalls and streams of rainwater, is well-marked. It's a pretty view from the summit, which measures just under nine hundred feet in height, with the Wentwood stretching off to the north and west. The forest is impressive, largely consisting of conifers, with blocks of russet larches bringing colour to the greenness. Up here, at the plateau of the hill, the palette is mainly brown rather than grey, a wide carpet of dead bracken punctuated by leafless dark-branched birches. From somewhere nearby a willow warbler's slurred song tries to mask the growl of distant traffic – the first of these returning songbirds I have heard this spring.

I search among the undergrowth for the hill's stone circle; eventually I locate it, surrounded by the stumps of hacked-off trees. According to Hando's guidebook it is 'older than Stonehenge', and although low-key – there are just two standing stones, with the rest of the boulders lying close to the ground – it is humbling to have such history to myself. The tallest menhir is plastered with lichens of varying colours – lime green, mustard, black – and pockmarked with penny-sized indentations that hint at its age.

The stream of consciousness of 'The White People' continues in the same vein as the girl progresses through her mythic hilltop world, before descending into a secret wood where she glimpses something 'so wonderful and so strange'; we learn only later, in the clumsy framing epilogue, what this cryptic thing is. The girl goes on to recount the dark fairy tales her nurse used to tell her, as well as stories handed down from the nurse's great-grandmother, who lived alone in a cottage on a hill. Some of the witch-craft-like rituals the old woman used to partake in, and the archaic secrets she knew of – like how to create the power-imbued figure of a clay man, or of the archaic maze game of 'Troy Town' – are passed on to the girl, who at the story's end, more than two years after her nurse has unaccountably gone away, returns to the pool in the wood.

I love 'The White People', partly, I think, because of its sheer elusiveness. I still don't know what exactly is taking place – and it's better for that. As to whether Machen actually wants us to believe the girl is privy to real forces of witchcraft and fairy other worlds, or whether the story is more of a parable about the loss of innocence, I'm not sure. (It could, of course, be both.) What isn't in doubt, however, is the peculiar, lingering impression 'The White People' leaves.

> All these are most secret secrets, and I am glad when I remember what they are, and how many wonderful languages I know, but there are some things that I call the secrets of the secrets that I dare not think of unless I am quite alone, and then I shut my eyes, and put my hands over them and whisper the word …

They lied.

She hadn't won.

My mother's tumour had not been completely cut out, despite that second visit to the Pilgrim, and the targeted sci-fi radiation, which did not have the desired effect. The secret word had not been defeated. Instead, over time, it re-emerged and mutated. Metastasised. Like the spreading phosphorescent speck at the end *The House on the Borderland*, or the creeping spot of fungus from 'The Voice in the Night'.

I cannot produce an exact mental map of when and where the all-clear became unclear, the distance is too long. But I remember Dad taking me aside, telling me Mum's illness had come back, and that she was going to have more treatment. This time chemotherapy in some form was involved, and steroids, which left her face bloated and caused her to put on weight. I know I didn't want my friends to come round and see her like that. Because I didn't want them to be callous, didn't want other people to know my mother was unwell. So, I said nothing.

I was a master of secrecy.

Perhaps it was a kind of denial – a magical thinking that by not giving the illness mention, it would be kept at bay – though I think it was more me being protective: she was my mum and I didn't want anyone else gossiping about her, or offering up false platitudes. It was us against the world.

Me against the world. And fuck all those others wanting to stick their noses in.

There were definite peaks and troughs over the next few years – around three years if my estimations possess any validity. Dark moments when Dad would take me aside and talk about a setback, then more positive episodes when the treatment had seemingly taken effect, when the bad cells were shrinking away. At some point, however, Mum became much more frail. I think her lungs had become involved, making her wheezy; she started carrying an inhaler – *your puffer you called it* – that she would turn to with increasing regularity. And that was when she got a wheelchair, so if we went shopping I could push her – though she would still scoot out, surprising onlookers, if we reached a high kerb or some similar obstacle.

Then came the secondary tumour in her brain that pushed down onto her optic nerve, causing her to lose the sight in one eye. She wore a patch sometimes when she was out, and didn't care what people thought – once a little boy asked his own mother why that lady was like a pirate and you could tell the woman was mortified, loud-whispering to him to be quiet, though Mum just laughed and told him it was because her eye was poorly. She was good like that.

You were a ghost pirate, I think.

Later still, the cancer in her brain caused occasional epileptic fits, which were terrifying to witness, and which I hadn't thought about for years until I started writing this. But she was determined. She would keep battling on, just like my nan had with her arthritis, even though her body was starting to disengage from the world around her.

And she did keep going. Until the sky finally fell away.

Down below me to the south, I see the curve of the Severn Estuary; somewhere to the east will be the border between Wales and England formed by the Wye, though the haze is too far-reaching to make that out, even if the contours of the land were to allow it.

A slant of sunlight angles down from a dark-grey cumulus cloud, like a ray from the heavens drawn in a comic strip.

In a clearing among the Wentwood a white farmhouse glimmers in the vaporous air.

The scene is akin to one in the 1944 Ealing Studios film *The Halfway House*, a ghostly piece of wartime propaganda (not dissimilar in tone to the previous year's *Thunder Rock*) that I first saw aged about ten or eleven. I watched it after returning from Sunday dinner at Nan and Grandad's – I loved settling down in front of black-and-white afternoon matinees on the telly, sprawled on the sofa knowing that Dad was pottering about outside in the garden. It's a film that lingered with me long after that initial viewing: it must have had something about it to lodge so firmly inside my head because I didn't watch it again until a week before

I came to the Grey Hill, yet I had retained a vivid sense of its odd ambience.

I've always associated the distinctive chimes of the inn's clock with the near-identical 'Westminster Quarters' sounded by the clock in my other aunt and uncle's front room (they lived in Boston, where that fateful cormorant had alighted – we only visited them a couple of times a year). The doorbell on my current house gives out a simple two-tone chime if somebody rings it, but it has another setting – the full eight-note Westminster Quarters – which can only be activated by fiddling with a tiny switch inside. Something I never do. Very occasionally – as first happened in the early hours of the morning, causing me, illogically and in a state of fright, to search each room for intruders – these troubling tones play of their own accord; I'm almost used to it now, though the sporadic sound causes a wide-eyed, raised-ear look of surprise to appear on my cat's face, and a slight quickening of my heart. I guess it must be the result of some random radio-wave interference, but it is odd that the standard chime never plays for these phantom rings, nor the other unselected sound the doorbell is capable of playing.

The Halfway House is a low-key production that has an out-of-time quality a world away from modern films. It's set around the Halfway House of its title, an inn (that has nothing whatsoever to do with the lonely watch-house on Blakeney Point) nestled in a Welsh valley close to the village of Cwmbach. The name translates as 'Little Valley', though I suspect it's chosen here for the play on words of how it sounds in English: 'Come back'.

The war is in full swing and a disparate group of travellers are making their way to the place for a summer weekend break: the well-known conductor David Davies, returned to his homeland after a long absence, harbouring the secret that he has been given only a few months to live; a couple in the process of splitting up, though their daughter (the young actress Sally Ann Howes from *Dead of Night*) is doing her best to prevent it; an Irish diplomat keen to defend his country's neutrality, despite the rift this causes with his English fiancée; a gruff Merchant Navy sea captain and his French wife, both struggling to come to terms with the loss of their son; and an ex-con army man and his black-marketeer friend – they scan the scene from the hillside with their binoculars as they approach, the inn shimmering into view where an instant before the valley was empty. All the guests are attended to by the innkeeper Rhys – played by Mervyn Johns, who also features as the figure haunted by a recurring, nightmarish sense of déjà vu in the central framing device that so effectively links together the disparate stories of *Dead of Night* – and his daughter Gwyneth, Johns' real-life daughter Glynis. From early on we realise there is something odd about this pair – Rhys seems to materialise out of the air when he first appears, neither of them cast a shadow, and both have a good line in portentous dialogue.

'Quite a lot of people who don't know where they're going end up here,' Rhys says to Fortescue, the disgraced army man, as he waits to check in. 'You were expected, sir.'

The Halfway House is a quiet film full of poignancy, its beautifully shot scenes adding a magical quality to the proceedings, though the location work was actually carried out on Exmoor – another of our childhood summer holiday destinations – rather than Wales. It's a film, I think, at least partly about living in the moment, and reminds me a little (although it's far less flamboyant and smaller in scope) of Powell and Pressburger's *A Matter of Life and Death*, which was to be released at cinemas eighteen months later.

As *The Halfway House* draws to its conclusion, we learn that time has flipped back and become frozen in a repeat of the weekend a year before when the inn was bombed and destroyed: Rhys and his daughter are well-meaning shades.

Standing on top of the Grey Hill I feel like one of the guests in the film. Drawn to a place offering a fleeting hope of reconciliation with the ghosts of the past.

Chapter 8

LONELIER THAN RUIN

The sea sizzles, its brown waves churning and depositing fine shingle in an endless spin cycle. I'm crunching along the strandline set down by the last tide. My steps take me into a mild, though breezy, southerly that's whipping up the restless surface. A desiccated plant fragment blows beyond the reach of the breakers, like tumbleweed in a western.

I walk up the beach, out of the sun and into shadow, a drifting mist of spray in close pursuit. In places the cliffs have subsided beneath gullies of cascading sand. Layers of yellow-brown strata are exposed to the elements where

brambles and grasses have been unable to get a grip. A raft of sea cabbage at my feet is trying to gain a foothold between the larger pebbles, and a sycamore sapling has sprouted to almost my height; it will not attain maturity before the waves once more overwhelm this meeting point of water and land. Fragments of masonry – one of them, carved and grey, has the look of the ecclesiastical, which here, below the ruin of Dunwich's Greyfriars Priory is not unlikely – lie among twisted lines of rusted metal.

A sign warns CLIFF FALLS ARE FREQUENT AND DEADLY.

In the distance I see a group of three figures. Through my binoculars I make out a middle-aged couple and their son, a rangy teenager, heading towards me; the woman is to the seaward side of the man and holding him by the hand, skipping aside when a surge overshoots her expectations. The lad's further back, striding alone, his hands in his pockets.

We too walked this same stretch of beach, all that time ago, though then the crumbling cliffs would have extended metres beyond where now they collapse in on themselves.

Do you remember?

I stare into the haze. How did we miss its approach? A figure formed of sea spray that must have hung there, unseen, for a moment – a play of the light above the shingle – before it dissolved to nothing.

The ephemeral pied piper who whistled you away.

On my twenty-eighth birthday, a writer I was then unfamiliar with died in a car accident a few miles outside Norwich, where at the time I was living. I remember reading the news in the local paper, the *Eastern Daily Press*, a day or two after, wondering why I had not come across the work of this man who had lectured for three decades

in my adopted city, at the university I was myself, five years later, to attend. (He even, for a single semester before his untimely death, taught on the Creative Writing MA I was to take.)

Winifred Georg Sebald was known on his books by his initials, W. G., and, throughout his adult life, as Max to his friends (he disliked his first two given names). He was born in 1944 in Wertach im Allgäu, a village in the Bavarian Alps. His father, who had been a soldier in the German *Reichswehr*, the 100,000-strong army Germany was permitted under the terms of the Treaty of Versailles, became part of Hitler's *Wehrmacht* when it was formed in 1935; he fought in the Second World War, not returning to his family until 1947. By this time he was a stranger to his son, having been held since the end of the hostilities in a French POW camp; later, his father's own complicity with history was a source of discomfort to the young Max, who grew up in a bucolic world close to the Austrian border where the conflict and its atrocities were not spoken about. This silence was to feature at the heart of Sebald's non-academic work, all of which was written after he passed the age of forty. Finding a form that could adequately encapsulate so much loss – so much wilful amnesia – took him that long to hone. Or, perhaps, to stumble upon.

After finishing his schooling, Sebald undertook a degree in literature at the University of Freiburg, one of the oldest educational establishments in Germany, founded in 1457. The small city on the western fringe of the Black Forest is where the great Dutch scholar of the Renaissance, Erasmus, came after fleeing the Reformation in Basel. For two years

(1529–31) he lived at the striking Haus zum Walfisch ('The Whale House'); this red-plastered, Gothic residence, which these days is a branch of the Sparkasse Bank, was the inspiration for the 'celebrated Academy of Freiburg', the bewitched school of dance in which a young American, Suzy Bannion, decides 'to perfect her ballet studies' in Dario Argento's 1977 horror film *Suspiria*.

The movie wasn't actually filmed in the city, but a convincing approximation of the building's façade (complete with a replica of its commemorative plaque marking Erasmus's residency) – and a dreamlike,

fictionalised Art Nouveau interior featuring Aubrey Beardsley panels and Escher-like murals – was reconstructed on a studio lot in Rome. *Suspiria* is a technicolour visual feast, which, along with Roger Corman's adaptation of Poe's *The Masque of the Red Death*, has perhaps my favourite use of colour in a horror film: its lurid vermilion rooms, and the bright scarlets of its corn-syrup blood, virtually burn themselves onto the viewer's retina, while the electronic soundtrack by the aptly named Italian prog rock band Goblin leaves a similarly deep aural scar.

Like Suzy Bannion – albeit in less dramatic circumstances – Sebald's stay as a student in Freiburg was also cut short. After two years he left the stuffy confines of German academia because, as he later wrote, he found it impossible to study the things he was interested in there, transferring instead to the university in the near-namesake, French-speaking Swiss town of Fribourg: like many of his family before him, Sebald had become an emigrant. This disorientating break with his past gathered pace when he took up a teaching post in German literature at the University of Manchester in 1966, despite at this point having little knowledge of English. Four years later he moved to Norwich and the fledgling University of East Anglia. Here he lectured on European literature, though it was nearly two decades before he began to produce the poetry and, in particular, the 'prose fiction' (Sebald's own classification of his hard-to-define work) for which he is now so lauded.

The book of Sebald's that most resonates with me is *The Rings of Saturn*, a meandering journey around the East Anglian coast and the lives of various imagined and historical figures, along with digressions that include the long-ago deforestation of Britain, the natural history of the herring and the silkworm, and the liberation of Bergen-Belsen – all of which take place within a strangely hypnotic atmosphere of ennui and entropy. While researching this chapter I found one of my father's few old letters that I possess, written to his aunt and uncle in Australia while he was undertaking National Service in Germany as a young man of nineteen. Looking up the address (BFPO 30) where the 1958 communication was sent from, I discovered the camp was Hohne in Lower Saxony, built four years before the war by the Nazis, and the location to which, at its liberation, the skeletal survivors of nearby Belsen were moved.

I'm staggered by this new-found knowledge, because Dad – like one of Sebald's characters – never once mentioned his youthful proximity to such a grim, infamous place. I feel the need to share this information, and instinctively reach for my phone to call my brother even though I know he won't answer.

Three staccato beeps.

Our line's dead.

One of the most notable episodes of *The Rings of Saturn* occurs at the very beginning of Sebald's melancholic walking tour. Though, to be more accurate, I should say the journey undertaken by the unnamed narrator who acts as a *version* of the German writer – because he is a figure who is similar to, yet not quite Sebald – in the same way that places in the book are not-quite-correct approximations of where they pertain to be.

It was on a grey, overcast day in August 1992 that I
travelled down to the coast in one of the old diesel
trains, grimed with oil and soot up to the windows,
which ran from Norwich to Lowestoft at that time.

Just inside the Suffolk border, Somerleyton Hall is located
in a wooded pocket of hinterland, less than five miles
inshore from the most easterly point of the British Isles
and the faded seaside grandeur of Lowestoft. Yet unlike
Sebald's melancholic narrator, I do not arrive here by train
– though it is an overcast August morning, and those same
diesel-spewing locomotives, now a quarter of a century
older, continue to belch out their noxious fumes into the
big skies that overlay the floodplain of the River Waveney
– but by car, driving through what Nikolaus Pevsner
describes as the hall's namesake 'weird village', before
turning through the understated gate and along the

protracted cattle-lined drive. The residence, when it eventually comes into view on my left, is impressive: a sprawling mix of red and cream bricks, with various squared-off, church-like towers jutting skywards.

Somerleyton Hall is Victorian, though the building work, which began in 1844, incorporates elements of the Jacobean mansion that previously occupied the site. The architect, who also designed the – to my mind – attractive houses in the village that Pevsner disparaged, was the upstanding John Thomas, more famous as a sculptor, and buried in Arthur Machen's 'goblin city' of Kensal Green Cemetery.*

Sir Samuel Morton Peto was the man responsible for funding the hall's transformation into grand spectacle. Peto had hauled himself up from humble origins, starting out as a fourteen-year-old apprentice for his uncle's London building firm, where he learned practical bricklaying, masonry and carpentry skills, and developed his talent for technical drawing. After his uncle's death in 1830 he inherited, along with his cousin, half of the company. The firm's stock rose rapidly thereafter through the winning of numerous high-profile tenders for public works, including the rebuilding of the Lyceum Theatre (where Bram Stoker was to work for two decades as manager), the construction of the Reform Club (the start and end point of Phileas Fogg's fictional eighty-day journey around the world), and,

---

* Coincidentally, though perhaps aptly, John Thomas also happen to be the forenames of my errant airman grandfather, who vanished from my nan's life shortly after fathering my dad and his two younger brothers.

later, in 1843, the definitive monument to Norfolk's 'Hero
of the Nile': Nelson's Column in Trafalgar Square.

The coming of the railways was to bring still greater
prosperity Peto's way, with the undertaking of building
work for the new form of transport – including the nearby
line and station Sebald's narrator alights from in *The Rings
of Saturn*. During the 1840s Peto held thirty-two line-lay-
ing contracts worth an estimated £20 million, making him,
according to Isambard Kingdom Brunel, the richest
contractor at the time in the world. But British rail was not
enough, and soon Peto was carrying out construction works
in Scandinavia, Canada, even Australia. However, an
underfinanced and unsecured deal to extend the London,
Chatham and Dover Railway into Victoria Station was to
be his downfall, resulting in bankruptcy and something of
a fall from grace. In 1862 Peto moved from Somerleyton,
and the house was sold to a Yorkshireman, Sir Francis
Crossley, whose own fortune had come from the more
genteel manufacture of carpets. Crossley's son Savile was
to become the first Lord Somerleyton, and their descendants continue to own the hall; the two women guides point
out various ostentatious portraits of contemporary family
members as they take a paying group of us on a tour – a
variant of the same one I imagine Sebald must himself at
some stage have participated in – of the public parts of the
building's interior. Childishly, every time the current Lord
Somerleyton is mentioned (it happens frequently) I can't
help picturing Lord Summerisle from *The Wicker Man* –
especially when we all mill around the bottom of the grand
staircase above which the walls are decorated with

numerous sets of vast deer antlers, like those that adorn
Christopher Lee's ancestral castle in the film.

I feel disproportionately young. Everyone else on the
tour is a pensioner, including a jolly woman in her sixties
who, at one o'clock in the afternoon, seems already at least
half-cut, amusing herself and the rest of us (though not in
the way she thinks) by asking various irrelevant questions
and then guffawing. I'm writing in my notebook, an action
I'm conscious has been noted by the guides, as one of them
makes a comment to me that 'you don't need to worry,
you're not going to be tested.' Shortly after the other sidles
over and asks if I'm interested in anything in particular. I
almost wonder whether they think I'm casing the joint –
noting down the pieces of china or taxidermy I have my
eye on – so I explain I'm here to research a book (I give no
clue as to what it's about). 'I've worked here for forty
years,' she tells me convivially, 'so just ask me at the end if
there's anything you want to know.'

The Rings of Saturn describes the hall's 'incomparable
glasshouses', part of its Winter Garden, no longer extant,
but which, according to a lavish spread in *The Illustrated
London News* of January 1857 (the periodical owned by
the unfortunate Member of Parliament for Boston drowned
in Lake Michigan), was lit by jets of gas and adorned with
'eight wire baskets, from which hang in graceful negligence
lovely creepers'. Sebald makes much of this now-vanished,
glass-domed wonder, which he contrasts with the faded
glory his melancholy narrator sees everywhere about the
hall and its motley collection of 'bygone paraphernalia'. He
concedes, however, that the Winter Garden must have

been a tremendous sight, and embeds into the book's text an indistinct, doctored etching of the illuminated nocturnal spectacle.

As the two guides lead us further through the ground floor of the hall there's much from them too about the old glasshouses; the courtyard once enclosed by their intricate structures is now a white-flowered garden where newly married wives and husbands can pose for their wedding photographs. Currently, two large mallard-type hybrids that have taken over the small square pond at its centre are the only ones posing; both are in their moulting, eclipse plumage, so it's hard to tell whether they are indeed a happy couple, though they seem inseparable. Sebald's narrator delights in telling us of the demise of the former pleasure palace which, a little over a century before, would have framed the sky above where the ducks are sitting: 'Somerleyton strikes the visitor of today no longer as an oriental palace in a fairy tale. The glass-covered walks and the palm house, whose lofty dome used once to light up the nights, were burnt out in 1913 after a gas explosion and subsequently demolished.'

And here I am given notice of the traps hidden in Sebald's method. Not everything his narrator says can be taken at face value. Truth and fabrication are hard to distinguish. I should know this already of course, but *The Rings of Saturn*'s languorous, almost-reportage style is tricksy, and has a habit of making me want to believe its every word. The book's rambles around the byroads of Norfolk and the Suffolk coast present themselves as an autobiographical work of narrative non-fiction – though my copy categorises itself in small lettering on its back cover as FICTION/ MEMOIR/TRAVEL – and perhaps my own familiarity with many of the locations has lulled me into letting my guard down to a greater extent here than when reading his other great works, *The Emigrants* and *Austerlitz* (although the same approach is employed there too). This detail, however, reminds me that Sebald's narrator is unreliable: because the story the two guides tell about the last days of the Winter Garden does not end in a gas-filled conflagration, but a more gentle dismantling of the structure at the start of 1914, the titanic glassed area having become too uneconomical to continue to heat.

Sebald goes on to describe in the most beautiful of phrases an unlikely apparition he encounters in the house.* As our tour meanders further through the rooms, I am pleased to find that it, at least, does indeed exist, still positioned in the place he describes: 'The stuffed polar bear in the entrance hall stands over three yards tall. With its yellowish and moth-eaten fur, it resembles a ghost bowed by sorrows.'

What *The Rings of Saturn* does not point out is that there are in fact not one, but two near-identical lifeless bears guarding either side of the hallway's inner door (of course, both may not have always been on show). They are indeed

---

* Although Sebald lived in the UK for over thirty years, he continued to write his books in his native German, and therefore we also have to remember that the words we're reading on the page have, in addition, been passed through the filter of one of his translators – perhaps another factor that adds to the oddly beguiling quality of the prose.

massive – three yards is no exaggeration – and posed in a
mirror image of each other, both holding out a giant front
paw in a slightly camp wave. Four faded, torn Indian tiger
skins hang on the walls, and the skull of a hippopotamus
rests on the floor's Minton tiles, its huge molars giving it a
jaunty smile. But it is the bears that hold my attention.
They're captivating.

The giant Arctic-dwelling predators were taken by Sir
Savile Crossley in 1897, in eastern Svalbard. Fifty-five were
shot during the expedition, of which three complete
mounted specimens remain (the third is on display in
Norwich's Castle Museum), as well as various skins and
skulls. In addition, two live polar bears were brought back
to Britain – it's believed one may have survived for several
years in Regent's Park Zoo. A contemporary newspaper
account described one of Sir Savile's subsequent talks
about the grim adventure, in which he detailed how the
killing was carried out:

> The general method of shooting bears is to stalk them,
> but they may be found occasionally in the round beds
> they make in the snow, or may be decoyed by a man
> lying on his back and waving his legs in the air, in
> which case, after getting his wind, they come slowly at
> first but with a final rush on what they imagine to be
> their prey.

A set of magic lantern slides was produced on the expedition's return (presumably to be used by Sir Savile to illustrate the talks he gave) and remains in Somerleyton's

archive. Alongside its picturesque seascapes of hundred-and-fifty-foot icebergs, the slides show various pathos-filled scenes. In one we are looking at the protruding, dirt-splashed head of a live bear in a cage anchored to the deck of the ship *Victoria*, on top of which lies a dead walrus; an earlier one shows three hunched men skinning a bear; and, most graphically, in another, two half-grown cubs consume the viscera of their mother on an ice floe. Her body is positioned on her back, her forelimbs at her sides like a portly human corpse waiting on the marble of the mortuary slab.

In one of *The Rings of Saturn*'s most noteworthy encounters, Sebald's narrator details a long conversation he has with William Hazel, the gardener at Somerleyton. Hazel recalls as a teenager how 'his thoughts constantly revolved around the bombing raids then being launched on Germany from the sixty-seven airfields that were established in East Anglia after 1940', picturing in his head the destruction taking place across the North Sea. Hazel later served in the army in Germany during the 1950s, learning the language so he could read 'what the Germans themselves had said about the bombings and their lives in the ruined cities'. To his astonishment he finds an absence of contemporary accounts of the time – it is as if, like in Ishiguro's *The Buried Giant*, 'everything had been erased from their minds'. This exchange cuts to the heart of Sebald's work and his exploration of how we, both individually and collectively, come to forget (or at least suppress) the losses we have suffered, the memories of people and events that once came to us

with such clarity, and the atrocities to which we are in
some part complicit.

I have thought a lot about the conversation between the
Sebald character and William Hazel. So, at the end of the
tour, I ask the guide – the one who has worked at the house
for the past four decades – whether a William Hazel was
ever Somerleyton's gardener. There are puzzled looks and
a discussion as the two women try and recall the name I've
given. I tell them I've seen it in a book in which the hall
features.

'Just a minute, I'll check I've got it right,' and I fish the
copy from my bag.

'Is that *The Rings of Saturn*?' they say.

I nod.

'Well … that's a load of rubbish – you don't want to
believe anything in that. He made things up!'

I'm amused at their response – and at myself, having yet
again half-trusted in the verisimilitude of Sebald's book
enough to wonder whether someone with the same name
as one of his characters previously tended the hall's flower-
beds. We chat some more, and I learn that the long-time
head gardener who would have been here when the
purported August 1992 visit took place is now retired.
Later, on the internet, I discover he was not born until
1949, so could not have harboured any imagined remem-
brances of Germany's carpet-bombing by the Allied air
forces: William Hazel is a fiction, a device.

Emerging from the hall I find myself in front of the
aviary, where Sebald's narrator also found himself lingering. In the book, poignantly, these cages are empty except

for a single Chinese quail described as 'evidently in a state of dementia, running to and fro along the perimeter of the cage and shaking its head every time it was about to turn, as if it could not comprehend how it had got into this hopeless fix'. The mental image it evokes reminds me of footage I have seen of polar bears transported from the boundless white Arctic to dreary, grey terrestrial confinement in Western cities – a destiny perhaps experienced by the two live animals brought back by the first Lord Somerleyton from Svalbard.

Sebald includes a photograph of the gamebird, taken through the narrow mesh of the aviary's cage front. In the foreground, sure enough, is 'a solitary Chinese quail', but, looking closer, the background reveals a second half-hidden individual I've not noticed before. Sebald, however, is correct about their identity: the two birds, both males, are indeed *Synoicus chinensis*, sometimes known by the common name Chinese quail, but more frequently as the king quail. What the monochrome photo doesn't show is the bird's chestnut belly and dark-blue face. It's a beautiful species, and one I've seen just once in the wild, in eastern Queensland when birding in a coastal swamp with my brother as we searched for the rare, crepuscular ground parrot. I am reminded of that trip to the far side of the world a decade ago because, although there are no quails in the aviary today, it is filled with noisy Australian bush birds. These are mostly zebra finches and budgerigars, as well as a miniature diamond dove whose airy, piping calls sound like a primary school child blowing into a recorder.

Poo-tee-weet?

As I watch the budgies, long-tailed and flutter-winged, chasing the length of the ornately decorated structure, it seems by and large a happy place. The one note of discord that brings me back to *The Rings of Saturn*'s forlorn aviary passage is that I notice a frantic immature great tit – its colours a muted version of what they will become – which has managed to get itself trapped inside, its constant flight from one end of the cage to the other reminiscent of the quail's 'hopeless fix'. The native songbird clings and picks at the mesh of the different skylights, trying to find its way out to the freedom it can remember. Its distress contrasts with the ignorant bliss of its exotic new companions: they know of nothing else.

I arrive beside the imposing yew maze, designed and planted in 1846 for Peto by the landscape gardener William

Andrews Nesfield. Sebald's narrator gets lost within its walls, having to draw lines in the gravel floor with his boot as a navigational aid. I struggle even to find my way in, as there is both an outer and inner entrance to the fiendish semi-circular structure. Walking around the maze is a frustrating experience, as it seems so simple, particularly when I notice that the couple who were at one point only marginally ahead of me have now reached the rotunda at its heart. Eventually, I get there too; I wait a while until the others have started to head back out and then contemplate the silence. Did M. R. James ever visit here? There is no mention of the hall in his *Suffolk and Norfolk* (just a puzzled reference to the old painted screen in the village's church, which, mysteriously, includes 'someone with a saw'), nor of any acquaintance with the Crossley family in either of his two biographies. Yet Somerleyton is not far from Aldeburgh, where James was a frequent visitor both in his childhood and in his later years, and it is not inconceivable that the maze filtered into the writer's imagination as a model for the yew hedges at the centre of 'Mr Humphreys and His Inheritance', which appeared in his second collection, 1911's *More Ghost Stories of an Antiquary*.*

---

* 'Mr Humphreys and His Inheritance' is one of James's most intriguing (though least frightening) stories. James seemingly buries much of his knowledge of the classics and biblical apocrypha within the tale, which itself is something of a maze. Some scholars of his work have speculated as to whether there's a puzzle hidden at its core that involves more than the restless spirit of Mr Humphrey's great-grandfather, and whose solution requires an expertise in early Gnostic sects.

The dank labyrinth in the story captures the sense of unease and fascination that these living structures elicit; certainly, I've always felt that way about them. A 'Jubilee Maze' (though *leylandii*, not yew) was planted in the formal bulb-industry show garden, Springfields, located on the eastern limit of the town where I grew up, to commemorate the twenty-fifth anniversary of the Queen's 1952 accession to the throne. A contemporary article in a local magazine made a grandiose claim about the upcoming attraction: 'This maze, which should grow by three feet per year, by 1979 should lose the most energetic of children and will rival in popularity the famous Hampton Court maze.'

Its dark green walls, which, when I visited during the early 1980s, were already taller than a man, could be surreptitiously accessed via a door in the side of my dad's neighbouring office. Once or twice in the evenings after the gardens were closed to the public he would let us both through and we would walk around the maze together. I came again in my later teens – the first time I'd been back since I was at primary school – climbing over a gate to gain illicit access. I hoped, indeed believed, it would still be exciting; I think I was expecting it to be vast and impressive, as that was how I remembered it, but the experience left me empty, producing nothing of the earlier childhood thrill: people had made shortcuts through some of the now-patchy hedges and the place seemed small and unkempt compared to how it was fixed in my mind.

A few years after my return visit the straggly *leylandii* were grubbed up when the gardens were built over and

remodelled to become a retail park (though a fragment of the planted area was retained). My father's stark 1960s office block is still there, but today has an air of dilapidation out of place against its new surroundings, the white paintwork of the wrought-iron railings of the balcony that led off Dad's room and overlooked the long-gone maze now tainted with rust.

We started coming to this stretch of the Suffolk coastline for family holidays in 1988, by which point Mum's cancer was a familiar companion. Over the next four years we stayed for short breaks in the same rented holiday home not far from Lowestoft and Somerleyton, and the polite seaside resorts of Southwold and Aldeburgh – two of my mother's favourite towns. Keeping me occupied was the flagship nature reserve of Minsmere, where I was happy to be left for hours. During the Second World War its

low-lying grazing marshes were flooded to deter the spectre of German invaders; as a result, in 1947, the country
gained its first nesting pairs of black-and-white avocets for
more than a century.

When these once- or twice-yearly holidays began my
brother was studying French at university in the Midlands,
but because the visits tended to be during Easter or the
October half-term he would often join us. Sometimes my
older cousin Patrick would come along, or one of Chris's
friends. I have fond memories of those trips, though my
diaries tell me little about what we did, detailing only the
birds I encountered: on our initial visit in April 1988 my
notes gushed that a 'brilliant Great Grey Shrike was showing well (for over twenty minutes) on Westleton Heath'.
The shrike, a scarce silver-and-black passage migrant and
annual winter visitor to Britain in small numbers from
Scandinavia, remains among my favourite songbirds. Its
evocative, monster-like name had drawn my attention
years earlier, when I first read about it in one of my books.
I can still picture that same individual as it surveyed the
brown heather from the top of a birch sapling; I remember
Dad, who was not particularly interested in wildlife but
enjoyed having attractive or interesting species pointed out
to him, got into a minor argument after he looked through
a birdwatcher's telescope without permission – an incident
that we'd joke about for the remainder of the holiday.

Nearby, where the land meets the sea, lies another strip
of heather and gorse: Dunwich Heath. This is the place
where, just over halfway through *The Rings of Saturn*,
Sebald's narrator gets lost, imagining himself to be trapped

in a yew labyrinth like the one he visited earlier in the book, before experiencing a vision not dissimilar to the astral flights of fancy taken by the Recluse in William Hope Hodgson's *The House on the Borderland*:

> It was as though I stood at the topmost point of the earth, where the glittering winter sky is forever unchanging; as though the heath were rigid with frost, and adders, vipers and lizards of transparent ice lay slumbering in their hollows in the sand. From my resting place in the pavilion I gazed out across the heath into the night. And I saw, to the south, entire headlands had broken off the coast and sunk beneath the waves.

Today, with the warm breeze, the clear blue sky, and the bright, late-afternoon sunshine that caresses the back of my neck, it's hard to imagine a less claustrophobic place – though there are a few more shadowed pockets among the heathland's shallow dips, and some of the paths do seem to meander counterintuitively, leading you away from where you wish to go. On a grey day with no one in sight and with the skies pressing in the feeling might be different, of course. Certainly the dome of Sizewell's nuclear power station in the distance adds a slight frisson.

A mile or so to the north is the village that gives the heath its name, with its shingle beach along which we used to stroll on those long-ago holidays. Dunwich, too, can seem a melancholy place, though its history could be seen to justify such thinking. Once it boasted up to twelve churches and two monasteries, a Domesday Book population of three thousand souls, and, until the beginning of the fourteenth century – before longshore drift did for it – perhaps East Anglia's finest harbour.* Fierce storms coupled with the wrong geology, however, meant the town's flaking cliffs were prone to be washed away by the unrelenting waves, with hundreds of houses and, today, all but one of the churches lost below the waters.

Legends say you can still hear the ringing bells of the submerged places of worship – a folk tale repeated at various other sites around the British Isles. Dunwich's sunken chimes are apocryphal, but stories of bones protruding from the cliff face beneath the old graveyard are not. A few years ago, the man running the village's charming museum tells me, a Norwegian television crew were filming by the site of the last surviving memorial from the now-vanished All Saints – the clifftop headstone is dedicated to Jacob Forster who departed this life in 1796, aged thirty-eight years – when the cameraman looked down to see half a skeleton laid out on a ledge. The story of an over-excited dog racing down the street with a human skull clamped between its teeth is probably not to be believed, however, though bones do have a habit of finding their way back decades later, when people come upon their labelled remains ('discovered on Dunwich beach' on such and such

---

* I suspect the fictional town in 'Ringing the Changes', Robert Aickman's excellent tale of the church bell-awakened dead, may have been inspired by Dunwich: 'Before the river silted up, Holihaven was one of the most important seaports in Great Britain.'

a date) in a loft or cupboard when clearing out an elderly relative's possessions.

They tend to be placed in the next open grave to be dug in the churchyard, the museum man says: a disembodied eternity in the intimate company of a stranger.

The settlement's decline lent the place a certain cachet for Victorian writers, including the Decadent poet Algernon Charles Swinburne, who features in *The Rings of Saturn*. He lodged nearby in 1875 (and again two years later), walking the brittle cliffs with his friend, the critic and poet Theodore Watts-Dutton. Here he wrote the poem 'Where Dunwich Used To Be', which details the slow destruction of All Saints Church;* Sebald shows us an

---

* Walter de la Mare's wonderful 'All Hallows' puts me in mind of All Saints – a remote, but grand, clifftop church miles from anywhere. As well as being under assault by the sea there are 'devilish agencies at work' that are gradually rebuilding the place of worship in a darker image: the ruinous tower mysteriously contains a new sculpture of a 'two-headed crocodile' and a sinister 'vulture-like' eagle.

underexposed old photograph (taken around 1909) of the same structure, highlighting the fictionality of his text by also including – along with a nonsensical explanation of how it remained standing – one of the ruined Eccles Church. The beach-marooned tower stood, in reality, some thirty-five miles to the north on the Norfolk coast, until the waves took it too, in 1895; the last vestige of All Saints (its north-west buttress) was moved from the adjacent cliffs in 1923, relocated a few hundred yards inland to the graveyard of the village's sole current church, St James's. Dunwich also inspired Swinburne's long poem about mortality, 'By the North Sea'; its evocative opening line – 'A land that is lonelier than ruin' – seems apt on a deserted winter's day, but not on this Indian Summer Sunday, when the top end of the beach is busy with cheerful family gatherings who fill the air with their chatter and the smell of barbecuing charcoal.

Swinburne was not the only writer or artist to be attracted by the romance of the place's faded glory. Painted around 1830, J. M. W. Turner's storm-riven scene titled simply *Dunwich* looks south towards the cliffs atop which All Saints still (at this point) stands, fully intact, beside the ruins of Greyfriars Priory. The poet Edward Fitzgerald, translator of *The Rubaiyat of Omar Khayyam*, spent his summers here during the 1870s. During his own 1897 visit – the same year he wrote *The Turn of the Screw* – Henry James stayed in the cottage that previously had housed Fitzgerald, noting later in his travel book *English Hours* that 'Dunwich is not even the ghost of its dead self; almost all you can say of it is that it consists of the mere letters of its old name.'* And Arthur Machen, though I have no idea whether he himself ever came here (the *Evening News* did send him to East Anglia in 1915), mentions a fictitious Welsh village called Dunwich in *The Terror*, his 1917 novella (serialised in the previous year) about how the First World War was causing nature to turn against mankind.†

M. R. James too was familiar with Dunwich and its long history of religious houses and subsiding cliffs, with the remains of its Templar church possibly finding its way into one of his best stories, 'Oh, Whistle, and I'll Come to You, My Lad'. Although the town's Preceptory of the Knights Templar is thought to have been irrevocably lost to the waves during the seventeenth century (the order itself had been disbanded some three hundred years earlier), a local geographic feature bearing the name 'Temple Hill' evaded erosion by the sea for a good while longer. Indeed, an archaeological dig was carried out at the site in 1935. So when, around 1903, James wrote his story, the preceptory's location was almost certainly still extant, as were the atmospheric nearby ruins of the Franciscans' priory, which today continue to cling to their clifftop field behind the gravestone of Jacob Forster.

---

* The American's masterful psychological ghost story was adapted into a 1954 opera by Benjamin Britten, this stretch of coastline's most famous son. Britten resided just a few miles to the south of Dunwich at Snape, another of my mother's favourite places.

† *The Terror* is probably where H. P. Lovecraft came across the name, borrowing it for one of his most notable stories – the corrupted, decaying New England settlement of 'The Dunwich Horror' (first published in *Weird Tales* in April 1929).

The title of 'Oh, Whistle, and I'll Come to You, My Lad' comes from a light-hearted love song of the same name whose lyrics are by Robert Burns. But in James's story it is not a lover who is coming, but an apparition swathed in bedsheets – an archetypal image of the ghostly rendered here, for all of its seeming familiarity and physical impotence, as terrifying as any of the revenants and medieval demons that haunt his other tales.

Parkins, a neat young Cambridge professor, is about to spend one of his vacation periods in Burnstow, a place modelled on the south Suffolk resort and port of Felixstowe, combined (I suspect) with elements of Dunwich. I wonder whether the town's name is a nod to Robert Burns, though it may just have been chosen for its ring of desolation; the fictional location also features fleetingly in James's later tale 'The Tractate Middoth'.

Parkins is going away to improve his fledgling golf game on Burnstow's links, as well as hoping to catch up with his research.* In a telling exchange with colleagues at the start of the story, much is revealed about Parkins' character; he comes across as a sincere but humourless young don with an outwardly strong disbelief in all matters supernatural: 'I hold that any semblance, any appearance of concession to the view that such things might exist is equivalent to a renunciation of all that I hold most sacred.' The testing of this antipathy towards the otherworldly is what drives the narrative.

---

* Parkins lectures in Ontography, a philosophical subject invented in the story by James – presumably related in some way to *ontology* and the nature of 'being' – which has now been co-opted as an actual term by some academics.

Taking a break from his golf to examine the Templars' ruin, Parkins decides to dig with his pocket knife beneath a bare patch of earth. The topsoil collapses inwards to reveal a void into which Parkins reaches.

As he withdrew the knife he heard a metallic clink, and when he introduced his hand it met with a cylindrical object lying on the floor of the hole. Naturally enough, he picked it up, and when he brought it into the light, now fast fading, he could see that it, too, was of man's making – a metal tube about four inches long, and evidently of some considerable age.

Heading back for the evening to his accommodation, the Globe Inn, he notices 'a rather indistinct personage' further along the beach, which appears to be trying to catch up

with him; he outpaces the figure, not keen on a twilight meeting on the lonely shore.

After dinner, where he eats with his playing partner, the no-nonsense Colonel Wilson, he returns to his room and, after noticing perhaps the same shape staring up at him through his window from the beach, remembers the metal object he dug up earlier. Once cleaned, it's apparent that it is an aged whistle, with letters inscribed on both its front and back. The longer inscription reads QUIS EST ISTE QUI VENIT, which Parkins translates as 'Who is this who is coming?' In order to answer the question he – foolishly, as the Colonel later comments – decides to put it to his lips.

> He blew tentatively and stopped suddenly, startled and
> yet pleased at the note he had elicited. It had a quality
> of infinite distance in it, and, soft as it was, he
> somehow felt it must be audible for miles round.
> It was a sound, too, that seemed to have the power
> (which many scents possess) of forming pictures in
> the brain.

Parkins begins to see a vision in his mind of a dark night-time expanse, broken up by the appearance of a solitary form. His reverie is disturbed by a sudden gust of wind that makes him look up through the glass – the flash of something, a gull's wing illuminated in the moonlight perhaps – before the window swings inwards. Later, as he struggles for sleep, he has more unsettling visions of a shingle shoreline edged by sand and the presence of a black, bobbing shape that pursues him as he flees across the groynes that bisect the beach.

The next day, after more rounds with the Colonel on the links, events gather apace as the pair accost a terrified boy outside the hotel. The lad swears he has seen a white-sheeted, waving figure in the window of Parkins' room. No explanation is forthcoming – no one has been in the room other than the maid to make it up, and nothing has been taken or displaced, except for the bedsheets on the super-fluous spare bed which are 'bundled up and twisted together in a most tortuous confusion'. Having shown the Colonel the curious whistle, the professor turns in.

And here comes the visitor he least desires.

After an hour or so of fitful sleep Parkins stirs, certain he can hear movement in the empty bed across the room. He rises to the window, where he has propped a makeshift curtain with a stick to block the moonlight, grabbing the pole to fend off whatever is alongside him.

> Parkins, who very much dislikes being questioned
> about it, did once describe something of it in my
> hearing, and I gathered that what he chiefly
> remembers about it is a horrible, an intensely horrible,
> face of *crumpled linen*. What expression he read upon it
> he could not or would not tell, but that the fear of it
> went nigh to maddening him is certain.

The academic is saved from the blanketed embrace of this apparition by the timely entrance of the Colonel. The animated air dissipates beneath the now-fallen sheet and

Parkins, out cold, is watched over for the rest of the night by the older man. The next day the whistle is cast into the sea, the sheets burned in a bonfire behind the hotel. 'There is really nothing more to tell, but, as you may imagine, the Professor's views on certain points are less clear cut than they used to be.'*

In James's story the Professor gets off relatively lightly. Yes, his nerves are thereafter never quite the same, but he has survived his encounter with whatever it was he summoned, even if his outward philosophy has not. It's a tale that is at once terrifying, but also playful and, at times, comedic – as well as offering up all sorts of unanswered questions for those attempting to divine more of James's subconscious psychology from what he may, or may not, give us of himself within its fifteen pages: because, rightly or wrongly, it's difficult not to discern Parkins as a version of James himself (albeit one stripped of his obvious sense of humour), and the text as a comment on his familiar world of high academia. In Burns's poem that provides the story's title, the woman implores her lover to be discreet in his courting, to pretend in public that he cares not for her. This, it strikes me, mirrors Parkins' own true opinion about ghosts – 'A man in my position cannot, I find, be too careful about appearing to sanction the current beliefs on such subjects.' It is, however, a charade his colleagues do not seem convinced by.

---

* James gives his own view on the subject in the introduction to his *Collected Ghost Stories*: 'Do I believe in ghosts? To which I answer that I am prepared to consider evidence and accept it if it satisfies me.'

Here again, as in so many of James's stories, we have all sorts of allusions to the terrors inherent in touch, and of how awful it is to have the sanctity of the bed where one sleeps shattered. Yet, like the lover in Burns's song, does Parkins – and perhaps by extension James – protest too much?

Does 'Oh, Whistle, and I'll Come to You, My Lad' conceal a yearning for companionship to mitigate the loneliness of the long night's upcoming darkness?

Chapter 9

WHO IS THIS WHO IS COMING?

Early April 1991, and we were about to return to Suffolk. I was seventeen by this point and in the lower sixth at school. I'm sure a break felt much needed, though not because of the usual concerns I might have been expected to be preoccupied with: how I would do in my A level mocks; whatever delicate social dynamic was concerning my clique; and girlfriends – or, at least, my lack thereof. Because since the end of the previous year – what L. P. Hartley might have referred to as that 'Golden Age' of 1990 – things at home had taken an unexpectedly grim turn.

A situation soon to get darker still.

Mum had been sporting her pirate's patch for several months, the vision in one eye now gone. (I have a sudden temporary sense of panic as I realise I cannot remember which side was affected, but how can I be expected to recall such details, I tell myself in defence.) Her face was puffed-up and swollen too, by the steroids meant to be keeping the tumour in her head at bay. Still, she took setbacks like these with fortitude, at least publicly. Looking back, I don't know what her prognosis was at the start of 1991. Whether, in secret, she and Dad already feared the worst, whether they saw any kind of future that stretched beyond the immediate? (I believe they were thinking ahead: a permanent move to the Suffolk coast had been mooted, with Dad taking early retirement.) He was fifty-two at this point and had undergone a health scare of his own a couple of months before, experiencing a terrible, tearing pain in his groin that had put him in Boston's by now familiar Pilgrim Hospital for a worrying week – the first time I'd ever known him to experience any serious signs of illness. Nothing, however, was found and no explanation was proffered by the medical staff, and by the end of January he appeared fine again; he'd resumed playing golf at weekends, so must have felt well on the mend.

And then I came home from school and into the lounge one afternoon to find Dad in a choking tide of tears. I don't think I'd ever even seen him cry before, let alone sitting there raging against life – I could just about make out his words – about how it was so bloody unfair. Chris, he told me, when at last he became coherent, had been to the doctor's about a lump in his neck and the blood tests had come back to show he had something called Hodgkin's lymphoma. Which was a type of cancer. So now it wasn't only my mum who was ill, who had *that* word.

But my brother too.

Chris had graduated from university in the previous summer and was working nights in the nearby bread-distribution factory, a short walk from our house – taking a year out and saving up for an extended trip he was planning to Africa in the spring. He seemed outwardly at peace with his diagnosis – even then he shared Mum's stoicism. But he told me not to look up the disease in the black leather-bound *Encyclopaedia Britannica* set Mum and Dad had purchased a few years before, figuring it would be a useful, albeit ridiculously pricey investment to keep us well-informed. I looked anyway, of course – and from what I understood of the medical jargon his prospects didn't seem great. Ignore what's there, Chris said, the doctor reckons the treatment's better now.

'It's one of the good ones to get.'

This is the time when I started going on those walks through the deserted night land – where I glimpsed that silent, white-haired old woman – to try and clear the thoughts convulsing around my head. And to be away from Dad, whose all-consuming sorrow was so difficult to witness. Who himself was trying to reconcile, I suppose, how to cope with a slowly dying wife (because that is what she was) and an eldest son about to embark on various treatments and operations from which there might not be a way back.

I'd stopped reading ghost stories by this point. Suddenly they didn't seem as entertaining.

Who is this who is coming?

Jonathan Miller's 1968 adaptation of James's story for the BBC arts series *Omnibus* curtailed its title to *Whistle and I'll Come To You*. The stripping out of the flourish of the original's Burns-inspired name is mirrored in the film's pared-down, black-and-white scenes, filmed on the cliffs at Dunwich and in the marram-guarded dunes of Waxham on the north-east corner of the Norfolk coastline. Where James's story playfully examines the nature of our belief in the irrational (though allowing the possibility of the existence of things beyond everyday comprehension), Miller's take is very much a psychoanalytical one that transforms Parkin – renamed from Parkins in James's original – into an ageing don on the threshold of a nervous breakdown. Indeed, as the film progresses we start to hear, in voiceover, the expressed thoughts of Parkin – played by Michael Hordern – who, as he lies unable to sleep, turns over the phrase 'Who is this who is coming?' in his head.

I love the look of the film, especially the scenes where Parkin pokes around the clifftop graves and uncovers the cursed whistle; I can't decide if the headstones are elaborate props or if, in 1968, more memorials were still to tumble to the beach below. Hordern's performance, with his blank expression, his verbal tics, his indifference to and difficulty with engaging other people in the hotel, is particularly adroit. And yet, I find I prefer the playfulness and the pacing of James's original. For me, its terrors stand the test of time better than Miller's interpretation, which leaves us reasonably certain that what we are witnessing is the mental collapse of a vulnerable man. (James would argue that a good ghost story can 'leave a loophole for a natural explanation', but that such a way out should 'be so narrow as not to be quite practicable'.)

That said, when the sheets rise from the spare bed in the darkness of Hordern's room – accompanied by his guttural, open-mouthed baby sounds – their simple horror is still perhaps the most powerful image of a ghost in any film I have seen.

There is another, later tale by James also set in coastal Suffolk. 'A Warning to the Curious' was the title piece of the collection of the same name dating from 1925, the final of the four separate volumes put out during James's lifetime (though his *Collected Ghost Stories* of 1931 did include four lesser works which had not appeared in book form before). The story, which takes place in the fictional Seaburgh, a counterfeit copy of the upmarket Suffolk resort of Aldeburgh, shares a number of parallels with 'Oh, Whistle, and I'll Come to You, My Lad'. A notable addition is a fragment of invented folklore about the last of the three lost crowns of East Anglia. Buried in a secluded tree-lined hillock away from the town, the legendary object is said to confer protection on the nation in times of trouble – a little like Machen's Agincourt archers in 'The Bowmen'.

'A Warning to the Curious' is a good story, and on the face of it contains greater menace than James's earlier tale

in the shape of the crown's guardian, the spirit of the late
William Ager, who is capable of inflicting more than
bed-wetting night fears (we can see the potential source of
John Gordon's subconscious inspiration for *The House on
the Brink*). But it does feel a bit of a rehash, and I can't help
wondering whether by this point in his life James, saddened
by the toll of the Great War on the young men of
Cambridge and Eton (and the more general toll that the
passage of time was taking on his friends and contemporaries), had his best stories, his best days, behind him.*

---

* One of the stories contained with James's last standalone
collection is most certainly a reworking of a previous tale ('The
Mezzotint', one of his finest). James modestly admits as much in a
brief afterword to 'The Haunted Doll's House': 'I can only hope
that there is enough of variation in the setting to make the
repetition of the *motif* tolerable.'

Lawrence Gordon Clark's adaptation of 'A Warning to the Curious', the second in the BBC's then annual 'Ghost Story for Christmas' strand, was broadcast during the final hour of Christmas Eve, 1972.* It's a very different beast from Jonathan Miller's film, and one I have come to prefer; in fact, I'd choose it over James's original text. Clark's version doesn't include the elements of scepticism about the supernatural that pervade Miller's piece – the rational, very much open 'loophole' – and keeps the ghost 'malevolent or odious' as James would deem necessary. The setting does, though, shift Seaburgh from Suffolk to Norfolk, the harbour and pine woods of Wells-next-the-Sea – where we often went for the day with my parents and my nan, and where Chris and I would subsequently spend many hours birding – providing the main locations. Later in the film we see a church and lighthouse; these distinctive landmarks were filmed further east along the coast around the collapsing cliffs of Happisburgh, where in 2013, archaeologists uncovered a set of 800,000-year-old hominid footprints – the most ancient marks of primitive humanity found outside Africa.

Wells Woods manages to look both beautiful and menacing in Clark's *A Warning to the Curious*, shot in grainy colour 16mm beneath a wintry sun that causes the near-sculptural trees to cast long, sinister shadows. As for

---

* The first, *The Stalls of Barchester* (shot on location at Norwich Cathedral), aired on Christmas Eve, 1971, with my introduction to M. R. James, *Lost Hearts*, following in 1973.

the night-time scenes, they rival *The Blair Witch Project* for
the creepiness of their glimpsed torchlit horrors among the
shadowed trunks. Although its seemingly unending
expanse of sandy beach – which features in the opening
sequence and again, briefly, to devastating effect at its
climax – is now, even in the heart of the winter, a busy
tourist destination, the belt of dune-strengthening,
Victorian-planted Corsican pines can be disconcerting
once you get away from the crowds; I certainly remember
feeling unsettled as I wandered around on my own birdwatching as a teenager while Mum and Dad pottered
about the town. Pine needles smother the thin grey soil,
the knotted trunks and thick canopy block out the daylight
and, apart from a few hard-to-see goldcrests and coal tits
calling listlessly from somewhere above, the woods often
appear lifeless. And though the narrowness of the strip of
trees means you shouldn't become disoriented, it's still
easy to lose your bearings and find you've walked much
further than you intended.

The adaptation of *A Warning to the Curious* features a
wonderful central performance from the late Peter
Vaughan, who at this point in his career was best known
for his role in Sam Peckinpah's *Straw Dogs* – though he
later would gain greater recognition for playing the elderly
butler, Stevens senior, in the film version of Kazuo
Ishiguro's *The Remains of the Day*, and as the comically
menacing criminal godfather Grouty from the sitcom
Porridge. Vaughan makes Paxton a sympathetic figure,
aided by changes in the script from the original that trans-
form him into a lower-middle-class clerk who's recently

been made redundant, rendering his search for the crown more forgivable.*

Another major change to the story is the film's opening. During the Great War, twelve years before the action of the present, we witness a previous archaeologist's attempt to dig up and steal the artefact; as a result he is hacked to death with a billhook by William Ager, the guardian of the legendary object, who at this point is still flesh and blood. I think this scene perhaps reveals a little too much too

---

* The main supporting actor, Clive Swift, does a fine job in the role of Paxton's fellow hotel guest Dr Black. Two decades on he would play Hyacinth Bucket's put-upon husband in *Keeping Up Appearances* – it feels somewhat incongruous that both of the film's leads would end up becoming best known for their roles in two cosy English sitcoms.

soon, though Ager undoubtedly presents a scary-looking figure – albeit the violence we watch him carrying out is more suited to Leatherface from *The Texas Chainsaw Massacre* than something we'd normally expect from one of James's avenging angels. But the altered opening does give us a memorable line absent from the original, as the consumptive Ager rasps from the top of the pine-clad hillock at his imminent first victim, his cloak fluttering ominously in the breeze: 'No diggin' 'ere!'

Paxton, of course, comes to discover where the crown is hidden, though the cost to him is prodigious, causing him later in James's original to lament, '… the worst of it is I don't know how to put it back.'

Digging up the past can be a dangerous pursuit.

When W. G. Sebald moved to Norfolk in 1970, to take up a post as a lecturer in European literature at the University of East Anglia, he lived, to begin with, in the small market town of Wymondham, my own home now for several years. Enquiring as to the whereabouts of Sebald's residence, in a strange coincidence I discover that the rooms he initially took were within a house owned by a friend of mine, which I was due to be visiting for the first time later that week, to attend a meeting of a local arts group. The building is a grand, late-Georgian mansion in view of the west tower of the town's looming medieval abbey.

I arrive early and am greeted by my friend Christine at the door; the pair of us head inside and sit at the oversize table that dominates the high-ceilinged entrance hall, where we begin to talk about the man who lived here, for a short spell, almost half a century ago.* Christine never knew Sebald, having moved in with her husband a few months after the German writer left. However, the story soon becomes far more convoluted than I had anticipated, as I learn that the house the narrator and his wife Clara (not the name of Sebald's actual wife) come to in the opening chapter of The Emigrants, Sebald's first 'prose fiction' work, is clearly modelled on this one and not, as described in the book, a chateau-like residence in the small town of Hingham, some seven miles to the west. (The key clinching architectural detail, now demolished, was the former presence of a strange bathroom on stilts, accessed across a kind of footbridge – Christine shows me where its iron supports used to stand.) Moreover, it transpires that the character of Dr Henry Selwyn, the subject of the book's first chapter, is in many aspects a thinly disguised and easily recognisable version of Christine's father-in-law (their names are very different, and of course, being Sebald, it is not an accurate biographical portrait). He too was a rural doctor, and his wife, Christine's mother-in-law – who is rather unflatteringly painted by Sebald – was indeed a Swiss woman of redoubtable business acumen responsible for the household's wealth, like her equivalent in the novel.

Christine tells me about the authentic Dr Selwyn, and as she talks he comes alive again within the walls he would have once walked. Her father-in-law was a polymathic

---

* The same huge table – 'at which thirty people could have been seated with no difficulty' – is described by Dr Selwyn in The Emigrants.

classical scholar, oarsman, amateur dramatist and keen naturalist (Sebald's initial encounter with the grass-counting Dr Selwyn is not far wide of the mark), never happier in his final years than when growing the delicious fruits and vegetables that Sebald's not-quite-himself narrator so vividly describes. Later, as Christine walks me around the extensive grounds, pointing out the vegetable patch that has now been left to go to seed, she herself takes on the role of Dr Selwyn, presenting me with two gnarled, furry-skinned quinces to take home; they do indeed prove to be delicious. The book locates a tennis court to the side of the house, but the photograph of it Sebald uses in *The Emigrants* was not taken here – the wall and trees are wrong, and the court is aligned in the opposite direction. However, I'm more disappointed to find that the castellated, flint-studded folly depicted as the doctor's almost full-time retreat – Sebald includes one of his characteristic grainy photographs of the fairy-tale structure – never existed here, and that the actual corner of the garden given over to him is occupied by a rather more mundane brick outbuilding, which is gradually being subsumed by ivy and other creepers.

One Sunday afternoon last winter I stepped out of my own home, a ten-minute walk away, for what I had planned to be a quick circuit of the town. However, for some reason I ended up pressing onwards much further than I intended, following the course of the small river, the Tiffey, downstream along its valley to the imposing Kimberley Hall – its grounds landscaped by Capability Brown – which stands two miles north of the town. Once into the estate I walked alongside a bare-leafed wood into which mysterious deep, brick-lined pits were dug, perhaps, I wondered, part of an old drainage system. (Though, briefly, I also questioned if there was a more outlandish or darker purpose to which they had ever been put.) A rusting iron ladder was angled into the dark sludge at the bottom of one of them, begging the thought as to why anyone would want to climb down: presumably it was there more as a means of escape? In any case, I did not investigate.

A line of poplars inadequately decorated with giant pom-poms of mistletoe straddled the sheep field crossed by the path, and at some point I passed through the walled gardens of the hall which were, if not exactly derelict, then decidedly unkempt; they seemed like a location from a book or film – at the time they brought to my mind the

lost domain of Alain-Fournier's *Le Grand Meaulnes*. Looking today at the photographs of Dr Selwyn's gardens in the first section of *The Emigrants* and comparing them to my own taken on that afternoon, I now think that Kimberley may well be where Sebald's images were obtained; certainly, at least, the one that shows, through out-of-focus foliage, the outbuildings and greenhouse.*

The whole atmosphere of the place, with its air of winter decay and the oddness and emptiness of the various locations – I saw no one else on my walk – put me in mind of Sebald. This feeling was heightened when, on retracing my route back towards the town, I found the initials 'W. G.' scored into a fence post next to a stile I had to climb; coming from the other direction I'd not noticed it. I wondered whether this was evidence that the writer had passed this same way years before, but almost as soon as the thought came I had to dismiss it, because below the two letters was inscribed the year '2008', meaning that if Max Sebald had added it then it must have been carved by the hand of his white-moustached ghost.

As well as the semi-fictionalised Selwyn and his wife Elli, the opening chapter of *The Emigrants* also features the house's maid, Elaine – and it should come as no surprise that she too had a real-life counterpart. The similarly named Eileen was of Anglo-Indian origin and came to the

---

* Christine later confirms that the book's photos are not of her garden and that Kimberley Hall could indeed be a good candidate, though there is no shortage of walled estates in Norfolk and Suffolk that might have provided Sebald's anonymous photographic backdrop.

family, in somewhat mysterious circumstances, during the
1950s. From what Christine remembers, she seems an even
more interesting and enigmatic subject than the few lines
of description given over to the novel's stand-in suggest.
For instance, Eileen would barter for goods with the local
shopkeepers (on more than one occasion she was picked
up by the police for alleged shoplifting, before being bailed
by her no-nonsense Swiss employer), and would loudly
lament the length of her working days and the conditions
in which she had to live – a mischievous, dramatic public
act she loved to perform, but which had little basis,
Christine assures me, in reality. One thing Eileen, who died
over a decade ago, did share with Sebald's Elaine was her
collection, which takes me back to that creepy New Forest
guest house bedroom my brother and I had shared:

> Only once did I manage to snatch a glance, and saw
> that her small room was full of countless dolls,
> meticulously dressed, most of them wearing something
> on their heads, standing or sitting around or lying on
> the bed where Elaine herself slept – if, that is, she ever
> slept at all, and did not spend the entire night crooning
> softly as she played with her dolls.

Christine admits that when *The Emigrants* came out she
was annoyed by the way Sebald had stolen, without attri-
bution, a version of the family's history – his words often
misrepresenting the people concerned – and particularly
by the portrayal of her mother-in-law (Sebald's Elli) who,
throughout our conversation, she touchingly refers to as

Granny. At the time of the book's publication Christine's
niece was especially upset, and that made Christine herself
take against Sebald. The passage of years, however, has
softened that sentiment, and she no longer has strong feelings about the subject.

She fetches two photographs of Dr Selwyn's doppel-
gänger: one of him in, I would guess, his sixties, and another
as a much younger man – a handsome figure with an exotic
air. Ironically, Selwyn's stand-in did not have a hidden,
foreign past (nor an earlier interest in mountaineering): he
was, like M. R. James, the son of a Suffolk vicar, and

likewise educated at Cambridge – in his case Sidney Sussex College. In real life the true emigrants of the house were its women, over whose presence Sebald rather skims. The similarity of the names he bestows upon them, Elli and Elaine, adds to the sense that he is conflating the two, deliberately trying to confuse the reader.*

I've been skirting around the key passage in *The Emigrants'* opening chapter, but feel the time is right to address it.

'Can I ask what happened to your father-in-law?'

'He killed himself,' Christine says, almost matter-of-factly, as if the subject is both ancient history and common knowledge – and I suppose if I were older and had lived in the town longer I would be aware of the story.

'Did it happen the way Sebald writes?'

'Yes,' she says. 'A shotgun.'

His reasons, in so far as we can try to second-guess the mind of another, were not the tale of regret that the doctor shares with Sebald's narrator at their last meeting (though the opening chapter of *The Emigrants* does, correctly, capture a sense of the fractured relationship the real Selwyn's counterpart had with his wife). Christine's father-in-law had been plagued by severe arthritis and associated health problems for a number of years. As a doctor he would have known his prognosis, Christine tells me, known he would not be getting better. Doctors, she says, have a higher rate of suicide.

---

* To compound the alliterative name confusion, Selwyn's visiting entomologist friend is called Edwin Elliott.

As we sit at the vast table contemplating the way things end, the silence is scattered by a rap on the door. The other members of our meeting have arrived.

Earlier, I said that events in my own story were going to get worse.

Perhaps by now you might have guessed how my father was to meet his maker? All his gut-wrenching sorrow when my brother was given his diagnosis. All his built-up stress from years of trying to reconcile himself to my mother's illness.

You would forgive a man in such circumstances for taking his own life. For stepping into the space below from a tall headland, or for putting an antique shotgun to his head like Sebald's Dr Selwyn. Looking back, I think I might have forgiven my father too if, at that critical point, confronted with the despair of what was happening around him, he had decided he could no longer bear to watch things unravel.

But that is not what happened.

My father had no agency in what was to follow. He was as helpless as the German who, at the time of his death, was being tipped by some as a future winner of the Nobel Prize for Literature. In December 2001, only a few miles from his home, Max Sebald suffered a massive heart attack at the wheel of his car, which ran into the path of an oncoming truck. In 2005, close to the point on the A146 where the accident occurred, the artist Jeremy Millar set off, in an act of ritual, a firework to commemorate Sebald's passing. He photographed the event, interested in the Sebaldian transience of the liberated smoke. Four of the

images he took showed a rising pale plume beside the roadside railings and, if we trust it has not been manipulated, the last of these can perhaps be seen to contain (depending on how your brain wishes to process it) a face-like outline that sports a wide, white moustache.* Though when I stop at the spot en route to Dunwich I, unsurprisingly, see nothing.

Afterwards, on my way home, I visit Sebald's final resting place in the village of Framingham Earl. It's late when I get there and the day has almost gone. I'm about to give up when I find it – the last grave I examine, cast in shadow by the adjacent Norman church, the overhead branches of an enormous pine tree, and a sculpted, globe-shaped bush.

---

* In Grant Gee's elegiac 2012 documentary film *Patience (After Sebald)*, a still of the writer is cleverly dissolved over the top of this smoke ghost to emphasise the resemblance.

Across the top of the headstone a row of rounded
pebbles has been balanced – almost identical in their shape
and smoothness to the stones on Dunwich beach. 'W.G.
MAX SEBALD' reads the name, below which are his dates
and an arrangement of lilies that steals the last of the light.

During the opening months of 1991 my brother was
admitted to the Pilgrim Hospital for various procedures for
his Hodgkin's disease. Dad and I drove through the darkness to see him shortly after he'd had the lump in his neck
excised. (I don't know why Mum wasn't with us – perhaps
she was already there, waiting at his bedside?) Chris was in
a ward high in the hospital, to which we had to take the
oversized lift. There he was, among a room of old men, a
scared twenty-two-year-old left groggy by anaesthetic. By
early April, however, he appeared remarkably on the mend.
He was fit to go on holiday, though Suffolk must have
seemed scant consolation compared to the cancelled
African safari he was supposed at that point to be
enjoying.

As it transpired, it was my father who failed to make it
to the coast.

My recollection of the exact timing of what took place
is sketchy; I suppose I've blocked much of it out. A day or
two before we were due to depart Dad began complaining
of abdominal pains. He identified a kind of firm lumpiness,
a mass, he could feel in his chest; I recall him asking Chris
and me to see if we thought it was normal. At his insistence
we both prodded it, reluctantly, but couldn't discern
anything that, to us, seemed unusual. I can't now

remember if he saw the doctor then – I think he might have done and been told not to worry, it was probably stress – but the sensation wouldn't go away. When it came to the Saturday we were meant to be setting off for Suffolk we went in two cars, because Chris's then girlfriend was coming too, along with our cousin. Dad must have been driving Mum, who by this time because of the loss of her sight in one eye and the onset of her epilepsy could no longer operate a vehicle. I'm not sure precisely what happened, but I know we didn't get far – to the brooding pinewoods of Thetford Forest, in fact – when Dad had to stop, because the pain was making it impossible to continue. Various scenarios were debated and it was decided we should proceed as planned, with Dad and Mum waiting there, in a woodland car park, for my aunt and uncle (who we called from a telephone box) to relay them back to Lincolnshire. We hoped – I think assumed – Dad would feel better in a couple of days and the two of them would then join us.

Genuinely I think we did, though it seems naïve and ridiculous now.

The four of us carried on to the Suffolk coast, and my parents were ferried back to the flatlands. Soon after – that night, or if not, the following morning – Dad was admitted to the hospital where Chris had recently resided. We spent the week birdwatching: the highlights recorded in my bird diary were an exotic hoopoe in the dunes at Kessingland – the location of an earlier, unrecollected family holiday from when I was a toddler (I have here its yellow box of slides) – and watching a great skua, a dark-brown piratical *bonxie*, muscle its way north past Dunwich's decaying cliffs.

During the week I remember, too, climbing Orford's castle, where, during the twelfth-century reign of Henry II, local fishermen out in the estuary were said to have caught a Wild Man – a merman – in their nets. He was naked and bearded, and seemed to prefer raw fish to other food. They imprisoned him in the castle and tortured him – the same polygonal keep features as a place of cruelty at the brutal climax of *Witchfinder General* – though the creature did not appear capable of speech (at least, not in any language they could decipher). Eventually, his captors began to view him as less of a threat (either a supernatural one, or as a

foreign spy), growing tired of the rigmarole of guarding
him. Their routines became more slapdash and somehow
he slipped back unnoticed to the sea.

Years before, at Bournemouth on a summer holiday,
Dad had helped me to make a merman of my own. We
rendered him from the beach itself, using seaweed for his
hair and shells for his eyes. Two other boys I had been
playing with assisted – they were both a little older. While
I fetched seawater to help sculpt the sand, I could see they
were giggling and pointing: they had given the figure
breasts (one of them whispered to me later what they'd
done). When Dad saw, he was annoyed at how, to him, the
innocence of the moment had been sullied. He didn't realise I was aware something had happened, but I was. I stayed
back, watching, as he spoke to them, both boys looking
suitably chastised as they flattened down the figure's chest.

'Let's get this merman finished then,' he said cheerily, as
I returned with my bucket.

Each evening on that final Suffolk holiday my brother
rang for an update from the village phone box. As the week
wore on it must have dawned on us that Mum and Dad
would not be coming. They were checking his heart in the
hospital, I recall being told, blithely expecting the whole
thing would end up being a warning episode of angina
brought on by all the recent stress. We returned home the
following Saturday, having enjoyed the break to an extent
– though it was nothing like the same without them both
there, nothing like the same when we couldn't take the
mickey out of something Dad had said, or some awful tank
top he'd insisted on wearing. He was still in hospital when

we got back: at his bedside I tried to tell him about the birds we'd seen and the places we'd visited, but he was distracted, understandably, his interest not rising above the perfunctory.

Days after he'd first been admitted (months if you count his unexplained pre-Christmas episode), the doctors finally decided what was the matter with him. He had lymphoma. Not the type Chris had.

The bad one.

They didn't seem to have a plan to do anything about it and Dad came home, in escalating discomfort; within a day or two we'd made him a makeshift bedroom in the front room so he wouldn't have to climb the stairs. And I remember picking up a stash of nutritional milky drinks from the chemist, because his appetite had eroded to next to nothing. Not that he wanted those either.

I undertook increasingly long, late-night walks through the sodium-lit streets. And still – and this seems incredible to me now, makes me wish I could fucking shake my seventeen-year-old self and tell him not to waste one minute of that dwindling time that could've been spent with Dad – Chris and I went on birding trips. Though, in fairness, I suppose they were a way of distracting ourselves from the awful reality.

Because the reality was like some nightmare out of weird fiction. Like the chaotic, unspeakable horrors in a William Hope Hodgson or H. P. Lovecraft story.

Dad was readmitted to the Pilgrim. Perhaps finally they'd start treating him? I would go after school, sometimes taking Mum and Chris myself, because by this point

I had L-plates and was learning to drive. And we would sit there by his bedside, among all the tubes and drips, but it was hard to chat because he was in so much pain. So broken. One day he asked me to dampen a flannel and dab it on his forehead because he was unbearably hot. The man in the bed next to the sink I had to use looked at me kindly; he had, I suppose now, a good idea of what was happening, of how it would end. Another time, after we arrived hoping for something positive, Dad told us that the chap opposite had flailed up in the middle of the night before crashing onto the floor – the huddle of doctors couldn't revive him. And one afternoon, the paper I brought up featured a front page headline that Bernie Winters, the comedian, had died of stomach cancer – not an item of news, in hindsight, that Dad needed to read. Instead I tried talking about cricket, or football, or whatever safe subject I could think of. But all of it was hollow noise.

Who is this who is coming?

They cut you open, then. To see what, if anything, could be done. Afterwards your belly was distended, with an ugly, jagged scar. It seemed an unnecessary, cruel act. Too little, too late.

Like already you were a cadaver to practise upon.

They put you in your own room on the ground floor. Though it was not just the one room, because I remember your bed facing in different ways, with different views of the real world which must have lain outside, so they must have kept moving you around – unless the view itself magically changed. You were barely talking by this point, transformed into an emaciated silent stranger in six weeks. They hooked you up to a cube-shaped machine that churned some yellowish, viscous fluid through your veins, which the doctors said offered you a last hope. We brought you in a fan because the room was so warm, leaving it there afterwards for someone else to feel its dubious benefit.

At school one morning (I still went in each day, still carried on as if nothing at all was amiss, telling none of my friends what was happening), my geography teacher fetched me out of an English lesson and took me home, because Mum had rung and we needed to get over to the hospital: the doctors were saying it would not be long (Chris must have been away). It was the first sizeable drive I'd done since I passed my test less than a week before, but we made it there intact. This time you were in the room at the back with the hawthorn hedge outside. Its branches shifted in the wind, silhouetted through the window against the bright May sky. And I held your hand – which was clammy, yet bony as a skeleton's – as the machine pumped its strange fluid, and as you lay there, looking up occasionally with a terrified expression before your eyes closed again. I thought it would be better, now, if you were to die. Because you looked so very ill.

A nearly-ghost bowed by sorrows.

But nothing changed, and we came home in the darkness. I started to cry as I waited to turn across the traffic into the top of our road, and I could not stop myself, because I remembered that I hadn't brought you anything for your birthday, which had been only a few days before.

'It's all right,' Mum said. 'He knows. He doesn't mind, silly. There's nothing he would want.'

And the next morning I was brushing my teeth ready to go back again when Chris and Mum came in and said through suffocating sobs that the hospital had called. We clung together for support, crowded beside the turquoise sink.

Who is this who is coming?

I am writing this with streaming eyes, my face, I should imagine, red and contorted. I think of a scene late on in Kurt Vonnegut's *Slaughterhouse-Five* – the copy my brother was to give me seven months later for my eighteenth birthday – where Billy Pilgrim is moved to rivers of tears by the performance of a barbershop quartet singing a song called 'That Old Gang of Mine'. He looks awful, and his wife asks him if he is all right (you must bear in mind the horrors of the war he has witnessed, how he has become unanchored from the traditional rules of time and space). He's okay, he says, the reason he is so affected by the banal ditty a mystery to him: 'He had supposed for years that he had no secrets from himself. Here was proof that he had a great big secret somewhere inside, and he could not imagine what it was.'

I had not forgotten my own buried secret.

Only I hadn't wanted to blow the whistle.

Not wanted, till now, to hear its sound of infinite distance.

Not wanted to picture you lying there that morning – your eyelids pulled shut, your skin tinged blue, your mouth agape – when the three of us came to see you for the last time.

Chapter 10

NOT REALLY NOW NOT ANY MORE

I interrupt a pair of elderly, grey-haired women who are eating their picnic to check whether I've reached Stormy Point.

'It's Alderley Edge.'

I smile, half in frustration. 'I mean the name of this actual spot.'

'I only live five minutes away and I haven't a clue ...'

'And I'm just a visitor,' chips in her companion. 'Ask someone with a dog. They'll know.'

Thanking them, I head to where the bare sandstone lips over the tree-lined cliff and fiddle with the leaflet I picked

up earlier, studying it to make sense of how far I've come. Seeing the slit in the shelf of rock behind me, I conclude this must indeed be Stormy Point, the location in the early part of Alan Garner's first children's novel *The Weirdstone of Brisingamen* where the threat facing the pair finds form and the two young protagonists are surrounded by a horde of goblin-like *svart-alfar*. The creatures emerge from the cleft in the pink-tinged stone known as the Devil's Grave, which I'd previously managed to overlook. Today, unlike in the book, iron railings guard the opening that leads down into the copper workings; peering through their prison bars all I see is a litter of dried-out oak leaves and discarded fag and crisp packets.*

---

* In silent contrast to Alan Garner's cousin Eric, I hear no bagpipes sounding from the space under my feet; in 1941, seven-year-old Eric, along with a friend, claimed to make out strange music that emanated from and moved beneath Stormy Point – a story not dissimilar to one I'd heard in Edinburgh about an unfortunate ghost boy who plays the pipes in a tunnel-bound limbo below the castle and the Royal Mile.

In *Where Shall We Run To?*, Alan Garner's 2018 memoir looking back to his childhood growing up on the plain directly below Alderley Edge, he tells of the time his father brought him to the Devil's Grave one Sunday and explained to him how, if you ran three times anti-clockwise ('widdershins') round the square stone known as the Devil's Gravestone, Lucifer himself would emerge. Alan excitedly asks his dad if he can try, before proceeding to enact the ritual – exactly what I too would have done as a boy:

A screech came out of the ground beneath my feet, and screams and groans and cackling and moaning, and pebbles flirted from under the stone and out of the trench, and sand and bits of twig, and there was a stamping sound in the cave, and more screeches.

Hilariously (though I'm sure to him it wasn't while it was taking place), the young Alan had been set up by his father and uncle in a well-planned prank: 'They reckoned it was time, and I was old enough to learn the Edge.'

Published in 1960, *The Weirdstone of Brisingamen* was Garner's first book, drawing on his family's centuries-old local roots and his love of the surrounding countryside – the novel focuses on stories about this geological outcrop in the Cheshire landscape a few miles south of Manchester that were relayed to the young Alan by his grandfather. Stories of a farmer on his way to Macclesfield to sell a white mare being stopped, at Thieves' Hole, by a bearded old man who wishes to purchase the horse, an offer the farmer refuses, thinking he'll do better at the market. 'None will buy,' says the tall newcomer. 'And I shall await you here at sunset.' The prediction proves correct. Returning that evening the farmer meets the striking figure once more and agrees to the deal. He follows the buyer to Stormy Point, then to nearby Saddlebole. Here, the stranger touches the staff he's carrying onto one of the giant boulders in the hillside, which splits apart with a sound like thunder. The bearded man, clearly a wizard of impressive magical powers, leads the farmer down into the tunnels below where an army of time-frozen knights lie sleeping beside their steeds; the farmer's horse will provide the missing piece for the final horseless slumberer.

According to Jennifer Westwood and Jacqueline Simpson's comprehensive survey of English legends, *The Lore of the Land*, versions of this story date back to at least the eighteenth century, the first print reference appearing in the *Manchester Mail* of 1805. The local curate of Alderley from 1753 to 1776, the Reverend Shrigley, apparently also relayed the tale of the wizard and the farmer, stating it to be true and to have happened some eighty years before. In Garner's retelling of the legend, which opens his novel, one hundred and forty knights are ready to come to England's aid in time of need; in comparison, a Victorian historian spoke of 'nine hundred and ninety-nine horses that are standing in its caverns'. Earlier versions do not identify these guardian warriors, but the Victorians, with their love of all things Arthurian, could not help but see King Arthur and his slumbering soldiers. In a letter to a friend, Elizabeth Gaskell wrote in 1838: 'If

you were on Alderley Edge, the hill between Cheshire and
Derbyshire, I could point out to you the very entrance to
the cave where Arthur and his knights lie in their golden
armour till the day when England's peril shall summon
them to her rescue.' A comparable story is told in several
places around England, and at Arthur Machen's Caerleon.
The similarity of the tale's theme to that of Machen's 'The
Bowmen' or M. R. James's 'A Warning to the Curious' is
telling too, while Susan Cooper's *The Grey King*, which
would follow fifteen years after Garner's book, also features
sleeping subterranean guardians beneath a hillside who
wait in readiness to come to humanity's aid.

I first read *The Weirdstone of Brisingamen* when I was at
primary school, around the same time I was enjoying
Tolkien's *The Hobbit* and shortly before I embarked upon
The Lord of the Rings. I used to stay up way later than I was
meant to after I went to bed, thinking my parents couldn't
see the light from my reading lamp through the gap of the
doorframe when they came upstairs; once I almost caused
a fire because, on hearing Dad's ascent, I quickly took off
my polyester pyjama top and smothered it over the bulb
to deaden the glow. A burning smell and smoke soon
started to emanate from the fabric, which now sported a
melted hole.

Garner's abortive spell studying Classics at Magdalen
College, Oxford coincided with Tolkien's literature profes-
sorship in the city (at Merton) – he once found himself in
the same room as the creator of Middle Earth, alongside
C. S. Lewis, another icon of children's fantasy fiction.
Garner left after his second year, to write *The Weirdstone of*

Brisingamen – being amused to find out decades later that
Tolkien had apparently read his book and hated its 'trivial
use of language'. And although his Edge-set novel shares
with Tolkien Gandalf-like wizards, goblins, elves, magical
charms and journeying quests, the thing about Garner's
debut that made it stand apart for me, and which I loved
when I first read it, was its blurring of the real and the
fantastic: even though I'd never been to Alderley, I instinctively realised it was an actual location. Indeed, all of the
book's place names except the fabled cavern beneath the
hillside, Fundindelve, can, according to Garner, be found in
the local vicinity (or at least on old Cheshire maps). That
in turn lent the possibility to me as a young reader that
other episodes within its pages might also be true.

It's a sunny April Monday morning when I set out onto the
six-hundred-foot Edge. Despite another local legend Alan
Garner tells of that says no birds sing there, plenty of noise
is coming from the trees on my visit, even though they are
not yet in leaf and the majority of summer migrants have
yet to return. Although the weather is pleasant and warm,
I'm still surprised by the number of people who are stroll-
ing, or running, around the tracks that meander among the
predominant covering of beeches and Scots pines. Now I
have my bearings and don't feel the need to ask specific
directions, every other person I see seems to be exercising
a dog. Most seem too smartly dressed for a woodland walk,
perhaps reflecting the large proportion of expensive, oversized SUVs and sports cars in the parking area – the village
of Alderley Edge, down the hill beyond the Wizard of Edge

pub, is regarded as one of the most upmarket, gentrified outer suburbs from which to commute into Manchester.

Never having visited before, and being such a fan of the two Alderley books from childhood, I'm slightly disappointed by my surroundings. It's not because of how they look: they're beautiful, and nearly every bit as filled with mystery – with their enigmatic rocks, sheer cliffs, and sudden mineshafts – as I would expect; in one spot I stand transfixed by the carved graffiti that peppers a reddish sandstone outcrop, trying to discern a meaning from the timeworn jumble of letters.

However, having been in the gift of the National Trust since 1948, the Edge is far more managed, far less wild than how it is fixed in my mind. And although menace and adventure probably still do exist here, they're harder to picture than in the pre-war landscape Garner was looking back to and writing about as a young man in his early

twenties, during the second half of the 1950s. Today's clement weather and the time of year don't help – a duller morning later in the season with more leaves on the trees would close me in and insulate me from the people out casually enjoying the views and fresh air.

I begin to wish I hadn't come.

In the afternoon I drive ten miles to the south-east, to the fringes of the Peak District and the setting for *The Weirdstone of Brisingamen*'s climax. Despite the traffic noise drifting from the nearby A54, with no one else in sight this feels altogether more in keeping with the land-scape of the book – and the landscape of my imagination. At the far side of a bright-green pasture of spring grass rises a rounded hummock fenced off from the grazing sheep. It's crowned with beeches, bare-leaved and reddish against the whiteness of the sky. I peer at it through my binoculars – signs on the gate in front state there is no access. I consider traipsing across the field in any case, but think better of it; for one thing, it would be wrong to disturb the mother ewes and their lambs. Besides, I don't need to get any closer to appreciate the scene – the view from where I am is enough, and through the glass held to my eyes I can make out the dark gritstone pillar, thought to date from Anglo-Saxon times, that crests the mystical hill. This is Clulow Cross (spelled Cluelow on my map), the location at the end of the book where the dwarf Durathror makes his heroic last stand against the forces of darkness.

The hummock has the archetypal appearance of an ancient barrow. With its grove of sacred beeches it reminds me of similar sites that dot the South Downs and Thames

Valley, like the isolated hilltops captured in a number of early works by one of the great English artists of the first half of the twentieth century. Paul Nash, who talked lyrically about the *genius loci* – the spirit of the place – paints this enigmatic sense into his 1912 depictions of Wittenham Clumps and the neighbouring Brightwell Barrow (at the time located in Berkshire, today in Oxfordshire). He refers to its landscape as 'full of strange enchantment. On every hand it seemed a beautiful legendary country haunted by old gods long forgotten.'

From this distance Clulow's cross among the trees reminds me, just a little, of the monolith from Kubrick's *2001: A Space Odyssey*, or of some antique phallic symbol that I could imagine Summerisle's residents dancing around in *The Wicker Man*. Indeed, later, while looking up its possible purpose on the internet, I find theories are in circulation about it being a fertility stone (though most sources suggest it acted as a more mundane wayside marker) and that women wishing to conceive perhaps would circle the base of the cross in a ritualistic fashion.* Certainly, even from my vantage point, the spot has a definite sense of enchantment, and I can see why Garner places it at such a pivotal moment.

Six miles to the north-east, as the Wild Hunt flies – this northern European folk tradition features prominently in Garner's second book, as it does in Susan Cooper's *The Dark is Rising* – I come to another atmosphere-laden location where I'm the only person present. Behind me lies Errwood Reservoir, barely more than an idea when Alan Garner's follow-up to the adventures of Colin and Susan, *The Moon of Gomrath*, was published in 1963, being completed a few years later to provide a new drinking supply for Stockport. The waters that nowadays engulf this stretch of the Goyt Valley are uninviting, with pine plantations running down to the far bank from the yellowed slopes above. There's little life, just a pair of Canada geese that are picking at some clumps of sedge on the near shoreline. I head away from the drowned world of former farms concealed beneath the calm surface, following a well-worn track up the west side of the valley that leads to the ruins of Errwood Hall. The cobbled path rises steadily and soon enters an area of mixed woodland and introduced rhododendrons, crowding the gullied stream on my left that feeds into the reservoir. I proceed until, on a levelled-out

---

* The website doesn't mention whether this should be carried out in a clockwise or a widdershins direction, though I suspect the first option might be safer in terms of what might result …

platform above me, sprawl the remains of a once-grand Victorian country seat.

Errwood was constructed around 1840 by a wealthy Manchester merchant, Samuel Grimshawe. The hall was Italianate in style, with a tall central tower, a sweeping drive and decorative fountains set among its extensive

grounds; as I walk between the blackened stone remnants it's not easy to imagine how striking – incongruous even – it would have seemed when it was built, more suited to the hills of Florence than the borderland of Derbyshire and Cheshire. Because there's little left now to picture, only low walls, disembodied steps leading nowhere and empty archways that frame the sky. Briars twist through the stonework, and the charred residues of old bonfires scar what can be seen of the flagstone floor; during the early 1990s the site was, for a time, a popular venue for illicit late-night raves. At the boundary of the house's footprint, on the cusp of a steep downward slope, I discover a collection of offerings: an oversized red paper-and-plastic Remembrance poppy; a withered heather seedling, its supermarket price label still attached; and a bag containing a hard-to-identify pot plant, waterlogged and dead, from which a small white teddy bear perches on a stick beside a handwritten card that reads 'HAPPY grandmother DAY grandma'.

Towards the end of *The Moon of Gomrath*, Susan visits the ruins in order to attempt to rescue her brother, who has been entrapped by the Morrigan – the shapeshifting female villain of the two books – in a spirit house in another plane that appears, in this world, only under moonlight:*

---

* A shadow land accessed from our own flesh and blood one – in its case, via the slum clearances of post-war Manchester – featured in Garner's next novel for children, *Elidor* (1965).

The moon rose a long time before it was seen, and it shot high from a cloud, an ugly slip of yellow, taking the watchers by surprise. And though the light it gave was small, and could not even dim the fires, the moment it touched the ruins they shimmered as in a heat haze, and dissolved upwards to a house. The windows poured their dead lustre on the grass, making pools of white in the flames.

Susan's own fate at the sequel's end is left up in the air – although the books were conceived as having a concluding third part it was not until 2012, almost fifty years after the release of the second, that Garner produced the final book in the trilogy. Perhaps fittingly, given its themes, *Boneland* seems a world apart from the childish, mythic pleasures of its two predecessors. It's a difficult, adult novel about memory and loss, with the now middle-aged Colin – a professor at the nearby Jodrell Bank astronomical observatory – trying to connect with his forgotten, intangible past.

At Crewe Services I turn off the M6 motorway. As my phone has decided to stop offering me directions, I'm not entirely sure which way I should be heading. Using guesswork and sneaked glances at my atlas I manage to navigate to my intended destination, the village of Barthomley. On the higher ground in front of me, obscured by trees, is a parish church dedicated to a now-obscure Anglo-Saxon saint. St Bertoline's isn't, to my mind, a picturesque building, but this may be because its style is so different to those

I'm used to in East Anglia.* Its red sandstone blocks would look rusty in most lights, but this evening's sunset lends the stonework a particularly Uluru-esque hue. It's a squat structure that was rebuilt in the fifteenth century, though a church has stood here since at least Norman times – before that the name of the rise on which it's situated, Barrow Hill, hints at an earlier sacred use. This previous incarnation as an ancient burial mound has ramifications in Alan Garner's fifth novel *Red Shift*; it's where, in the book's Roman-era timeframe, a talismanic Bronze Age axe head is laid to rest.

Red Shift is a difficult book that offers few concessions to its readers. When it came out it was marketed for children, yet it has the structural complexity that a modernist such as Faulkner would be proud of with the way its three interwoven storylines, mainly consisting of dialogue, merge into one another. (In the case of *Red Shift*, unlike with Faulkner, there aren't even chapters to help break up and make sense of the writing.) I can't say now how I got on when I originally tackled it, a couple of years after I'd read the Alderley Edge novels. I imagine, though, that I skimmed through it at pace, something I tended to do with more demanding titles. Certainly, it hadn't lingered in my head like the earlier books, so when I pick it up again it's like I'm reading it for the first time.

---

* According to the Reverend Alban Butler's *Lives of the Saints* (1756–9), Bertoline (also known as Bettelin and, most commonly, Bertram) was the favourite disciple of Guthlac at Crowland Abbey – the romantic Fenland ruin close to where I grew up, and which John Clare and L. P. Hartley wrote about.

History has a way of repeating itself in Alan Garner's work. Sites in the landscape interconnect with chosen characters to ensure events (or, at least, a version of them) rerun their course, reaching through time to produce echoes of what's gone before – or what has yet to take place. The majority of the action in *Red Shift* occurs close to Rudheath (near Northwich) and in the countryside around the Cheshire–Staffordshire border, converging on Barthomley Church and another distinctive local landmark, the summit of Mow Cop. Analogous incidents from three well-spaced periods come together: the present of the early 1970s (or perhaps the late 1960s – although *Red Shift* was published in 1973, the year of my birth, it took Garner six years to write); the English Civil War; and the Roman occupation of Britain and the lost 'Spanish' legion also commemorated in Rosemary Sutcliff's children's classic *The Eagle of the Ninth*. At the novel's heart is the modern-day Tom, a bookish, troubled youth whose intense first relationship with his girlfriend, Jan, is on the verge of collapse. His angst seems to spill backwards into the past and the atrocities that two equally sensitive, isolated young men in the second and seventeenth centuries are tangled up with.

Red Shift's universe is an unforgiving one. It's a bleak book (though it does emphasise the stubborn resistance of the human spirit) that explores relationships, betrayal, the British class system, humans' propensity to repeat patterns of destructive behaviour, the meaning of existence – and, probably, much more. *Red Shift* is a dazzling achievement that requires several readings to do it justice and attempt to decode what Garner is saying: it even includes its own scrambled message, printed on the end pages of the first edition, which can be cracked using Lewis Carroll's 'Alphabet Cipher' and the keyword 'TOMSACOLD' – a phrase from Shakespeare's *King Lear* that the main character repeats throughout:*

> I love you. If you can read this you must care. Help
> me. I'm writing before we meet, because I know it'll
> be the last. I'll put the letter in your bag, so you'll find
> it on the train afterwards. I'm sorry. It's my fault.
> Everything's clear, but it's too late. I'll be at Crewe
> next time. If you don't come I'll go to Barthomley. I
> love you. The smell of your hair will be in my face.

Given the intricacy of the novel's structure, it's something of a surprise to find that *Red Shift* was adapted (by Garner himself) into a compelling one-off, eighty-four-minute film transmitted in January 1978 as a BBC *Play for Today*. Although Barthomley Church itself didn't feature as one of the locations (the disused stand-in was in Yorkshire), the Cheshire landscape – particularly Mow Cop and its crowning folly – remains at the film's heart. The adaptation is easier to navigate than the novel because, on the screen, the transitions between the different time periods become clearer. The television version also loses a few of the more

---

* Charles Dodgson (Lewis Carroll was his pseudonym) lectured in mathematics at Christ Church, Oxford. He developed the Alphabet Cipher – one of a number he invented – in 1868, three years after the publication of *Alice's Adventures in Wonderland*.

extraneous episodes from the original – such as the conversations Tom (Stephen Petcher, in his major broadcast role)
and Jan (Lesley Dunlop) have with the rector – as well as
shedding something of the book's undoubted, complex
power.*

Above me, a clattering of jackdaws are squabbling
around the decorative pinnacles that top St Bertoline's
castle-like tower. I love these sociable small crows, though
I'm always haunted by the memory (or, at least, the
memory of being told about it by my mother) of the dilapidated aviary – like the one at Sebald's Somerleyton – that
stood in my home town's public park. At the end of the
1970s its shit-spattered cages still contained various budgerigars and canaries, as well as a solitary jackdaw with a cell
all to itself. It could mimic 'hello' and a smattering of other
words, until some thoughtful soul decided to feed it a
lighted cigarette.

One of the grey-naped birds lands noisily on the algae-
stained gargoyle of a lion that leers out from a corner of the
turret, calling me back to the present not in approximations of English, but with its excited cries. I half-fancy it
recognises me and wonder whether it could be the individual I liberated from *Penda's Fen*'s Chaceley church a few
days ago – until I realise how ridiculous the thought is.

---

* Perhaps the biggest surprise is that *Red Shift*'s director John
Mackenzie would, shortly afterwards, helm the seminal London
Docklands crime thriller *The Long Good Friday*. Mackenzie also
directed an extended 1977 public information film in the tradition
of *Lonely Water* whose body count approaches that of his best-
known work. *Apaches* highlights agricultural dangers to unwary
children – a warning to the farm-curious.

The tower plays a key role in *Red Shift*, for it is on its roof that the villagers – including Thomas Rowley, the finder, in this time of civil war, of the talismanic axe head – hole up against a company of Royalist troops recently returned from Ireland. Garner was inspired by a real, documented historical massacre that took place here on Christmas Eve, 1643: Cavalier soldiers set a fire at the base of the tower to smoke out those sheltering above, forcing them to come down into the churchyard. Accused of siding with the Parliamentarians, twelve of the local men were then stripped naked and executed where they stood. (In the novel, Thomas is deliberately dealt a non-fatal blow by his former friend Venables, which allows him to play dead and subsequently be taken to Rudheath, and later Mow Cop, by his wife.)

I try the door but it's locked, so I have to be content with meandering around outside, searching among the gravestones for a memorial to the men who were murdered here during the atrocity. There's nothing obvious, despite several impressive headstones almost of the correct period that lie horizontal and flush with the grass.

On the back wall of the church I notice that a small triangular fragment from one of the opaque leaded windows is missing. It's too high for me to see through, so I hold up my camera to it. The image of the hidden interior is unnerving, revealing what appears to be a sleeping woman with a white sheet draped across her midriff: she is nothing more than lifeless alabaster, an effigy to the thirty-year-old wife of the first, and last, Marquess of Crewe.

The flock of jackdaws on the tower calls out in sudden, metallic unison. As I look up, the whole party alights, lost to my view in the flame-orange sky.

After leaving St Bertoline's, I drive seven miles to the north-east, navigating my way through a maze of houses up to Mow Cop Castle, a folly built in 1754 that dominates the towering outcrop and provided the striking cover image for *Red Shift*'s hardback first edition. The sun is already sinking beneath the horizon as I arrive, and the evening has taken on a bitter chill, so any leisurely plans I had to explore the summit's rocks and gullies no longer seem so appealing.

I am, however, afforded a panorama of the Cheshire plain: the white of Jodrell Bank's giant parabolic radio

telescope is still visible in the distance but I cannot make out the Edge in the gathering darkness. Astronomy plays an important role in *Red Shift* (and in *Boneland*) – Garner's own fifteenth-century house is situated very close to Jodrell and he has a keen amateur interest in the subject (though he's an even more accomplished archaeologist). The book's title, at least in part, refers to a complicated phenomenon concerned with the observable properties of starlight: essentially, as far as my rudimentary grasp of physics goes, more light is *red-shifted* – that is, it appears redder (of a longer wavelength) to human eyes – as it becomes more distant.

At the conclusion of the novel, his relationship with Jan on the brink of coming to an end, Tom says prophetically: 'Red shift. The further they go, the faster they leave. The sky's emptying.'

In contrast, the sky above me, above Mow Cop, is filling with new stars that flicker into my vision. I ought, I think, to search for Orion, the constellation that, early in the book, Tom and Jan promise to stare at simultaneously every night at ten o'clock whenever they're apart.

Only I can't remember what it is I'm supposed to look for.

"'Not haunted," said Gwyn after a while. "More like still happening?"'

If, when I first encountered it, *Red Shift* left me a little cold, then the same could not be said of Alan Garner's previous novel, *The Owl Service*, which was then, and remains, my favourite of his works. I read it soon after I started at my local state grammar school (an education I shared with the book's central character Gwyn), and it's another challenging novel that blends the events of the past – in its case drawing on medieval Welsh folk tales – with a present doomed to repeat itself. Like *Red Shift* it's a complicated piece of richly textured writing that refuses to disclose what's going on with layers of exposition, but it is, nevertheless, more accessible than its successor. It too is a book purportedly aimed at a teenage audience, and containing strong main characters on the cusp of adulthood – but its themes and the sheer quality of the writing make it equally relevant to adult readers.

Published in 1967, *The Owl Service* had a long genesis, with various factors and seeming coincidences coalescing to provide its inspiration. While Garner was working on *The Weirdstone of Brisingamen* he'd become familiar with the *Mabinogion*, a collection of stories first written down in the fourteenth-century *White Book of Rhydderch* and *Red Book of Hergest*; the tales contained within the two antiquated volumes were part of an earlier oral tradition.* One story in particular (the fourth tale, or 'Fourth Branch', of the collection) interested Garner: that of Lleu Llaw Gyffes, a local lord of Gwynedd, and his adulterous wife Blodeuwedd. It's not a straightforward narrative of a woman who marries the wrong man and then commits a desperate act to try and rectify the situation, but one complicated by layers of myth and shape-shifting magic.

Due to a destiny placed upon the illegitimate Lleu by his mother that 'that he shall never have a wife of the race that now inhabits this earth', Blodeuwedd has in fact been conjured by the wizard Gwydion out of 'the blossoms of the oak, and the blossoms of the broom, and the blossoms of the meadow-sweet' into 'a maiden, the fairest and most graceful that man ever saw'. In effect it is an arranged marriage the ethereal Blodeuwedd has no say over – so we shouldn't judge her for falling for the charms of the stag-slaying Gronw Pebyr, very much a man of flesh and bone. After meeting and becoming lovers one heady night while her husband is absent, Blodeuwedd and Gronw plot to kill Lleu, a task complicated by various magical protections his mother earlier laid on him. Lleu can only be killed by a wound delivered by a spear that has been crafted over the course of a year – as long as the craftsmanship has

---

* Over a decade at the start of Queen Victoria's reign, a woman originally from my own south Lincolnshire, Lady Charlotte Guest, brought together and published for the first time the entirety of the tales in their native language (she had married a Welsh husband, the Member of Parliament for Merthyr Tydfil), and introduced them to a wider audience by translating them into English.

exclusively been carried out on Sundays. In addition, he cannot be slain either inside or outside a house, on horseback, or on foot. Today, it might be easier to get around these stipulations – the fatal blow could be struck in the office or perhaps in a car – but in medieval Wales the options were narrowed down to a particular set of vulnerabilities that the gullible Lleu readily gives up to his wife:

> 'By making a bath for me by the side of a river, and by putting a roof over the cauldron, and thatching it well and tightly, and bringing a buck [a male goat], and putting it beside the cauldron. Then if I place one foot on the buck's back, and the other on the edge of the cauldron, whosoever strikes me thus will cause my death.' 'Well,' said she, 'I thank Heaven that it will be easy to avoid this.'

To cut an ancient story short, a plan is duly hatched and carried out, with Gronw waiting in ambush by the river and casting the Sunday-forged spear at his unguarded love rival. The consequences are not exactly as intended, for Lleu's own godlike nature is now revealed; when the projectile's poisoned tip pierces him, he undergoes metamorphosis into an eagle and flies away. Still, the lovers assume they have seen the last of him, ruling over his lands in his absence.

But it is, of course, not the end of things.

The wizard Gwydion relocates the injured raptor, turning him back into a man to undergo a period of recuperation under the care of the region's finest physicians. After that, Lleu, along with a huge army, marches on his former home. Blodeuwedd flees but is captured by Gwydion, who as punishment transforms her into an owl:

> For I will turn thee into a bird; and because of the
> shame thou hast done unto Lleu Llaw Gyffes, thou
> shalt never show thy face in the light of day
> henceforth; and that through fear of all the other birds.
> For it shall be their nature to attack thee, and to chase
> thee from wheresoever they may find thee.

In recompense Gronw reluctantly agrees to suffer the same riverside, spear-tinged fate as Lleu. The returning husband allows his rival to hold a large stone in front of his body as the projectile is hurled. However, the shield is no match for the weapon, which pierces straight through the unfortunate Gronw's back. 'And thus was Gronw Pebyr slain. And there is still the slab on the bank of the river Cynvael, in Ardudwy, having the hole through it. And therefore is it even now called Llech Gronw.'

Alongside an interest in this ancient tale of lust and revenge from the *Mabinogion*, in 1960 Garner was eating a meal at his future wife's house in Cheshire. The food was served on a Victorian dinner service with an unusual petal pattern that, when rotated, resembled owls.* The author perceived in them the story of Blodeuwedd, the woman

---

* The pattern is thought to be by the influential designer Christopher Dresser (1834–1904).

made from flowers who is transformed into the cursed bird of the night – and in *The Owl Service* the plates become a receptacle in which the valley's menacing force is held until the introduction of the three young protagonists, who provide the catalyst which leads to it once again being unleashed.

In a further coincidence, Garner's future mother-in-law described to him the circumstances under which she had received the china: her sister had been storing the set in a barn because she thought that the owls they depicted were watching her eat and causing her to have indigestion. Later, during the 1969 filming of *The Owl Service*'s TV

adaptation, there were a number of further coincidences, including a rescued tawny owl that was sheltering in the stables where shooting took place. Garner ascribed these twists of fate to 'selective perception', adding: 'It seemed at times that I was discovering, not writing, a story. It was all there, waiting, and I was like an archaeologist picking away the sand to reveal the bones.'

Red Shift, too, came to Garner as a result of various stories, deep-buried memories and found objects, including the tale of the lost 'Spanish' legion who might just have ended up atop a south Cheshire quarry, the Civil War massacre at Barthomley Church, and even 'Bunty' – the name given to the axe head by Jan after her fondly remembered budgerigar – which was what Alan's own childhood pet was called. Most tellingly in its effect on Garner, however, was this:

> In 1966, four months after hearing about the Spanish
> slaves on Mow Cop, I was reading graffiti in the waiting
> room at Alderley Edge Station. One, done in chalk,
> was: 'Janet Heathcoat = Alan Flask. It is true.'
> Somebody had added, in silver lipstick, without
> punctuation or a capital letter: 'not really now not any
> more'. And the sky fell on me. The result was the novel
> *Red Shift*, six years' work, finished in 1972.

The final stimulus for *The Owl Service* came in 1963, when Alan Garner holidayed with his family in southern Snowdonia. They stayed in an isolated, rather grand, seventeenth-century house, Bryn Hall (it was, of course, said to be haunted), just outside Llanymawddwy. The seventy-five-year-old caretaker and gardener, Dafydd Rees, had worked at the hall since 1898, when he was ten, and possessed an intimate knowledge of the local area and its timeworn stories. He became the inspiration for the character Huw Halfbacon – in the book a kind of idiot savant intricately tied up with the doomed, repeated events of the gloomy valley – who offers up enigmatic declarations and is treated with surprising deference by the locals in a way that seems far above his station as a handyman. Huw, it turns out, is an unwitting version of Gwydion, the wizard from the *Mabinogion* – the meddling trickster whose actions precipitate the tragedy that will unfurl now that the late-teenage Gwyn (Lleu), Alison (Blodeuwedd) and Roger (Gronw) have been brought together, once more, in the valley. 'Always it is owls, always we are destroyed.'

The afternoon is grey when I arrive in Llanymawddwy. I have come in from the west, across one of the highest passes in Wales, Bwlch Oerddrws – a lonely wind-raked spot that in earlier centuries was notorious bandit country – before the route drops me into pine-clad, almost Scandinavian scenery around Dinas Mawddwy. As soon as I turn north off the main road, following the left bank of the River Dovey, the landscape opens up and takes on a kind of familiarity: I am entering the haunted, insular location which, more than half a century ago, provided the canvas for the book. With one key character, Huw, in situ, and with the perfect setting in which to anchor its events, over the next three springs and autumns, Alan Garner and his young family returned for their holidays to Bryn Hall: the place where the strands of the idea mingled together and took strange, silent flight on the way to becoming *The Owl Service*.

On the face of things there is little to see in Llanymawddwy. It's not much more than a hamlet, a scattering of slate-roofed houses that hug the old drovers' road, looking across to the low, sheep-grazed fields that line the narrow waters of the fast-running Dovey. There's no shop and no pub, though at one time, when it was a stop-off on a pilgrims' route, there were seven inns; the contemporary focal point is the simple, plain church. I potter around its graveyard, annoying a barking sheepdog with my presence, hoping to find the last resting place of the giant Llywelyn Fawr o Fawddwy who's said to be buried beneath its hallowed ground, but no obvious oversized headstone stands out (nor indeed any smaller one). None the less, it's an attractive, peaceful spot, with the hillside at the back of the church-yard sloping upwards and away to wilder country.

Carrying on, I cross a bridge that marks the edge of the settlement, after which the road starts to rise. The trees become thicker and on my right is the shade-filled entrance track to Bryn Hall. Frustratingly, it's hard to see anything more than the back wall and sloped roofs of the house, as the building sits below the road in the lee of the hillside. I'm excited, however, to see on the crest of the ridge up to my left the pine copse that plays such an important role in *The Owl Service* – the spot from which the fateful spear is hurled: 'He is standing on the bank of the river, see, and the husband is up there on the Bryn with a spear: and he is putting the stone between himself and the spear, and the spear is going right through the stone and him.'

The Stone of Gronw is a real historical object, though it's not found in this valley, but further to the north, close to Ffestiniog;* close to where we stayed on our own family holiday. A trip of which I possess no solid memories, just those contained within the small yellow plastic box – which I have beside me now on the passenger car seat – labelled 'WALES 78' in handwriting that's still achingly familiar despite the passage of time.

Sunlight illuminates the image on the Kodachrome slide I pull from the box, bringing the past out of shadow. A slate-roofed, single-storey cottage somewhere in Snowdonia fills the frame, and a low stone wall angles across the foreground. Behind this stands a small boy, his hands in his pockets. He's wearing orange shorts, a white T-shirt emblazoned with cartoon zoo animals, rust-brown sandals from Clark's and a blond pudding-bowl hairstyle. He looks serious. A woman is at the boy's back, her legs hidden by the wall, her hair cut in an up-to-the-minute, centre-parted feathered bob, with big Jackie Onassis-style sunglasses covering her eyes. She is pretty, with a kind face. The ghost of a smile pulls at the edges of her mouth, which is fitting.

She is my mother; the boy is me.

---

* Another Stone of Gronw does still stand nearby along the Dovey – a near-replica that was made for the 1969 ITV television adaptation. Unfortunately I did not have time to search for it during my visit.

Despite criticism from some that Garner's setting of the
story's events didn't chime with the source material, he
knew perfectly well that he was relocating the action to a
place better-suited to allowing him to tell his own version.
The Owl Service is not a simple rehash of the Fourth Branch
of the *Mabinogion*, but a re-imagining that adds fresh ingre-
dients into its potent mix, including the confusion and
immediacy of teenage relationships, class and societal
tensions between the holidaying outsiders and the house's

Welsh staff, and the complicated dynamic that exists between parents and children – particularly where second marriages are concerned.

We see, too, a near-perfect example of the distancing that education can bring, in the fraught relationship between Gwyn and his emotionally controlling mother – something that's also vividly on display between Tom and his parents in the present of *Red Shift*. Alan Garner was the first member of his family to complete a formal secondary education, getting a scholarship to the prestigious Manchester Grammar. But what should have been a triumph had the unfortunate consequence of closing him off from those dear to him – a moment movingly captured in his memoir when the mother of one of his friends says, after he has won his scholarship, that he won't want to speak to them any more: 'I didn't understand. I felt something go and not come back.'

It would be good to be able to see more of the place that had such a bearing on the story. But Bryn Hall is a private home and I have the distinct sense that its occupants wouldn't appreciate unsolicited callers. The building was meant to feature as the key location in Granada Television's version of *The Owl Service*, adapted by Garner (who has a minor non-speaking cameo in the drama as a tall local) into eight twenty-four-minute episodes. Shortly before production began, however, the owners refused permission to film. The series producer and director Peter Plummer, who had visited the hall while Garner was writing the book, described it as, 'A house among dark trees, a house without electricity, but a house with more electricity than most

people found comfortable.' A suitable last ditch stand-in was procured on the Wirral and used for the interiors, though many of the outdoor scenes were shot in the valley (and nearby Dinas Mawddwy) that I passed through on my way here.

The series does a great job of capturing the book's atmosphere – particularly in its striking title sequence, which assaults the viewer with the jagged silhouette of the fir trees up on the Bryn, accompanied by the discordant sounds of a motorbike, an emptying bath, and the scrape of claws, all set against lilting harp music. Although *The Owl Service* was shot in colour, when it was first shown (at the very end of 1969, running into February 1970) it was transmitted in black and white due to a union disagreement; the colour version wasn't aired until the summer of 1978. It has an art-house feel, with strong production values and performances from its cast – and to my mind it dates well. Like so much television of the period, it seems surprisingly adult in its content for a Sunday tea-time children's drama – if anything the sexual tension that simmers between the three main characters is more heightened here than in the book.*

Much as I enjoyed the adaptation, for me it can't compete with the novel, though perhaps, as is often the case, if I'd seen it before I read the print version the opposite would be true. What really strikes me when reading *The Owl Service* again is how it snaps along. A great deal of the book, like *Red Shift*, is made up of dialogue: talon-sharp exchanges between the sympathetic, working-class Gwyn and the harder-to-like Roger and Alison. Yet where we do have passages of description, they are succinct and poetic. The ending is clever, too, in the way our previous sympathies are brought into question. All the teenagers feel real, quite a feat given that they represent figures from a mythic folk tale. Certainly, by this point in his writing career – more than a decade in – Garner had learned to capture believable, rounded characters on the page. Figures far removed from the flatness of Colin and Susan in the Alderley Edge novels: not that their deficiencies were something I noticed as a boy, because the atmosphere of the setting – the half-real, half-imagined world the siblings

---

* The presence of Gillian Hills, the twenty-four-year-old actress who played Alison, probably adds to this. At fifteen she'd starred in the lead role of the cult Soho-set film *Beat Girl*, going on to have a stint as a French pop star before appearing in a notorious naked scene with Jane Birkin in Michelangelo Antonioni's *Blow-Up*.

were sucked into – was, and remains, the thing that beguiled me about those first two books. Here, though, in *The Owl Service*, that authentic sense of place comes together with memorable characters in an alignment as perfect and cryptic as the flower-owl plate design.

I'm loath to leave this curious valley. An afternoon seems inadequate even to begin to become acquainted with its bewitching scenery, its brooding secrets. When finally I go, I head out on the old pilgrims' route, past sedge-filled rough pasture streaked in shadow by scattered ancient oaks, turning off at the steep pass of Bwlch y Groes – where at the end of the TV adaptation Gwyn's mother abandons him. A moorland track takes me alongside the waters of Lake Vyrnwy and the half-submerged willows that rise from the shallows of its north-eastern corner like the trees in Algernon Blackwood's story. I keep expecting some hidden force, like that in *The Owl Service*, to turn me back towards Llanymawddwy. But nothing comes.

So I beat on, against the encroaching darkness.

Past events reverberated in my own family too. Nine months after Dad, you followed. Out-of-season sunflowers travelled beside you on the slow drive and, for a time, until they began to fall apart in the February dampness, lay on the mess of earth that covered the space the two of you shared.

That you still share.

'What's the point?' you asked your doctor, a sympathetic man younger than I am now, as he visited you in the emptiness of the house after Dad died. It wasn't a general question about the nature of existence – though it may as well have been – but a reaction to your own updated prognosis: he'd just told you, and this would not have come as a surprise, that your cancer was unremitting. That it could not be cured.

'But there are ways of fighting a battle, Lesley,' he said, which I think was meant to give you hope that the inevitable could be postponed. That it could be taken on nobly, with honour. And you tried, you really did, but it's hard when your body is breaking down: when you've lost the sight of an eye, when to walk more than a few steps makes you breathless and debilitated, when the epileptic fits that offer you no warning – a condition shared by Thomas Rowley in *Red Shift* – become increasingly frequent and terrifying.

But you carried on as best you could. Because what else is there?

Lying on your bed, you and I would enjoy films together on the tiny portable TV. And the three of us – you, Chris and me – tried to celebrate my eighteenth birthday, silently pretending the empty chair at the restaurant table didn't remind us about the fourth not present. Still we went together on drives along Our Bank, to look for owls.

Because always you wanted owls.

And we were lucky, because there were so many near where we lived – as least the way I remember things. We saw them often, too, as they ghosted those flat fields.

Towards the end, after Chris and I could no longer look after you at home, you did not have to become a pilgrim in Boston but were given your own quiet room in the skeleton-crewed Victorian hospital just up the road from my school; two kindly ambulance men carried you down our stairs in a wheelchair on the evening you left the house for the last time. I snuck across to see you in the few weeks that followed when I had free periods, though still I didn't tell any of my friends, any of my teachers, about where it was I kept disappearing to. About where you were.

So, when history's repetition reached its inevitable end point and you were no longer speaking, when we were no longer sure if you even knew we were there, at least you looked at ease. Hardly anything had changed in your outward appearance those past nine months – you weren't thin, or pale, or pained. We were lucky, I suppose. Because it wasn't like it had been with Dad and we were spared the agony of watching you erode before us. Only now, your breathing was metronomic, with a high-pitched, harrowing wheeze.

You'd fallen into a fairy-tale slumber from which you would never awaken – not even if Chris and I were in peril. Not even if we desperately needed you to come to our aid.

Yet, however hard I try, I cannot remember if, at that final moment – when you were no longer owls, but flowers – my brother and I were beside you.

Not really now not any more.

Chapter 11

TROUBLE OF THE ROCKS

Time passed lazily after my mother's death.

It was just Chris and me, the population of the house halved. Four months disappeared in a numb haze of exams before my A-levels were over, then off to begin university in September. My brother got a job as a trainee reporter on the local newspaper, a fledgling John Gordon. Not much sticks out to me now from that time of only the two of us, apart from one incident. Towards the end of my first term, I arrived back on a Friday evening for the weekend, knowing Chris was himself away and hadn't been home since he set off for his girlfriend's in Yorkshire that morning. As

soon as I unlocked the front door I could hear loud music
upstairs; I recognised the song, it was a track titled 'Babes
in the Wood' off the Irish folk musician Mary Black's
album of the same name. I was more than a little disturbed,
my immediate thought being that we'd been burgled,
although there was no sign of anything out of kilter when
I switched on the hall light. I made lots of noise, waiting at
the foot of the stairs and shouting up warnings; had someone emerged I'm not sure what my plan was, but nobody
did. After that I went around the house, opening every
door and checking no one was hiding under a bed or in a
wardrobe. My brother's CD was still playing when I
entered the room from which the sound emanated – our
old playroom, as we called it.

I was shaken, knowing that Chris wouldn't have left the
stereo blaring away when he'd gone from the house after
breakfast – and knowing there was no autoplay feature
engaged that would have made the album repeat in a
continuous loop. (When I told Chris later, he was adamant
he hadn't had any music on that morning, which I believe.)
The track wasn't the first on the disc, but the fourth, and
though I rationalised the whole thing as being the result of
a freakish power surge that happened to occur approximately twelve minutes before my arrival (and which solely
affected the CD player), at the time I definitely harboured
suspicions that some weird agency was involved. A small
part of me half-wondered whether it was an enigmatic
spirit message from my mother – I always came to associ-
ate the incident with her, and never with Dad: the 'Babes
in the Wood' theme was suitably allegorical, but the more

I considered it the more ridiculous that seemed. Setting aside my lack of belief in any kind of afterlife, it just wasn't a song that would have had any relevance to her (Chris bought the album after she had died), and I couldn't decode any Pheneas-esque meaning in what she'd possibly be attempting to say in such a cryptic fashion. Still, it was an odd occurrence – and it's understandable that I found it unnerving: I was eighteen and returning alone to an empty family home recently stripped of its two most longstanding inhabitants.*

By the autumn of 1994, Chris had completed his various bouts of treatment and was on the mend, so we went down together to the tip of Cornwall. It was a destination I'd come to with him five years before during October half-term, when I was in the fifth form. On that initial visit we were meant to be visiting the Isles of Scilly – an outcrop, some say, of the lost Arthurian land of Lyonesse – but gales around the Land's End peninsula marooned us on the mainland for several days. As a keen new birder this wasn't such an imposition: I got to watch my first firecrests – indescribably beautiful, miniature stripe-headed migrants that fed in the sycamores and thin elms of the sheltered seaward valleys – and a delicate, rare wader from North America

---

* It would be easier to ascribe a supernatural origin to the music I came home to if R. Dean Taylor's 'There's a Ghost in my House' had been playing – particularly as we didn't own the track on CD. My older, Northern Soul-loving cousin had introduced me to this slice of Tamla Motown when I was six, knowing the slightest suggestion of a ghost would be a siren song to me.

that I'd never before seen, a lesser yellowlegs.* We returned
to the area twice the following year, and again later on
sporadic long day trips or weekends from Chris's house in
Dorset. In this way, the Far West – a contrasting mix of
wild coastal moorland and granite tors that almost rival
Dartmoor, rough-walled fields that have stood unchanged
since the Iron Age, verdant valleys where giant *Gunnera*
plants overhang streams like it's the Cretaceous period,
and high cliffs that guard sandy smugglers' coves – became
one of my favourite parts of the country.

At the time of our 1994 trip I was in the grip of a fad for
ancient sites and monuments, fuelled by a copy of Janet
and Colin Bord's *Mysterious Britain*, a gazetteer of standing
stones and timeworn earthworks. The birding was quiet –
not unusual on the Land's End peninsula, where there are
seldom large numbers of autumn migrants, though interesting rarities from both America and Asia can be found
when weather conditions align. However, the quietness of
the valleys did allow us to visit a site in my book I was
particularly taken with: Mên-an-Tol.

Today, I drive a mile or two inland from the wild north
coast at Morvah, stopping off at Lanyon Quoit, an impressive table-like Neolithic structure – probably the remains
of a burial chamber, though it could feature as some sacri-
ficial faery altar out of one of Arthur Machen's stories.

---

* I was to encounter a lesser yellowlegs again on my latest visit,
nearly thirty years on from the first, feeding elegantly among the
mud of a Du Maurier-esque creek near Truro – a far more
picturesque backdrop than the flooded field next to a petrol
station in which that earlier bird had settled.

From the lay-by on the minor road where I leave my car I walk along a high-banked track bordered by autumn-browned bracken. It's a bright afternoon, but typically for this final Atlantic-jutting vestige of England, the weather is changeable and has already caught me out with a sharp shower; it may do again as storm clouds are hurrying across the sky. I pass a huddle of granite walls – a farm cottage in earlier days, I suppose, now being used to store hay – and on the horizon recognise the outline of a defunct tin mine's engine-house rising from the heather, its asymmetrically placed chimney giving it the characteristic silhouette of this landscape.

The area's copper- and tin-mining history can be better seen a few miles to the west around the clifftops of Levant and Botallack, now preserved by the National Trust and forming part of a World Heritage Site.* Terrifyingly, to me at least, the workings extended for more than a mile underneath the sea, reaching down to a depth of 350 fathoms (historically, mines used fathoms as a unit of measurement). The miners, however, had more to worry about than the weight of all that pressing water and the threat of tunnel collapses, given the shocking life expectancy that resulted from the caustic dust in their lungs, or the arsenic that was a by-product of the mining process. If you did somehow survive to middle age and beyond, then the longer-term effects of breathing in radon were another risk – when I take a tour of the remains of the Levant Mine and its beam engine (major excavations at the site began in 1820), the knowledgeable guide is obsessed with the radioactive gas, going off on a long and sad tangent about its effect on pet dogs and cats in local houses. He also tells us about the ghostly 'knockers' – spirits that signalled through their tapping where rich lodes could be located – before leading us along a narrow tunnel carved through the cliffs till we come to a metal grille that straddles an endless black space: the shaft in which thirty-one miners died in a devastating 1919 accident. Peering down into the darkness it's like the

---

* The Cornish mining industry sits at the heart of one of my favourite Hammer films, *The Plague of the Zombies*. It features a striking scene in which the undead, who are being used by the local Victorian squire as slave labour in his mine, claw their way up through the soil of the village churchyard. Its actors never came near Cornwall, however; the film was shot at Bray Studios and in the surrounding woods and heaths of the Home Counties. Levant and Botallack did, though, provide an authentic backdrop to the atmospheric Children's Film and Television Foundation production, *Haunters of the Deep*.

pit below the mansion in *The House on the Borderland*, a sombre spot in no way improved by my fear of heights.

It's good to emerge into the freshness of the cliffside air again, and as I poke around the remains of the mine's old office – beautiful, decorated tiles still adorn a roofless remnant of floor, fully exposed to the wind and the rain – I hear a familiar metallic pinging sound somewhere above me before I pick up the broad-winged, tumbling form of two medium-sized birds that alight on the top of the closest chimney stack. They are choughs: red-billed, cliff-dwelling crows that are the rarest British member of their family and a traditional symbol of Cornwall, appearing on the county's coat of arms. Yet this seeming esteem did little to preserve their status. The widespread removal of grazing clifftop livestock (choughs feed on invertebrates in the soil with their thin, curved beaks, so require a cropped sward) sparked their precipitous decline throughout the nineteenth century. The last successful nesting in Cornwall was

in 1947, though an aged, non-breeding pair was resident
near Newquay up until 1967, when one of them died; its
mate clung on, alone, for another six years. So, when I first
came here with Chris, there were none of these charis-
matic corvids to enliven the day. Cornish choughs were
barely more than a memory – like Dolly Pentreath, the
eighteenth-century Mousehole woman popularly regarded
as the last fluent speaker of the county's dead language.*

---

* Quite unexpectedly, in 2001 a pioneering party of these glossy-
black crows arrived across the water from Ireland; today small
flocks can be seen around the Land's End peninsula and the Lizard.

Back on the Neolithic moorland, I climb a stile and am into a short-cropped area of turf in the middle of which stands the holed circular stone of Mên-an-Tol. It's smaller than I remember – around three feet in height – flanked either side by two upright, round-topped slabs of granite that, originally, were arranged in a triangle. (I'm sure the distinctive stone and its two outliers appears in the top right-hand corner of Paul Nash's surreal, and rather phallic, 1938 painting *Nocturnal Landscape*.) There's no traffic noise, no man-made sounds, only the mumbling of the wind overlaid with the thin, overhead *seeps* of passing meadow pipits.

Virtually every field in this edge-of-the-world tip of England seems to contain some sort of noteworthy ancient stone, but this one is for me the most extraordinary. When I came here with Chris, having read in *Mysterious Britain* about how crawling through the hole was said to cure various ailments, I made him pass himself through, then followed myself for good luck. It can't hurt, I said, and I think I might just have believed – at least a little – the possibility that the stones possessed a magic that would keep Chris's illness at bay, even though we undertook the whole thing ostensibly as a joke. My book talked about 'powerful currents passing through the earth' that could conceivably be focused onto such sites. Elsewhere, according to the testimony of a Mrs Jane Tregurtha from Newlyn in W. Y. Evans-Wentz's 1911 *The Fairy-Faith in Celtic Countries*, a benign pixy (or Cornish 'pisky') is responsible for the site's health-giving properties:

At the Men-an-Tol there is supposed to be a guardian
fairy or pixy who can make miraculous cures. And my
mother knew of an actual case in which a changeling
was put through the stone in order to get the real child
back. It seems that evil pixies changed children, and
that the pixy at the Men-an-Tol being good, could, in
opposition, undo their work.

I decide to crawl through again now, something that, nearly
a quarter of a century on, is not so easy to accomplish – at
least with any kind of dignity. Fortunately no one else is
around (except perhaps the pisky), though a Dutch couple
turn up as I'm leaving; I'm relieved they didn't arrive a few
minutes sooner to witness my ungainly scramble.

After that initial traverse, Chris was given a clean bill of health – at least, until the end of 1996: the odd patches on his lungs that previously had showed up on his check-up X-rays and been dismissed as 'fatty deposits' were now deemed malignant. In a flourish he underwent pioneering stem-cell treatment in Bournemouth – a few days after getting married – that offered him a final hope.

It was a success.

My brother's shadows had been seen off – something confirmed each subsequent year when he returned to see his specialist, and matter-of-factly told me weeks or months later (if he even remembered to at all) that he was in the clear.

The pisky had come good.

A short drive from the doughnut-shaped stone, tucked back from the rugged northern coast, is Zennor. Alphabetically the last of England, this charming collection of cottages sits in a kind of dip, clustered around the Tinners Arms and the partly Norman church of Saint Senara. Like Orford in Suffolk, it has its own legend of a strange visitor from the sea – though in its case a mermaid, rather than merman – celebrated on a carved fifteenth-century bench inside the solid, grey-stoned place of worship.

This is a harsh, ancient country, full of such stories and superstitions. Walter de la Mare, on his first visit to Cornwall, felt its strange power, writing later that he didn't feel safe until he'd crossed back over the Tamar into Devon. A similar sentiment was expressed by the painter and sculptor Sven Berlin, who vividly describes this wild meeting of land and sea at the start of *The Dark Monarch*, his libellous 1962 memoir-cum-novel about the nearby St Ives artists' community:*

> Everywhere there was a brooding Presence over the hills, like Saul, emanating desolation, loneliness and destruction: the Dark Monarch who wrecked men's lives, smashed their ships on the rocks and cut off terror stricken fingers to snatch at the jewels of eternal life.

D. H. Lawrence had come to Zennor too, in February 1916, with his German wife Frieda, who happened to be the cousin of the 'Red Baron' – not a popular relative to possess in wartime Britain; they lived initially at the inn before moving outside the village to a house at Higher Tregerthen. Lawrence hoped to found an idealised writing commune called 'Rananim' and had persuaded the New Zealand short-story writer Katherine Mansfield and her future husband to occupy the neighbouring cottage; the pair lasted only six weeks before the landscape's bleak damp-ness and Lawrence's angry intensity became too much for them. In October 1917 the Lawrences themselves left, but not voluntarily: anti-German feeling was running high and accusations of spying were being whispered, though the

---

* The words were written after Berlin had left Cornwall (in September 1953) for a punishing two-month Romany caravan journey to the New Forest. He pitched up, a little like all those doomed Victorian seekers of Utopia, at Minstead, close to where Arthur Conan Doyle was to be re-interred.

intimacy of Lawrence's relationship with a Zennor farmer, William Henry Hocking, didn't help to endear him to the locals. Following a search of their property a military order was drawn up under the Defence of the Realm Act ordering the couple out of the county at short notice – events that are depicted in Lawrence's semi-autobiographical novel *Kangaroo*.

Two decades on, rumours of occultism swirled around the area following the puzzling death, in May 1938, of Rupert Brooke's Cambridge lover, Ka Cox (by this point married and known as Katherine Arnold-Forster), who lived with her politician and artist husband in a house on the hillside above the village. It was an incident in which, at least in the popular imagination, no less than the 'wickedest man in the world', Aleister Crowley, later became implicated – despite being in London at the time. He did come to Cornwall briefly during 1938 – the Lamorna-based artist Ithell Colquhoun's odd, compelling book about West Cornwall, *The Living Stones*, has a chapter devoted to the 62-year-old's eleven-day August visit, when he stayed at the Lobster Pot in Mousehole. And even if he didn't have the opportunity to partake in any of the black masses or orgies that it's rumoured he was involved in on that sortie to the south-west, then it's to be hoped that he at least got to enjoy the salty air and the county's famed light.

Lamorna, with its trout stream, lush tree-lined valley and picturesque cove, has its own special magic – and the clarity of that Cornish light played a big part in attracting the artists who followed in the brushstrokes of the

pioneering Samuel John Birch – 'Lamorna' Birch – who
settled here in 1892. In the early years of the twentieth
century over a hundred professional painters, sculptors and
potters, as well as a smattering of writers, lived in the
secluded valley a few miles south-west of the artists' colony
at Newlyn and the nearest sizeable town of Penzance. I can
see the appeal: turning off the winding B-road, the narrow
route runs beside the stream down to my left, with large
sycamores forming a dense canopy above. This Arcadia
carries on for almost a mile before the Atlantic emerges
dramatically before me – along with the daylight. A
comfortingly thick sea-wall offers protection to the cove's
right flank, while opposite are giant scree slopes of
oversized boulders left behind by former quarrying
operations. On both sides the cliffs crowd in, and now and
again a peregrine powers between them. The tide is high,
lapping just below the car park, and a whirling flock of
black-headed gulls in their winter plumage are hovering
over and swimming on the sea's surface in a frenzy of
feeding; I pick out two Mediterranean gulls, distinguishable
by their clean white wingtips and thicker, blood-red bills.
Later, I walk east along the coast path to Mousehole,
passing through the silent shadows of the clifftop nature
reserve of Kemyel Crease, where towering Monterey pines
rise from the steep slopes like I'm on the cusp of some
undiscovered Shangri-la.

Born in 1906 in India's Assam region, the daughter of a
British civil servant, Ithell Colquhoun was educated back
in England at Cheltenham Art School and the Slade (where
M. R. James's friend and illustrator James McBryde

retrained after passing up on a career in medicine).
Afterwards, she went to Europe, encountering André
Breton and her future husband Toni del Renzio; after their
acrimonious divorce in 1947, she turned from Surrealism
and devoted increasing amounts of time to her interest in
the spiritual and occult. Her first book, 1955's *The Crying
of the Wind*, is an offbeat account of her travels around
Ireland, and was followed two years later by the equally
hard-to-classify *The Living Stones*. It's about her quest for a

rural Eden away from the modern world, and about the ancient megaliths, folklore and customs that pepper this cul-de-sac of land. Even then, however, in the mid-1950s, she bemoans the growing number of cars coming to the valley – I'd hate to think what she would make of it nowadays in summer.

Lamorna becomes almost a character in its own right in *The Living Stones*, along with the ramshackle Vow Cave – sited alongside the sometimes trickling, sometimes torrential stream – that was Colquhoun's one-room studio and home in those post-war years (it was rebuilt in the 1990s using Cornish granite rather than the corrugated iron of her time). Her 1955 oil painting *Landscape with Antiquities*,

Lamorna acts as a kind of stylised treasure map of the menhirs and stone circles of the area, showing the Merry Maidens and the Pipers, found just off the road between Lamorna and St Buryan. Early on in the book she discusses the bird life of the valley but, perhaps predictably, my favourite chapter is titled 'Lamorna Shades'. Here Colquhoun tells of the potential studio (which I believe must have been attached to Rosemerryn House, the former home of the mysteriously drowned Cornish writer, Crosbie Garstin) she considered taking before discovering her 'mouldy little place' at Vow Cave. The American owners warned her that it contained 'spooks', which, although prone to walk noisily around the attic, were 'perfectly harmless'. She wonders whether they're quite as benign as the owners suggest, given the house's reputation for tragedy and strange happenings.* These include an apparently haunted mirror that could be straight out of the film *Dead of Night*: 'a lady looking into her mirror one day was horrified to see not the expected reflection of herself and her furniture but a mist forming within the "many dimensions" of the looking-glass and becoming denser every second.'

To add to the place's aura, in the grounds of Rosemerryn sits the sunken Boleigh fogou, an underground, man-made Iron Age chamber stretching about forty feet in length, which it's speculated was used for ritual or ceremonial purposes. In the local legend of 'Duffy and the Devil' – a

---

* Eventually Colquhoun rejects the Rosemerryn studio not because of its ghosts, but for more practical reasons: the owners use it as a lounge area each evening, meaning she would have to clear away her painting materials at the end of every day.

reworking of Rumpelstiltskin in which the Devil's unlikely name turns out to be 'Terrytop' – the *fogou* (from the Cornish word for cave) is the place where the neighbourhood coven summon their master; in real life, it was said to have been a Royalist hideout during the Civil War. This location is just one example of the charged nature of the valley – seemingly every other house has its rumoured resident shade. And, to Colquhoun, the woods themselves have their own unquiet guardian elemental spirits: 'Others think that the melancholy of Lamorna goes further back than can be imagined: some trouble of the rocks before humanity began may still impinge upon the vitality of the trees.'

Later in *The Living Stones* Colquhoun ventures further afield, away from West Penwith. She travels to various localities around the county including the annual May fair in Helston. There she watches a Spaniard called Alonso stick blades through an 'up-ended coffin' in which his assistant – a young woman resembling the girl in Robert Aickman's 'The Swords' – is entombed.* At the fair Colquhoun also comes upon a strange, sad sideshow featuring 'The Cornish Pixie': 'He looked rather like a leprechaun or goblin. His whole face had a certain pathetic beauty; his mouth was thin, and there was a tear at the corner of one his blue eyes.'

---

* 'The Swords', which contains one of the most casually disturbing scenes I've ever read, is from Aickman's 1975 collection *Cold Hand in Mine* – by which time the former chief of the Inland Waterways Association had honed his enigmatic style to near-perfection.

Colquhoun goes on to visit Padstow's own celebrated rite of spring with its famous Hobby Horse, known thereabouts as the 'Obba 'Oss: 'This, I thought, is the image of a demon or of some creature used in sympathetic magic to exorcise demons.' Robin Hardy, the director of *The Wicker Man*, had also stumbled upon Padstow's festive parade while filming in Cornwall in the sixties. The experience, which he found rather sinister, stayed with him and became part of Summerisle's own May Day festivities at the climax of the film: 'We saw the Hobbyhorse chasing the girls, everything. But they had seemed to put up a wall of evasion about it. And it was very unpleasant being a stranger in the town that day.'

These traditional Cornish rituals and gatherings bring to mind two of the books in Susan Cooper's *Dark is Rising* series, both set around the fictional fishing port of Trewissick, a version of the Mevagissey that Cooper had been brought to on holidays in her youth – at a parallel date to when Colquhoun was painting further down the coast. On my visit a flock of turnstones, busy brown-and-white wading birds that were a favourite of my father, are perched like carved wooden decorations – for once not scampering about the quayside like wind-up toys – on the gunwale of a rowing boat moored on the sheltered waters of the harbour.

Pleasant as the village is, I find it hard to square with the quiet little place Cooper holidayed at in her youth – though I do my best to conjure several of the gabled houses located on the narrow streets that twist up the hillside into the Grey House, where the Drew children's adventures with the wizard Merriman begin in *Over Sea, Under Stone*. In the novel Trewissick has its own summer carnival, complete with a costume parade and traditional dancing reminiscent of the fair at Helston that Colquhoun visited.

Greenwitch, the third in Cooper's sequence, is a darker book, replete with a dreamlike mood and striking pagan imagery. At its centre is the titular Greenwitch, a foliage statue made afresh by the women of the town each year to be given as an offering to the sea. It's an evocative and complicated creation that brings to mind the votive structure at the finale of *The Wicker Man*:

> 'Hazel for the framework,' the woman said. 'Rowan for the head. Then the body is of hawthorn boughs, and hawthorn blossoms. With the stones within, for the sinking. And those who are crossed, or barren, or who would make any wish, must touch the Greenwitch then before she be put to cliff.'

This is the novel in which Jane Drew emerges as a strong character in her own right, rivalling Will Stanton, the hero of *The Dark is Rising*, who appears for the first time here in tandem with the Drew children (all of them are also reunited in the last of the series, *Silver on the Tree*). Jane forges a kind of kinship with the Greenwitch, which is itself possessed of a complicated, angry life force that's disarmed by Jane's empathy and unleashes the Wild Magic of the town's haunted, burning past to defeat the darkness that, in Cooper's universe, is always waiting.

*

Lamorna wasn't somewhere that my brother and I tended to frequent as we went about trying to find lost migrants on our visits: all those trees and thick cover make birding there hard going. We concentrated our efforts on the valleys even closer to Land's End and St Just: Nanquidno, the Cot, Kenidjack, St Levan and Porthgwarra. These last two hamlets are tucked away to the west of Porthcurno, a village at the heart of Britain's early telegraphic communications industry – at one point fourteen submarine cables came in here from the Atlantic and connected the country to the rest of the globe. Later, until the closure of its engineering college in 1993, it became a hub for the training of telecommunications staff from around the world. This, coupled with the iconic open-air Minack Theatre that's hewn out of the very stones of the cliffs – a one-woman vision and feat of construction begun, in 1932, by the remarkable Rowena Cade – gives the place a somewhat surreal atmosphere. Fittingly, the opening theatrical performance in this most storm-lashed of backdrops was *The Tempest*.

The approach to neighbouring Porthgwarra, a high-hedged minor road that passes through several farms but little else on its snaking path down to the sea, reminds me of the fictional village in E. F. Benson's short story 'Negotium Perambulans': Polearn, a similarly sited place between Land's End and Penzance. The tiny, cut-off settlement is noted in guidebooks, Benson tells us, only for the interesting carved wooden panels in its church. Even the postman in Benson's 1922 tale doesn't bother to go all the way down the hill, dropping off and collecting his letters from a box beside the track above the village, while the fishermen take their catch by sea round to Penzance, rather than use the circuitous landward route. 'But they are linked together, so it has always seemed to me, by some mysterious comprehension: it is as if they had all been initiated into some ancient rite, inspired and framed by forces visible and invisible.'

And so Benson introduces us to an archetypal isolated and insular community, setting up readers to believe there will be dark secrets and, no doubt, strange, hostile locals. We fully anticipate that the villagers will reveal themselves as a corrupted, inbred lot like those we find populating H. P. Lovecraft's Innsmouth and Dunwich.* Yet, in contrast to our expectations, here in Benson's Polearn the village's inhabitants are decent, God-fearing folk. Certainly the story's narrator reckons so, remembering back with fondness to his childhood, when he was exiled here at the age of ten to stay with his aunt and uncle, Polearn's vicar, in order that the fresh sea air should cure him of a lung problem. Outdoor life – long days spent wandering the clifftops and playing with the local boys – turns him into a strapping lad when, at thirteen, after three happy years, he goes off to Eton and then Cambridge, and then into the wider world to pursue a lucrative law career.

Although the narrator's childhood stay was largely serene, Sundays were less so, as then, along with the rest of

---

* Or like the mob of Sam Peckinpah's 1971 violent Cornwall-set thriller *Straw Dogs*, which was filmed just a few miles away, around the village of St Buryan.

the village, he had to sit through his otherwise mild uncle's fire-and-brimstone sermons, delivered before those altar-rail panels mentioned by the guidebook, the last of which depicts Polearn's own churchyard and lychgate: 'In the entry stood the figure of a robed priest holding up a Cross, with which he faced a terrible creature like a gigantic slug, that reared itself up in front of him.' Beneath the carving is a Latin line from the ninety-first Psalm, which gives the story its title: '*Negotium perambulans in tenebris*', roughly translated as 'the thing that walks in the darkness'.

We soon get an idea of what this morbid tableau might refer to, when we learn that a much earlier place of worship stood on the flattened area of ground beneath the quarry. The owner of the land demolished the sacred structure and used the stones to build a house on the site, even co-opting some of the church's vestigial consecrated elements into everyday usage, such as substituting the altar as a table, which the fellow ate off and played dice on. As he grew older, the man developed a terrible fear of the dark and insisted that candles be kept burning all night. One evening a strong gale (not a rarity in this part of the world, from my experience) caused them to be extinguished, the screams emanating from the man's blood-streaming throat bringing his servants to an unholy scene in which 'some huge black shadow seemed to move away from him, crawled across the floor and up the wall and out of the broken window'. For a long time afterwards the dwelling by the quarry, unsurprisingly, was left empty. But during the narrator's childhood sojourn in the village it once again became occupied, by a man from Penzance. Despite the boy's

initial hopes 'that it would be intensely exciting to wake at
some timeless hour and hear Mr Dooliss yelling, and
conjecture that the Thing had got him', the new owner
kept himself uneventfully to himself.

When the narrator returns to Polearn – after two decades
as a barrister he wishes to escape the rat race – he moves
in with his aunt (his uncle has by this point died) while he
looks for a place of his own. The reclusive Dooliss, he
learns, acquired an identical night fear to that of his predecessor, and met his end, several years before, in a similar
fashion. However, the unhallowed quarry house has a new
resident, though the artist John Evans is almost unrecog-
nisable as the young man the narrator remembers. His
artistic (and personal) style has much changed in the inter-
vening period and he now creates dark works that bring to
my mind the paintings of the early twentieth-century
London artist Austin Osman Spare, a favourite of Aleister
Crowley. Like previous inhabitants of the house, Evans too
has developed a phobia of the darkness – and of the thing
that walks within it. At the conclusion of the story his
grisly demise is witnessed by the narrator, the sight of it
sending him away from the idyll in which he hoped to see
out his days:

> But I had made up my mind that when once I had
> provided for my own independence, I would go back
> there not to leave it again. And yet I did leave it again,
> and now nothing in the world would induce me to
> turn down the lane from the road that leads from
> Penzance to the Land's End, and see the sides of the

combe rise steep above the roofs of the village and
hear the gulls chiding as they fish in the bay.

'Negotium Perambulans' is a story rich in atmosphere,
with a convincing Cornish setting – though the agency
behind the creature that comes out of the night is difficult
to discern. Is it a vengeful force sent by God to punish the
defilers of the original church and those who come after, or
'some trouble of the rocks before humanity began' as Ithell
Colquhoun might suggest? Whatever the cause, the details
are visceral: 'there on the floor he lay, no more than a rind
of skin in loose folds over projecting bones.'

This physical repugnance is a feature of many of E. F.
Benson's stories, leading M. R. James – although an admirer
of his tales – to note of his long-time acquaintance that 'to
my mind he sins occasionally by stepping over the line of
legitimate horridness'. It is a characteristic taken to its
extreme in 'Caterpillars', in which a plague of horrific
claw-footed caterpillars inundate an Italian villa, apparently causing one of the guests to later develop and die
from some unspecified cancer. It's an awful image, with the
'greyish-yellow' insects representing the malignancy just as
effectively as the crab that ordinarily gives the disease its
name: 'Gradually, like some hideous tide of flesh, they
advanced along the passage, and I saw the foremost, visible
by the pale grey luminousness that came from them, reach
his door.'

*

Edward Frederic Benson, known to his family and close
acquaintances as Fred, was born in 1867 in Berkshire,
where his father Edward White Benson was headmaster of
the recently established Wellington College. Fred was the
second youngest of six siblings: four boys and two girls.
They were a remarkable, gifted and generally tight-knit
family – who would go on to move in the highest of circles,
including Queen Victoria and William Gladstone, and
count themselves friends of Robert Browning and the
Tennysons – yet emotional, physical and mental health
troubles stalked them all, like the lingering ancestral curse
in E. F. Benson's homoerotic 1930 novel of Cornwall and
the Great God Pan, *The Inheritor*.

The family's patriarch was a domineering, complex, changeable character, and wed his cousin, who was twelve years his junior, as soon as she was eighteen. Minnie, known later as 'Ben' to her close friends, spent the rest of her life falling in love with various women; none of the Benson children married, and all were far more comfortable in the company of members of the same sex. Tragedy struck the family early on too, with the eldest (and Edward White Benson's favourite) child, Martin, dying of meningitis aged seventeen, and the first of the two daughters, Eleanor Mary ('Nellie'), from diphtheria, at twenty-seven. Margaret ('Maggie') shared Fred's love of wildlife, and possessed her own menagerie of animals including a goat, canaries, collies and a large collection of guinea pigs. She grew into a brilliant scholar – though she attended Oxford at a time when women were not permitted to hold a degree – later going to Greece and Egypt with Fred, where she gained repute as an archaeologist. These good times were not to last, however, and in 1907, she was admitted to a mental asylum;* she died in 1916 from heart failure.

When Fred was five, the family relocated to Lincoln, his father being appointed chancellor of my home county's cathedral – that most gothic of buildings, with its underwhelming imp – before they were uprooted again, in 1877, when Edward White Benson was offered the newly created post of bishop of Cornwall. The eight of them moved to the vicarage at Kenwyn, a suburb on the hill above Truro,

---

* Maggie's physician, Dr George Stevens, had earlier treated Virginia Woolf's breakdown following the death of her father.

and work soon began on extending the house, now renamed Lis Escop ('Bishop's Palace' in Cornish), into a residence worthy of the title.

Half a decade younger than M. R. James, Fred Benson's formative life ran, in many respects, along parallel lines. He attended Temple Grove prep school in Surrey, as had James, and as had his brother Arthur – a friend of MRJ's.* However, Fred failed his scholarship for Eton and ended up as a fee-paying pupil at Marlborough, before following in his older sibling's steps and taking up a place at King's, Cambridge in the autumn of 1887. Arthur Christopher, the oldest of the three Benson brothers who reached adulthood, is best known for composing the words to Elgar's 'Land of Hope and Glory', though he was also a successful author, producing a large number of books including editing a ten-volume edition of Queen Victoria's letters, and two published collections of ghost stories. In addition, he had a career as a house master at Eton before becoming master of Magdalene College, Cambridge – where he continued to be one of James's closest, albeit most acerbic friends.

The youngest of the Benson children, Robert Hugh (known as Hugh), also trailed his brothers to Cambridge, afterwards entering the Anglican Church before

---

* On Christmas Day 1882 Edward Benson had been offered, and accepted, the position of archbishop of Canterbury – a promotion that led to the family leaving Truro. Monty James (during the holidays at the end of his first term at King's) happened to be visiting Arthur at Lis Escop when the offer of the archbishopric came through.

converting a few years thereafter to Catholicism. This was a scandalous choice for the son of an archbishop – though by this time Edward White Benson was no longer alive to suffer any embarrassment. Hugh was an author too, and wrote a number of supernatural tales, the majority of which make a point of referring to his Catholic faith (James thought them 'too ecclesiastical'). He died a few months after the start of the Great War from an underlying heart condition and pneumonia, followed a little over a decade later by Arthur.

Fred was the last of the family left standing.

The popularity of the writings of E. F. Benson has also outlived those of his brothers. He achieved instant success in 1893 with his first book, *Dodo*, a novel that satirised the frivolities of upper-class society and whose title character was a woman based on Margot Tennant, the future wife of Prime Minister Herbert Asquith, and mother of the film director Anthony Asquith. Like the rest of his family, Fred moved in smart circles. For instance, he knew Oscar Wilde, having most probably been introduced by his King's compatriot Robbie Ross (Wilde's lover and, later, the Irishman's literary executor), and attended the opening night of *Lady Windermere's Fan* with the novelist Max Beerbohm.*

After *Dodo*, the other big success in E. F. Benson's prolific career came between the wars with the *Mapp and*

---

* E. F. Benson's personal favourite of his own supernatural tales was 'How Fear Departed the Long Gallery', a comic but at times still frightening piece that reminds me of Wilde's 'The Canterville Ghost'.

Lucia books, the works for which he is now best remembered. They feature two snobbish, well-to-do women and
their comedic social rivalry and petty squabbles. Four of
the novels are set around Tilling, a version of Rye in Sussex,
the town where for many years Fred resided. He purchased
and lived at Lamb House, the former home of Henry
James, a family friend to whom his mother had sent an
early handwritten draft of *Dodo* for feedback; the American
was unimpressed ('He wrote me two or three long and
kindly and brilliantly evasive letters about it'). Years before,
at Addington Palace, the rural mansion near Croydon that
came, in addition to Lambeth Palace, with the role of archbishop, Edward White Benson had shared with James 'the
few meagre elements of a small & gruesome spectral story
that had been told *him* years before' – the tale of an old
country house, complete with 'some dead servants & some
children', that provided the inspiration for *The Turn of the
Screw*. The Tudor manor was Hinton Ampner in Hampshire,
though the National Trust property that stands there today
is a later reiteration and not the structure so troubled by
poltergeists around the year 1771 that it was subsequently
demolished.

Given that while at Cambridge E. F. Benson was a
member of the Chitchat Society – he was present on the
momentous evening of 28 October 1893 when M. R.
James read aloud his first two ghost stories ('Canon
Alberic's Scrap-book' and 'Lost Hearts') – and that the
family was associated with Henry James, it's little surprise
that Fred took to writing his own unsettling stories. Early
efforts appeared in periodicals such as *The Illustrated*

London News, *Hutchinson's Magazine* and *Pall Mall Magazine*; the latter contained 'The Bus-Conductor', a tale with a chilling premonition that formed the basis for the opening filmic episode of *Dead of Night* ('Just room for one inside, sir').

E. F. Benson's first book of supernatural stories, *The Room in the Tower*, was published in 1912. Its title piece is one of his most anthologised and features the vampiric, portrait-dwelling Mrs Stone. The actor Christopher Lee was a pupil at Wellington College when Benson visited his father's old school and read to an assembled hall of boys: Lee found 'The Room in the Tower' the 'most vivid' of the tales that Benson delivered to the rapt audience in his quiet voice, perhaps drawing on its atmosphere for his own later Hammer Horror depictions of the blood-sucking Count. In 1923 came *Visible and Invisible*, then *Spook Stories* in 1928, with Benson's last dedicated ghostly collection, *More Spook Stories*, in 1934. This contains my favourite of his tales, an atypically wistful, autobiographical work titled 'Pirates' that takes place at 'Lescop', a barely disguised version of his childhood family home in Truro.

The set-up of the story is not dissimilar to 'Negotium Perambulans'. Fifty-six-year-old Peter Graham, a successful businessman, is the chairman of a company that owns a number of dormant Cornish tin mines which, with the aid of a new, cheaper chemical process, have been deemed viable again. Peter, a hands-on chap, has come down to Cornwall to assess the properties and decides to stop off at Truro to take a look, forty years since he last saw it, at his

old house. Conveniently, Lescop has been unoccupied for some time and the local estate agent entrusts him the keys and tells him to inspect the place at his leisure.

Arriving at Lis Escop I'm not sure what to expect, though I've seen photographs of the exterior, so its architecture isn't a surprise. It's a grand building, dating originally from 1780, but extensively remodelled and added to thereafter; today it is known as Epiphany House, an ecumenical Christian conference centre and retreat. The manager, Janette, greets me and shows me around – pointing out the numerous changes since the Bensons arrived here in 1877 for their residence of a little over five years: here, Janette speculates, would have been Minnie's sitting room, here's the bishop's study. But, with the much-changed layout, it's not easy to picture the space described so vividly in Benson's story. The attic floor, for example, where, if the geography of 'Pirates' is to be believed (and I see no reason why not), Peter Graham, and therefore by extension Fred Benson, had his bedroom, is currently in a state of disrepair and not accessible. I content myself with peering out of the leaded window at the top of the curving staircase, perhaps the spot where the returned Peter remembers looking over the lawn as a boy, watching the clumsy antics of wood pigeons in the neighbouring tree – though there's no 'drooping lime' there now.

In 1953 the bishop of Cornwall's residence was relocated within the grounds of Trelissick House, a six-mile drive away. For three decades, until its financial failure, Lis Escop became part of Truro Cathedral School. The extensive gardens were parcelled up and sold, the house being purchased in 1983 to be used as a convent. The nuns were of a small, aged order and, when just two of them were left, gifted the place to set up the charitable trust now in operation; the last of the sisters, who was being looked after and living out her days at Lis Escop, passed away, Janette tells me, a couple of weeks before my visit.

'It's the end of an era,' she says.

On his return, Peter finds the house's emptiness and dilapidation rather mournful. He's pleased to be outside where he can familiarise himself, after such a long absence, with the extensive grounds he so loved to play in, where he used to search for birds' nests and moths. Like me, Fred Benson was a keen naturalist as a boy, an interest he kept for the rest of his life. He described his own lawn at Lamb House as 'bird-haunted' and writes beautifully about the ventriloquial starlings that he would feed bacon rind to, one of which would imitate a redshank as it perched on the garden trellis. Away from Rye, on numerous occasions he enjoyed birdwatching holidays to the north Norfolk coast, usually to Cley and Blakeney – hence how he came upon the isolated Halfway House on Blakeney Point, which provided him the inspiration for 'A Tale of an Empty House'. In *Final Edition*, the volume of autobiography completed just ten days before his death, he describes trips around those same marshes and reedbeds, detailing the 'sea swallows' (terns), bearded tits, the then rare avocet, and the 'three tall spoonbills standing aloof and meditative' that remained indelible in his memory. (My first spoonbill was also on the flooded scrapes at Cley, a typically immobile individual of this heron-like species.)*

Peter's initial euphoria at being within Lescop's gardens soon turns to despondency, as he realises how 'utterly neglected' they have become. However, his spirits are raised when he notices a familiar structure among the briars and thickets, which takes him back to a childhood game he used to play with his siblings: the 'Pirates' of the story's title. Pirates was a real game the Benson children invented in the grounds of Lis Escop. Its rules were somewhat involved but, basically, two participants hid in the garden's thick cover and maze of pathways, while the other three (though occasionally their mother joined in and, just once, the bishop) 'set forth at the order of the Admiral to

---

* Spoonbills so often seem to be sleeping when you see them, concealing their weird spatula-shaped beaks as if they don't want you to believe that such an instrument could have possibly ever evolved.

pick a trophy without being caught by the Pirates'. They
had to reach 'Plymouth Sound', the summer house at the
top of the garden. As Peter comes once more to this place
– its 'roof collapsed and its walls bulging' – he thinks he
hears one of his sisters calling out to him; earlier, walking
up from Truro, he experienced vivid flashbacks of fellow
Grahams, frozen in a time-shifted moment.

The last of these – the family on their way to a birthday
outing together – puts me in mind of one of the most
unsettling incidents of the New England author Shirley
Jackson's novel *The Haunting of Hill House* – perhaps the
ultimate haunted dwelling in fiction, and the one book I
read while researching *Ghostland* that caused me to feel
nervous about switching off my bedside light. During a
night-time argument, Eleanor and Theodora, the two
young women brought along to help test whether Hill
House is haunted, happen upon a menacing, spectrally lit
picnic in the grounds of that 'maniac juxtaposition' of a
place. Eleanor's dead mother is there, picking at a plate of
fruit, causing Theodore to scream. 'Don't look back,' she
cries out in fear, 'don't look back – don't look – run!'

Nothing so dramatic happens to Peter, who heads away
without incident and drops off the keys at the office in
town. Chatting to the man there it transpires that Lescop's
previous tenants have never stayed for long; there are
stories of the place being troubled, and it's available very
cheaply: 'It was just because it was haunted that he longed
for it, and the more savagely and sensibly he assured
himself of the folly of possessing it, the more he yearned
after it, and constantly now it coloured his dreams.'

Back in London, a newly acquired heart condition – and the subsequent warning from his doctor that if he doesn't take things easier he'll soon be dead – spurs Peter to action, and Lescop is inevitably purchased. The old furniture he's clung onto from the house is repatriated, repairs carried out, and rooms decorated as he remembers them from before. His own fondly recalled bedroom is restored in the attic, but there are strict instructions that no work should be started on the garden – Peter will direct that project after he takes up residence. He moves in, but, disappointingly, hears no more voices or whispers.

They're here though, he thinks to himself.

Having finished my tour with Janette I wander along the lane to Kenwyn Church, skirting what's left of the gardens (much has been turned over to new housing, or is awaiting development). There's still a dense, overgrown area to the rear of Lis Escop, however, where bamboo grows tall, where pirates could easily be hiding in ambush. Two goldcrests call from deep within a yew tree. In the story, one of the gardeners, the son of the cowman from forty years before – in the Bensons' time there was a cattle meadow at the side of the house – can recall the vast array of guinea pigs that Sybil would once have kept in their hutches somewhere out here, a clear reference to the pets E. F. Benson's troubled sister Maggie doted on.

After three weeks the work overseen by Peter has been carried out and the grounds returned to an approximation of their original condition. The house's owner is giddy, unable to take his now usual siesta in the restored summer house – 'Plymouth Sound' – because he can't stop himself from pacing the newly cleared pathways in an excited state of agitation. A tightness pulls across his chest and he retreats inside for an early night. Yet he wakes suddenly:

> The room was curiously bright, but not with the quality of moonlight; it was like a valley lying in shadow, while somewhere, a little way above it, shone some strong splendour of moon. And then he heard again his name called, and he knew that the sound of the voice came in through the window. There was no doubt that Violet was calling him: she and the others were out in the garden.

He follows their familiar noise, down to where they are waiting at the summer house, passing his mother who now is sitting in her room on her bed, saying to him how lovely it is, Peter, to have you home. (I don't think there's any malice in this ending, and yet, I find I cannot be absolutely certain ...)

His body is discovered on the gravel the next morning.

As to my own somewhat less grand childhood dwelling (c. 1960, rather than 1780) – the only house I had lived in until I went to university – it's still there. From the outside it doesn't appear very different, though the car port is covered by a garage door now and all the wooden windows have been replaced with uPVC ones. I thought hard about attempting to look inside again. About asking the current owner – the same man we sold it to two decades ago – whether he would show me around, but I realised that even if he agreed to my odd request I wouldn't want to see the place transformed into someone else's home. I want to keep its memory – its ghosts – to myself, not have it sullied by someone else's casual small talk. Still, I can't resist an occasional drive-by when I'm passing – but with the death of my elderly aunt and uncle (who'd continued to live in the town) during the writing of this book, the incentive for those already infrequent Lincolnshire visits is reduced further.

The last time, I dawdled in my car on the street out front before parking in the cul-de-sac around the corner – the way I walked each day to my primary school. On the grass by the old people's bungalows a green woodpecker is feeding – a bird that was near-mythical when I was young, as I'd never seen one locally, let alone right next to home. Buoyed by that, I follow the footpath along the route of the former railway line that ran past the back of the house, now lined with flimsy-looking flats where the bread factory my brother was working in when he got his Hodgkin's diagnosis used to stand. I peek over the fence at the rear end of the garden. The horse chestnut Dad planted to mark Chris's first birthday towers upwards, though most of the other flowers, trees and shrubs he spent his Sunday afternoons toiling over, while I sat inside watching strange old films like *The Halfway House*, seem to have been removed.

Will 'Babes in the Wood' sound in the distance, I half wonder. Will my mother be sitting at a picnic on the grass, like the family party outside Hill House or the one Peter Graham glimpses as he retraces his childhood steps? Somewhere behind the house's walls, might my parents' shades – like the ethereal, lingering trace of the couple in Virginia Woolf's tender two-page story 'A Haunted House' – be prolonging the 'hidden joy' of their relationship?

Nothing stirs, except the branches of the conker tree; silence lies steadily on the lawn.

It's not the house that is haunted. It's me.

And I want to be; I have to be. Because if I give them up – if I stop looking back – everything that ever happened to us will cease to exist.

Chapter 12

ANCIENT SORCERIES

Two skylarks perform their songflight somewhere above me. In the harsh glare of the late morning sun I can't pick them out, and it's no easier when the scene's temporarily thrown into eclipse by a fast-moving cloud. The breeze is forceful, shaking the foot-high grass and masking the faint radio-interference sounds of the larks.

Badbury Rings in Dorset, an Iron Age hill fort consisting of three concentric circles of chalk banks and ditches. A herd of brown and black cows graze contentedly alongside the earthworks. One of them coughs as I pass, the sound a little like the persistent throat-clearing my

brother couldn't stop himself from doing when we were last here. I don't know the exact date because I made no note of it and there are no corroborating pictures on my phone; that summer of 2014 I took few photos because I didn't want to document what was unfolding. But on that similarly sun-stoked day we watched – briefly, because they never stayed still – dark green fritillary and marbled-white butterflies. So I can date our visit to around the end of June, because that's the period those two species are on the wing.

You see, my brother was dying.

He had, within a few months, become frail and thin: a prematurely aged 46-year-old perched on his maroon electric mobility scooter, which he manoeuvred with gusto around the paths of this ancient fortification. He drove it with no self-consciousness – with little grumbling about the rapidity of his physical deterioration, his hacking dry cough, and his complete lack of appetite. I admired him for how he managed to keep it together, because he seemed so much mentally stronger and more dignified than I could ever imagine myself to be in that situation. But then he always was the stoic, sensible one, always just got on with things while I went flitting from job to job, off on travels to look for obscure rare birds, or half-heartedly tried to write books that never came.

Several weeks before – around the beginning of May – the doctors had finally determined what was causing Chris's breathing to become laboured, his heart to stop functioning correctly. He'd been admitted to hospital two years previously with related symptoms, which were eventually attributed to long-term cardiac damage caused by the corrosive therapy carried out to treat his Hodgkin's lymphoma. After that initial scare, following a spell of recuperation, he was back at work, back to becoming himself again. Yes, if we happened to be walking up a slope I would notice that he'd get breathless and have to pause for rests, but I was hopeful that with ongoing medication nothing much would substantively change. But as the spring of 2014 got under way he collapsed at home and was readmitted to hospital once more. This time they found the underlying cause: it wasn't only his heart that had been damaged by the earlier treatments – insidious cancer cells were concealed within his lungs, another little-known consequence of the chemicals, or the radiation, that had before kept his disease at bay.

Chris went home and every opportunity I got I came down to his house on the outskirts of Wimborne Minster – only a few miles from Badbury Rings – to help out in the small way I could, dropping my nieces off at school or at their dancing lessons (they were nine and twelve then), and to enjoy being with my brother: our expectations were finite, though we hoped he had a year or more left. Knowing his stubbornness, he'll hold on far longer, I thought, when I dared to wonder about that empty future at all.

When I reach the outer circle I head clockwise around the periphery of the Rings, just as the two of us did before. Here, higher up the hill, the wind is stronger and a swift is quartering uncharacteristically low over the grass and wild flowers. A swift once more – like the pioneering April bird that had sailed above the Southampton General car park; I follow its twisting flight through Chris's binoculars, which I have borrowed.

Later, I will see numerous common-spotted and pyramidal orchids, but none of the mimicking bee orchids that Chris and I did manage to locate that day. An elderly but sprightly Dutchman – from Friesland, in the north of the country, he tells me – asks what I'm looking at.

'Orchids,' I say.

'I don't know what they're called in English, but in Holland they grow taller,' he replies, then explains how he has been coming here for fifty years, as his late wife was from nearby Blandford. I sense his sadness – you are on a pilgrimage of sorts like me, I think. We move on to a safer topic of conversation for two strangers: the weather.

'We should be okay,' I say, glancing up at the fast-changing sky.

'Let's hope. I'm on the campsite, so need it to be good.'

He carries on, away into the woodland at the heart of the hill. I sit down next to the Ordnance Survey triangulation station that juts up from the bank – a modern monolith – and listen to the scratchy song of a nearby whitethroat. Few butterflies are on the wing – perhaps it's too windy? Just a handful of meadow browns, but none of the marbled whites or fritillaries I saw before. A stoat lollops past through the long grass, too fast for my camera, but I can make out its black tail tip, so am certain of its identity. I smirk to myself, like I always do when I encounter one of these agile little killers. Because my mother couldn't help but crack her joke: how do you tell a weasel from a stoat?

Weasels are weasily recognised and stoats are stotally different, of course.

I get to my feet. It's time to walk in the wood. When Chris and I were last here I was concerned that the foot-worn path up through the centre of the Rings to the apex of the hill was too muddy and his scooter wouldn't make it, but he didn't seem concerned. 'I'm not bloody carrying you,' I joked. And we were fine. Beyond the concrete plinth showing neighbouring landmarks, we watched a spotted flycatcher perform dashing sorties among the Scots pines, the first example of that declining migrant I'd seen that summer. They used to nest behind our house when I was at school – the newly fledged youngsters usually appearing at some stage on our washing line – but now I encounter them only sporadically (the species' British population has declined massively over the past fifty years). I wonder whether I might find one here again, whether even the same individual could show itself to me through my Chris's binoculars. The thought puts me in mind of M. R. James's 'A View from a Hill', in which Fanshawe is visiting his friend Richards on a sunny June day like today.* Fanshawe takes the loan of a strangely heavy, archaic pair of field glasses from his host and, from a nearby vantage point, can see people milling about on so-called Gallows Hill across the way.

'And now – by Jove, it does look like something hanging on the gibbet.'

The squire, when he tries them, sees nothing.

It transpires that the maker of the optics, a local anti-quary named Baxter, has been boiling down the bones of hanged men and incorporating the grim fluid into the instrument's lenses, in order that he can see through their dead eyes into a previous age. Predictably, events do not end well for him.

Through my rather less heavy borrowed Leica binocu-lars no flycatchers present themselves, no past visions or snatched glimpses through my departed brother's eyes

---

* The rural Herefordshire setting of the story was probably inspired by the landscape around Kilpeck, just south-west of Hereford, where the late James McBryde's wife Gwendolen and daughter Jane lived after the artist's death. MRJ was a regular visitor there over the years.

– though would I even know the difference, I wonder, as so much of what we enjoyed looking at was so similar.

So many things about us the same.

From out of nowhere a shower has started, so I make for shelter beneath a holly bush among the oaks, the sound soporific as the rain drops onto the leaves above my head; if I stay here for too long I might never want to leave. The place possesses a peacefulness – a sort of magic, I suppose. It's a sense described in reverential terms by the artist Paul Nash, who also captured the languorous undulations of the age-old hillside in an illustration included in his 1935 *Dorset* Shell Guide – an early title in the series of petroleum-sponsored guidebooks for the new breed of pioneering motorist that, under the editorship of John Betjeman, he compiled:

> I have read of enchanted places, and at rare times come
> upon them, but I remember nothing so beautifully
> haunted as the wood in Badbury Rings. Long
> afterwards I read of the tradition that King Arthur's
> soul inhabited a raven's body which nested there –
> indeed it is one of the last nesting-places of the wild
> raven in England – but I needed no artificial stimulus
> to be impressed.

I've not heard the croak of any ravens today, but driving around the local lanes that summer with Chris, we often saw their distinctive wedge-tailed silhouettes sailing above us and picked out their gruff croaks, and he told me how they'd been getting far more common in the county over the past few years.* The Arthurian raven legends at Badbury are a comparatively recent phenomenon, stemming from a late-Victorian, Cambridge antiquarian scholar, Edwin Guest, who hypothesised that Badbury was the location of Mount Badon, where the historical Arthur was said to have defeated the Saxons (though several other sites make a similar claim). This speculation seems to have become intertwined with the notable presence of breeding ravens – the last to nest in Wessex, some have claimed. From those two snippets of purported fact, it was not such a leap to have Arthur's spirit transferring into one of the shaggy-throated corvids, a species which had been popularised by Edgar Allan Poe's famous poem and Dickens's novel *Barnaby Rudge*; the tradition of keeping ravens at the Tower of London and the associated legend also first arose in the Victorian age. Yet other local folklore grew up too, involving the great king's midnight appearances at the Rings with his ghostly cohort of knights, superseding earlier stories of a golden coffin buried somewhere between the ancient fort and the neighbouring village.

The shower stops and I start down the hill. I try to think back to where else Chris and I went during those end days: we looked, unsuccessfully, for otters on the river in Blandford Forum; to Knowlton, not far from Badbury,

---

* This is borne out by recent data, which shows a sizeable increase in the raven's British breeding range during my lifetime. Yet our largest crows are still mostly absent from the east coast, so every time I hear their calls I'm taken back to our earlier holidays in the uplands, or weekends at my brother's in Dorset.

where the ruins of a Norman church sit within an even older circular earthwork in the chalk – a perfect example of the links between the pagan past and Christianity; to Corfe Castle, where we ate a cream tea (or at least I did, Chris having little appetite by this point) in the shadow of the now romantic ruin that was blown apart during the Civil War; and to Maiden Castle, a bare-hilled Iron Age fort overlooking Dorchester, whose size dwarfs all others in the country. John Cowper Powys's 1936 novel *Maiden Castle* was inspired by the impressive site, though it's a book I struggle to have much affinity with. Thomas Hardy wrote about it too – his short story 'A Tryst in an Ancient Earthwork' describes the place beautifully: 'At one's every step forward it rises higher against the south sky, with an obtrusive personality that compels the senses to regard it and consider.' This was another location Paul Nash painted and photographed, writing powerfully of the skeletal remains – lifeless objects in the landscape – that he'd recently witnessed being uncovered there (during the 1930s) by the archaeologist Sir Robert Eric Mortimer Wheeler:

The sun beat down on the glinting white bones which were disposed in elegant clusters and sprays of blanched sprigs and branches. Or some seemed to be the nests of giant birds; the gleaming skulls like clutches of monstrous eggs. It was a place, with these scattered groups of fantastic nests and long raised ledges on the open hills, resembling a bird sanctuary. A sanctuary for moas.

Chris and I only got as far as the parking area that day, hoping to see a corn bunting, a rattle-songed, streaky-brown farmland species that we came across often in our Lincolnshire youth, but has since been decimated by the onslaught of pesticides and changes in agricultural prac-tices. We didn't find any, but today, almost as soon as I leave the car, I hear one. And there it is, perched on a low fence post. Another, more distant male is on a telegraph wire, attempting to demonstrate the superiority of its own voice. Nash was right, I think: this is a sanctuary, only the birds it shelters have not quite yet gone the way of the flightless, extinct New Zealand moa.

From Maiden Castle I detour into Dorchester: Thomas Hardy's Casterbridge. The Dorset county town is where Hardy lived – in Max Gate, a house he designed himself

– for almost half of his eighty-seven years. It's also the setting for the culmination of one of the few uncanny stories he wrote, 'The Withered Arm' – a Wessex tale Hardy himself described as being 'of rather a weird nature'.* Its main protagonists are the milkmaid Rhoda Brook and her illegitimate son, a boy of twelve or thirteen fathered by Lodge, a local farmer. The story begins with talk of the imminent arrival of the farmer's recently acquired wife. Rhoda, understandably, is bitter about this turn of events and the way she's been cast aside. She sends out her son on a spying mission, though his reports back of the girl's loveliness are not what the older woman wants to hear. Two or three weeks later, as she lies in bed, Rhoda experiences an unsettling night terror: 'the young wife, in the pale silk dress and white bonnet, but with features shockingly distorted, and wrinkled as by age, was sitting upon her chest as she lay.' Feeling herself suffocated, she struggles and grabs 'the incubus' by its left arm, flinging the figure away from her onto the floor of her room.

It transpires that the picture the milkmaid has built up about the woman she views as a callous usurper is unfair. Gertrude Lodge has a pleasant, kindly nature: she brings new boots to the boy because she feels sorry for the state

---

* Although he rarely turned his own hand to writing tales of an overtly supernatural nature, ghosts (and memories of the departed) feature frequently in Hardy's poetry. Yet we know Hardy was a fan of the genre – his second wife Florence told of how he sent a Christmas card to M. R. James 'in a fit of enthusiasm' after reading the Cambridge don's ghost stories.

of his footwear, and strikes up an unlikely friendship with Rhoda. She confides in the older woman that she's recently been troubled by a strange mark – 'as if produced by a rough grasp' – on her left arm, which is beginning to cause her increasing discomfort. It appeared at the same time Rhoda cast off the creature in her night terror. As the summer draws on, Gertrude's odd condition deteriorates further, and she confesses that she believes her husband already loves her less due to her newly acquired disfigurement: 'Men think so much of personal appearance.' Rhoda has begun to feel responsible, wondering whether her own anger and jealousy have combined to 'exercise a malignant power over people against my own will'.

The arm begins to shrink and wither, and Gertrude persuades Rhoda to take her to a noted wise man said to be gifted with healing abilities. Conjuror Trendle is a grey-bearded local who lives in a remote cottage on the wild Egdon Heath, a place in Hardy's work of eeriness, magic, and the superstitions of a bygone age. Trendle makes a living selling furze (gorse, traditionally used for fuel), turf and sand that he harvests from the heath, yet also helps those who come to him regarding more esoteric matters. He tells Gertrude that 'an enemy' has caused the affliction, showing her the likeness of the person in a glass filled with the albumen of an egg. Although what she sees is not described to us, her later reaction to Rhoda confirms the identity of the glimpsed figure.

Over the course of that winter the farmer's new wife gradually loses the use of her left arm. Local gossip puts it down to her being 'overlooked' by Rhoda Brook – an old

term for the Evil Eye.* Rhoda and her son leave the neighbourhood, nobody knowing what has become of them. Six
years later Gertrude Lodge, by this point firmly trapped in
a loveless and childless marriage, goes again to see Conjuror
Trendle on the heath. One possible last cure remains: to
touch the limb against the neck of a recently hanged man.
'It will turn the blood and change the constitution,' he tells
her, so Gertrude makes a secret plan to visit Casterbridge
on the occasion of a forthcoming public execution.

This being Hardy, of course, things do not conclude
brightly.

Egdon is a location vividly rendered in this story, which
also plays a greater role at the heart of Hardy's novel
The Return of the Native. In the geography of his imagined
'partly real, partly dream-country' of Wessex it's a wild
expanse, stretching much further than the actual heathland areas, known as Black Heath and Duddle Heath, that
were within easy walking distance of the cottage in which
he was raised in the hamlet of Higher Bockhampton, three
miles east of Dorchester.

By the time I arrive, the rain clouds that tracked me at
Badbury have blown over and the heather-covered hill-
sides are gathering the afternoon warmth. I like to think
I'm following in the very steps the young Hardy himself
took, past Rushy Pond, a shallow 'heath-hemmed' water-
ing hole where I watch a pony silently emerge through the

---

* This archaic definition of 'overlooked', now I think of it, fits
neatly with the name chosen for the building at the heart of
Stephen King's *The Shining* – the Overlook Hotel.

scrub to drink. I follow the old Roman road to Puddletown, walled in on my left by a monotonous stand of Scots pines whose bone-like roots crisscross the surface, causing me more than once to stumble. Heat reflects back at me from the foot-worn chalk of the path and, at one point, I nearly tread upon the blackness of a red admiral butterfly that basks there open-winged; from the nearby furze two yellowhammers sing out to me about the paucity of bread and cheese. This ancient thoroughfare inspired a poem by Hardy, 'The Roman Road', in which the memory of his long-departed mother, who brought him here as an infant, is remembered and contrasted with those earlier, unseen legionaries.

The heath itself, though it doesn't cover a large acreage, is still easy to get lost in – like Sebald's mesmeric Dunwich – particularly as I try to locate the tumulus that's the setting for the evocative Guy Fawkes' Night bonfire at the beginning of *The Return of the Native*. The real-life location, known as Rainbarrows, consists of three now overgrown cavities – inside which, in 1887, urns containing the cremated remains of the dead were unearthed – rather than the more conspicuous singular 'Rainbarrow' whose 'blurred contour' obstructs the sky of the novel. This viewpoint is also, so the leaflet I picked up in the Hardy's Birthplace Visitor Centre tells me, the spot from where the author once witnessed a public execution – a hanging – down in the dip of Dorchester. Before that, as a young boy, he'd been haunted by a story his father told him, a story that provided the inspiration for the devastating ending of 'The Withered Arm': during the 1830s his father watched four men, including a starving lad of eighteen, put to the noose, for being mere bystanders when a haystack was torched.

I have a similarly vivid early recollection from my childhood which involves Thomas Hardy. Monday 27 July, 1981. I am lying on the bottom bunk of our Post House family hotel room at Heathrow the night before we embark on our maiden trip abroad, to Canada.* The main difference in my recollections, however, between Canada and all

---

* On our unprecedented three-week family holiday we stayed with friends on the outskirts of Toronto – not far from the location of Algernon Blackwood's failed 1891 dairy-farming adventure.

the holidays that went before or came after is that my mother kept a diary. The other trips are documented only by their ramshackle selection of slides housed in plastic yellow cases, or the unsorted photographs fading and crinkling in my loft – there's no key to help me decode the places and events depicted.

I have her diary beside me now. A white, blue-lined notebook, approximately A5 portrait in size, with a red Canadian maple leaf emblazoned on its board cover. It contains the only written words I possess from my mother, and is the only time, to my knowledge, she kept such a record – though I wonder whether her teenage self ever wrote about boys she fancied, or of an imagined future in Swinging London, a world away from the flatness of her Fenland home.

The opening page records that the four of us 'watched tv until 10.30', not saying what was on. But I remember. I've never been able to forget: it was John Schlesinger's 1967 adaptation of Hardy's novel *Far from the Madding Crowd*, starring Alan Bates and Julie Christie. In the semi-darkness of dawn, Bates's shepherd, Gabriel Oak, is sleeping in his hut. The younger of his two collie sheepdogs, inexperienced and eager to please, has freed itself from its chain and is now mindlessly harrying the sheep in their clifftop pen until they knock down one of their enclosing willow hurdles and pour forwards. I was plagued by the terrible thing that happened next – I still am – even though I was only half-awake and up to that point had barely been following what was taking place on the screen in the corner of the room.

Oak's dog harries the sheep one by one to leap over the side of the cliff; we see them fall, see their corpses lying on the chestnut sand as white-capped breakers roll in. The shepherd is roused and rushes out, but too late; his silhouette is framed from below as he cocks his shotgun and shoots the dog dead.

'We all spent a restless night,' Mum wrote.

In addition to occasional visits to the prehistoric remains that proliferate this part of the south-west when I was visiting my brother, our earlier unjournalled 1983 family holiday to the New Forest and its surroundings gave me my first glimpse of two of the country's most important ancient landmarks: Stonehenge and Avebury. I don't remember much about that initial trip to Salisbury Plain, other than perhaps being slightly underwhelmed – a feeling fostered by Dad's obvious disappointment at no longer being able to walk among the now fenced-off megaliths. He and Mum had come to the site on their honeymoon in 1965, the pair of them posing in turn for photographs in front of the CND-graffitied stones.

A different black-and-white view of the distinctive sarsens comes at the start of another of those old horror films I watched so keenly in my youth. *Night of the Demon* is loosely based on M. R. James's 'Casting the Runes', though it only really retains the central concept of the original story – the idea that a curse summoning some supernatural entity that will bring death to the victim can be enacted by handing them, without their knowledge, a slip of paper bearing certain runic

symbols;* likewise, the perpetrator of this dark magic will become its recipient if the transaction is reversed. Stonehenge doesn't appear anywhere near James's original

---

* *Night of the Demon* (1957) was directed by the Frenchman Jacques Tourneur, who, fifteen years earlier, was responsible for two of RKO's classic horror movies, *Cat People* and *I Walked With a Zombie*. Although it's an excellent film, most critics lament the ropiness of *Night of the Demon*'s unconvincing monster that pursues the recipients of those wind-wafted slips of paper. I'd tend to agree – I don't think there's any need for the audience to see the close-up of the demon so early on – but the flickering lights and swirling smoke that herald its arrival remain a chilling effect.

text, but *Night of the Demon* opens with an atmospheric scene of the monument – a low wide-shot filmed from behind a breeze-blown tussock – accompanied by a voiceover that informs us:

> It has been written since the beginning of time, even
> unto these ancient stones that evil, supernatural
> creatures exist in a world of darkness. And it is also
> said: man, using the ancient power of the magic runic
> symbols, can call forth these powers of darkness – the
> demons of hell.

Later, the lead character, an American psychologist named Dr John Holden, returns to Stonehenge to examine the writing on the stones – a scene performed in the studio, as no such symbols have ever existed there in reality (and the symbolic graffiti my parents were witness to has also long been removed). The rest of the action veers equally away from James's original tale of academic differences taken to their extremes, but in its way is no less memorable. Niall MacGinnis's goateed Karswell steals every scene in which he appears, becoming a much more prominent, fleshed-out character in the film.* At one point he conjures a mini-tornado to disrupt the annual Halloween party he's throwing for the local village children – a sharp contrast with the print version's magic lantern show of wolves, spectres and 'a great mass of snakes, centipedes,

---

* MacGinnis's first major role was the lead in Michael Powell's Foula-shot *The Edge of the World*, two decades before.

and disgusting creatures with wings' that sends the youngsters fleeing: in James's story the crowning horror is that 'he made it seem as if they were climbing out of the picture and getting in amongst the audience'.

Stonehenge also features at the climax of Hardy's *Tess of the D'Urbervilles*, and has long been a subject for visual artists too. Its first known depiction was in two fourteenth-century manuscripts, before a number of Elizabethan painters tried to capture their own imaginative response to the site's pagan mystery and grandeur, paving the way for those towering figures of early-nineteenth-century English art, J. M. W. Turner and John Constable. Turner visited the stones on several occasions between 1799 and the 1820s, his resulting output most dramatically including a watercolour dating from *c.* 1827.

In Turner's *Stonehenge*, a break in the storm-driven sky bathes the monument in a bleaching, white-brown light;

it's as if all of Heaven has directed its glory, or its ire, onto this heathen place, around which unsubstantiated associations of druidic sacrifice – popularised by the antiquarian William Stukeley in the 1740s – had subsequently grown. On closer inspection of the painting, many of the sheep grazing at the base of the stones are lying prostrate, as is their shepherd, struck dead by the lightning that has speared from the storm clouds. It is an image that reminds me of the final incarnation of Nigel Kneale's *Quatermass*, a story about societal breakdown and the clash between generations, which was shown on ITV in the autumn of 1979, following a technicians' strike that had kept the channel off air for seventy-five days.

It would be three or four years until I saw the series, watching it at my aunt's house during the summer holidays after she'd taped a repeat off the telly for me – it's clear to me now that I owe much of my love of sci-fi and horror films to her and those VHS recordings. Although this was the last appearance of Professor Bernard Quatermass, it was my first encounter with him, and so John Mills's elderly, worn-out version of the fictional scientist sticks with me, even though it isn't the strongest of the character's on-screen incarnations.[*]

---

[*] For me that honour is reserved for *Quatermass and the Pit*, which I watched one Sunday afternoon following Dad's recommendation. It's another story warning of the dangers of digging up mysterious objects – in this case a devilish Martian spacecraft that's intertwined with the dark history of humanity and which, in the 1967 Hammer film version of the earlier BBC series, is buried beneath the wonderfully named Hobbs End tube station.

The 1979 *Quatermass* is directed by Piers Haggard, the man behind the folk horror of *The Blood on Satan's Claw*. Soil-bound supernatural forces are not at work here, however, but a dystopic England gone mad, in which social order has been destroyed. In the opening scene the elderly professor, having travelled down from his home in Scotland, is dropped off by a cab in a decrepit, boarded-up London street, from where he has to make his way on foot to the fortified compound of the 'British Television' station, the only such facility still left. He is accosted by a gang, before being rescued by radio astronomer Dr Joe Kapp, a fellow guest on the same programme. Quatermass implodes on the show, where he's meant to be commenting on a historic link-up between the Russians' and Americans' space stations, using the broadcast as an opportunity to appeal for information about his missing teenage granddaughter. Shortly afterwards, live on air, the spacecraft-docking goes badly wrong. Both vessels are lost, along with twenty-seven lives.

Kapp takes Quatermass under his wing and the pair flee in an armoured van through the anarchic outskirts of the city, back to the younger scientist's house and Jodrell Bank-esque radio telescope in the West Country. En route they encounter their first group of Planet People, a hippyish youth cult that are mobilising in numbers towards various Neolithic sites, from where they hope and believe they'll be transported to a better existence on some distant world. At the end of the opening episode the two men (and Kapp's wife) visit the nearby stone circle, Ringstone Round, where they are helpless observers as a pulsing sound fills the air and a beam, like the light in Turner's painting,

descends upon the hundreds of young people who have
gathered there; everything within the stones becomes ash.
On the lip of the ring a girl survivor has been blinded and
left clinging to life by what she calls the 'lovely lightning'.

It transpires that analagous cases are happening around
the globe at increasingly large gatherings of believers
(culminating in tens of thousands at Wembley Stadium),
which now begin to include other disaffected converts
from the gangs we've earlier encountered. Quatermass
comes to believe that the incidents entail the harvesting of
youth by some kind of alien machine – the destroyed
spacecraft happened to be in the ray's line of transmission.
At the programme's denouement we witness the professor's attempts to enact a plan that will prevent further
materialisations of the death-bringing beam.

I cannot remember much of *Quatermass* when I sit
down to watch it again – it's been over thirty years since
that previous summer holiday viewing. In the meantime,
I've forgotten most of the dystopic stuff (and the amus-
ingly prescient vision of future televisual family entertainment), but can still recall nearly every word of the nursery
rhyme that's eerily intertwined with the stone circle
happenings:

Huffity puffity Ringstone Round,
If you lose your hat it will never be found.
So pull up your britches right up to your chin
And fasten your cloak with a bright new pin.
And when you are ready, then we can begin:
Huffity, puffity, puff.

A ray of extraterrestrial energy descends from the heavens onto a Wiltshire ring of Neolithic stones in a cult children's series transmitted after school on ITV two years before *Quatermass*, during January and February 1977. *Children of the Stones*, however, was set around Avebury, rather than Stonehenge. I recall little about the place from our 1983 holiday, yet of all the ancient sites we came to, this village, whose buildings are laid out among the monument, is the one I find most impressive today.

The settlement dates to Anglo-Saxon times, with the oldest building, the church of St James, built in the eleventh century but incorporating materials from earlier structures. Even though I'd been back once about fifteen years ago, I had forgotten the scale of the place, how the stones are so intertwined with the fabric of the village – as is the vast earthwork bank and ditch – and how so many sacred-looking groves crown the hilltops about the horizon.

As you make your approach you pass the weird cone of Silbury Hill, the largest man-made prehistoric chalk mound in the world. The massive standing stones themselves are weather-worn and pockmarked, repurposed today as scratching posts for sheep or oversized perches for birds. A jackdaw is on top of a taller sarsen; it allows me to draw near to the base, safe in the knowledge there's no way I can reach up. One of its glossy blue-black wings is stretched down in an ungainly fashion as it attempts to air it following the shower that began as I arrived. This close I'm struck by the clarity of its eye, its pale, silvery iris in which is set a tiny pinprick of a pupil that stares down at me with more than a hint of comprehension.

'Hello jackdaw,' I mutter, conscious that these agile undersized crows seem to have accompanied me at so many of the places I've visited while writing this book. But, unlike the aviary-imprisoned bird in my local park from when I was little, this one doesn't answer back.

I didn't see *Children of the Stones* as a boy (I would have been three when it was first transmitted – and it was only repeated on UK terrestrial television in the following summer), but can understand why the serial left such an impact on those a few years older than me who watched it at the time, because so much is contained within its seven episodes. There's the theme of the villagers becoming subservient 'Happy Ones', unnaturally cheerful, do-gooding automatons who greet each other with the phrase 'Happy day' and are gradually subsuming everyone inside the boundary of the circle into their cult;* the driving force behind this assimilation is the lord of the manor, Hendrick, adding a touch of 1970s class warfare into the proceedings.

We also have a cycle of events that repeatedly attempts to play itself out across the generations, like we saw in *The Owl Service* or *Red Shift*: 'Nobody leaves the circle!' a villager incredulously laments at one point. Actual history makes its way into the script too, by means of such details as the so-called 'barber-surgeon', a medieval skeleton (with an accompanying set of scissors) found beneath an unexcavated stone in 1938 – human remains which become integral to the unfolding drama.

Then there's the striking physical backdrop of the landscape itself, the furtive sense of history it holds. At ancient sites like this the deep past haunts our present – the unknowable lives and actions of previous inhabitants from

---

* This sinister takeover reminds me of the alien pod people from *Invasion of the Body Snatchers* or the robotic, docile women of *The Stepford Wives*.

so many generations before call out to us, begging us to understand their barely uncovered existences. Yet how can we? I've been able to conjure little more than a trace of my own vanished parents, let alone gain any meaningful impression of the people who toiled – for whatever impenetrable reasons, more than four millennia ago – to erect these gargantuan boulders ...

The opening credits of *Children of the Stones* begin with a sigh of synthesisers and the silhouetted close-up of one of the gnarled megaliths; the music – weird choral voices – builds to a peak, and we pull out to an aerial shot that shows us the scale of how the village (renamed Milbury in the series) is literally encircled by the past. In the first episode we witness the arrival of astrophysicist Adam Brake, here to further his research into the stones and their electromagnetism, and his teenage son, Matthew. The professor points out 'the hill' – enigmatic Silbury – as they approach, and Matthew confesses his understandable fear of moving to a new home.

'Suppose they all turn out to be nutters?' he asks, an eventuality that, of course, turns out to be the case.

Children of the Stones is not the only unsettling programme of its era to take advantage of Avebury. The penultimate offering in the original run of the 'Ghost Story for Christmas' strand, 1977's contemporary-set *Stigma*, was also filmed here. At the heart of its drama is the removal of one of the Neolithic stones from the garden of a cottage adjacent to the circle by workmen carrying out improvements. As it is lifted an ominous wind blows, and from that point everything changes for the occupants of the house. It's a pared-down, quietly effective, yet incredibly bloody piece, and the last to be directed by Lawrence Gordon Clark.*

Avebury, like Stonehenge, possesses a magnetism irresistible to artists. Paul Nash first came here in 1933, the rocks featuring in his 1937 lithograph *Landscape of the Megaliths*, while John Piper's 1940 *Avebury Restored* displays a brooding quality of light not dissimilar to Turner's shepherd-killing lightning storm. In a more abstract series of 1973 works (he probably derived their angular forms from photos he'd taken of marble surfaces), Derek Jarman places the stones he painted among a succession of coloured vertical and horizontal lines.

Better known now as a filmmaker, Jarman had trained, like James McBryde and Ithell Colquhoun, at the Slade (in painting and set design). I'd first happened upon arguably the most magical of his creations when my brother and I were birdwatching at Dungeness in Kent. Jutting into the English Channel, the Ness has its own magnetism to birds, its geographic pull aided by the heated outflow into the sea from the blocky Dungeness B nuclear-power station that attracts various avian visitors to feed in the raised temperatures of the water. In the middle of this most desolate of moonscapes, Jarman sculpted and grew a garden of sublime,

---

* *Stigma* was the first new work commissioned specially for the strand that was not an adaptation of an existing tale by Charles Dickens or M. R. James (though elements of the story are reminiscent of 'Oh, Whistle, and I'll Come to You, My Lad'). The following year's *The Ice House* (written by *Robin Redbreast*'s John Bowen) is strange to the point of distraction – more akin to Robert Aickman meets Flann O'Brien.

unlikely beauty around Prospect Cottage, a tin-roofed, black-varnished, yellow-windowed fisherman's hut.

Although I had little interest in gardening (my mum used occasionally to drag me to various plant nurseries, something I dreaded due to the boredom it induced in me), at some point after our visit I saw a television feature about Jarman that made sense of the strange oasis Chris and I had stumbled upon among the shingle.* I was mesmerised by the garden, so that whenever my brother and I subsequently went to Dungeness we stopped off to look. Our earlier visits would have been between 1990 and 1992, when Jarman was still alive and could conceivably have been present within the cottage, though we never

---

* I imagine the television piece was connected with the release of Jarman's 1990 film *The Garden*, which focuses on the existence-affirming plot of shingle situated in the shadow of so much that's seemingly at odds with the creation and sustenance of life.

met him; he was diagnosed with HIV just before Christmas in 1986 and died in February 1994. When the last book he wrote – about his garden – came out posthumously, my brother bought it for me. I'd forgotten that he'd written inside it, but there are his words on the title page:

To Ed, Happy Birthday 1995 from Chris

In the book, referring to the shingle that formed the topsoil of his seaside plot as well, perhaps, as to some of the menhir-like objects he positioned into the rocky ground of his last of England, Jarman writes: 'I invest my stones with the power of those at Avebury.' Clearly the Wiltshire monument had left its impression on him, as his Dungeness retreat had on me. Aside from his series of paintings of those famous standing stones, in 1971 he also produced a Super 8 film titled *Journey to Avebury* – part of his cinematic apprenticeship – which I find to be the most disconcerting visual portrayal of the enigmatic site. It's a hypnotic ten minutes of grainy footage consisting of mainly static, wavering shots of the landscape around the village and nearby downs, punctuated by old straight tracks and wind-stirred verges full of wild flowers and cow parsley that my grandad would've loved to put a match to.

Journey to Avebury possesses a Polaroid palette – oddly saturated, yet somehow washed-out colours beneath a tobacco-tinged sky (it appears to have been shot through a yellow filter). This, coupled with the absence of people, lends the film an almost post-apocalyptic look: it's as if everyone really has been vaporised by an interstellar death

ray. We're nearly halfway in before we get reassurance that
this isn't the case: a group of kids sitting on a wall in the
village wave to the camera. Apart from these 'Happy
Ones', the only living creatures are two distantly glimpsed
ridgetop walkers near the end of the footage (though even
they have an otherness about them, reminding me of the
strange boatman in Blackwood's 'The Willows'), various
loafing cows, and a sprinkling of birds.

Birdsong features too, at the start and finish of the
accompanying soundtrack – a 1990s addition, because
originally *Journey to Avebury* would've been a silent movie.
The band that bring us this later, beating-heart electronica
are Coil (they also contributed to the soundtrack for
Jarman's final cinematic offering, *Blue*), and its pulsing
psychedelia adds to the film's unsettling nature – it reminds
me, a little, of the music behind the opening credits of
Kubrick's *The Shining*, as the camera tracks above Jack
Nicholson's yellow VW Beetle as it heads to the Overlook
Hotel in the Colorado mountains. The journey in Jarman's
film, however, ends less destructively and dramatically: a
clumsy zoom towards three far-off groves of Nash-like
beeches, before a sudden cut to black.

Derek Jarman's Garden is a poignant book – my copy
made more so to me by that unremembered dedication
from my brother – filled with wonderful photography by
Howard Sooley of the garden's sculptural mixture of shingle, found objects and impossibly colourful plants. In some
of the photos Jarman is there tending his stony ground, his
clothes by this point far too large for his shrunken frame.
He's drowning in them, which reminds me of Chris in his

last months, when all of his things were too big for him too; he gave me his old jeans, but because he was that bit taller than me they dragged on the floor. I went shopping with him in Poole while he bought a new wardrobe – a couple of shirts, T-shirts and pairs of trousers – the final few clothes he would ever need. Towards the end of the book Jarman heartbreakingly records his time in St Bartholomew's Hospital, depicting the other 'exhausted, sick, trembling' young men, his fellow HIV patients, unwilling participants in Lou Reed's 'Halloween Parade'.

'Death stalks through the ward in this bright sunlight,' he writes, and I know exactly what he is describing – HIV back then, cancer still: the end result is the same. I would have known it in 1995 when Chris presented the book to me, but now the image is even more ingrained into the scar tissue of my psyche.

As the summer of 2014 slipped towards autumn my brother's physical form shrank further; the effect was striking, despite his better-fitting clothes. But still we continued to go out together on short trips. Often these would be to 'the Lake', Longham, his local birdwatching patch. One time, a busy sunny Saturday, all of us – the whole family – decamped to the beach at the far end of Hengistbury Head (a favourite spot Chris and I frequented on numerous, usually fruitless birding walks), my brother leading on his scooter while we straggled behind. On another occasion the two of us ventured around a nearby heath at dusk looking for crepuscular nightjars; he somehow managed to navigate the narrow, overgrown tracks as the birds' maddening churrs mocked from the gorse, always a wing-beat ahead.

And then, I remember my sister-in-law and I dropping him off in the centre of Bournemouth (the resort where my parents had spent their honeymoon), so he could meet his colleagues from the newspaper. By now my brother had taken the decision to stop his chemotherapy – the doctor deemed its effectiveness had come to an end and if he carried on there was every danger his weakened immunity wouldn't cope with any future infections. He was in remarkably good spirits, but I still harbour a suspicion that this was the moment – the point when he could no longer take proactive action – that his decline began to accelerate.

Chris and I watched a lot of films together that summer, though I can't recall most of them now. I brought books for him to read too; I know I introduced him to M. R. James at this point and he said he enjoyed the stories, but another supernatural anthology that I lent him left him singularly unimpressed. Certainly it wasn't as good, but I wonder whether the subject matter was too close to the bone for someone who was dying. Yes, ghost stories might largely function as what MRJ would describe as a 'pleasing terror', but inherently they are about how we reconcile ourselves with that ultimate of endings. Stephen King, in his extended meditation on how horror works, *Danse Macabre*, posits that scary movies (and by extension ghost stories) are not about death, but about life. They are 'the celebration of those who feel they can examine death because it does not yet live in their own hearts'. If there's anything in this, then it's little surprise Chris didn't feel the urge. And, I suppose, for me, continuing to read such tales was an act of defiance, an act of clinging to the life my brother still held onto, and the deeper-seated memories of our faded family that we both, at that point, could still share. I'm reminded of Ray Bradbury's children's novella *The Halloween Tree*, which seems to me to strike at the heart of what such stories are for. And why I've always been drawn to them:

> So in the middle of autumn, everything dying, apemen
> turned in their sleep, remembered their own dead of
> the last years. Ghosts called in their heads. Memories,
> that's what ghosts are, but apemen didn't know that.
> Behind the eyelids, late nights, the memory ghosts
> called, waved, danced, so apemen woke up, tossed
> twigs on the fire, shivered, wept. They could drive
> away wolves but not memories, not ghosts.

Two occasions from those final few months when Chris and I were out together stick with me in particular. In the first, we'd come to one of the tidal inlets that snakes inland from the south side of Poole Harbour. Middlebere. There's a bird hide that overlooks the water and the mud, and it can be a good place to observe waders and the odd egret. A narrow path leads behind some farm buildings before it becomes a boardwalk beneath the cover of trees. We proceeded along this to reach the hide, a typical shed-type structure with window slats that could be opened to allow a narrowed view of the inlet. On this afternoon there were few birds – probably the tide was wrong, or we were just unlucky – so I busied myself trying to turn a distant dot of a gull into something more interesting.

We hadn't been inside long when Chris stated that he needed some air. I went to go with him but he said he was okay and sat down on his scooter, which was parked outside on the boardwalk. 'It's too close in there. I'll wait,' he said, and it was clear he'd had a kind of panic attack, which was completely unlike him. I'm not sure what triggered it – probably he wasn't – but I wondered then, as I do now, whether the weight of his situation, his mortality, had struck him in that instant. I felt powerless – I was power-less – to do anything to help, and it was anguishing to see him that way. Because we didn't talk about what was happening, except in a jokey fashion – he'd asked me in a text, for instance, if I would say a few words at his funeral 'about what a great bloke he was' – but there were no deep, heartfelt conversations like you'd get in some maud-lin drama. We just tried to carry on, which was why seeing him in that moment was so hard. By the time we'd got back to the car he was fine again, and we continued as if nothing had happened. But something had, because I was now properly conscious, properly frightened about what I would do when that hollow future arrived.

The other occasion was a few weeks later, in the middle of September, when the two of us went to Portland Bill. Described by Paul Nash in his Shell Guide to Dorset as a 'solid and single block of limestone' that's 'inhabited by people distinctive in manners and customs', the Isle of

Portland is an impressive sight, joined to Weymouth by a low causeway, the harbour on your left, Chesil Beach on your right, before the land rises steeply to five hundred feet, then tapers off towards the Bill itself. Alongside its sixteenth-century castle, various naval buildings, and two prisons, Portland is full of quarries out of which comes its famous Portland stone, used to build St Paul's Cathedral, the British Museum and the Bank of England, among others.*

I first came here with Mum and Dad at Whitsun 1989 (Chris was away at university) – the last holiday the three of us took together before we started going to the far less solid-feeling Suffolk coast. On that visit I wandered off while my parents sat in the café, watching my first Manx shearwaters, miniature northern hemisphere relatives of the albatross that flashed by me, alternating white and black as they beat, then glided, past the lighthouse on their straightened wings. Portland's location jutting four miles out into the Channel makes it a magnet for migrant land birds too; almost invariably, when I came to Chris's in the spring or autumn, we'd end up here – though typically my timing was poor and all the good birds had come through

---

* Portland and Weymouth act as the backdrop to *The Damned*, an odd 1961-shot Hammer offering directed by Joseph Losey. In the film a group of radioactive children are kept imprisoned beneath the limestone cliffs as 'buried seeds of life' in readiness to repopulate the world in the aftermath of a nuclear conflict. An even more-ridiculous slice of sci-fi/horror – the laughably entertaining *Night of the Big Heat* (1967), starring both Christopher Lee and Peter Cushing – also features location footage of Portland (doubling for a fictitious northern isle).

the day before, or would arrive the minute I was home in Norfolk.

That mid-September afternoon in 1994 was another quiet one, apart from large numbers of hirundines – swallows and martins – that were flying south. There were the usual reports of rarities some lucky soul had happened on – a tawny pipit from southern Europe, a barred warbler from Scandinavia – but we didn't see much during our cursory examination of the area near the car park and bird observatory. I made my way around the bramble-fringed path that skirted the top of the miniature former quarry located between the two to check if the resident little owl was in its customary hollow in the rockface. Sure enough it was, though Chris couldn't see it from where he was on the main track.

'Do you not want a look?' I asked, but he said he wasn't bothered, that he'd seen it plenty of times before. So I borrowed his camera, which he had tucked into the bag on

the back of his scooter, and snapped off a photo that I showed to him on the LCD screen.

'That's nice,' he said. But it was all I could do to stop myself from dissolving in front of him, because the thought struck me that, most likely, he would never see that yellow-eyed owl again. Because by this point his decline had gathered a velocity that couldn't be stopped.

Always it is owls, always we are destroyed.

There is a final occasion. The hardest one for me to go back to.

A few weeks after visiting Portland, my partner and I called in to Dorset for a night or two on our way to Cornwall and the Isles of Scilly, where we were going for a holiday. Chris was in decent spirits, not different from how he'd been when I was last there ten days before. I felt okay leaving him, because I could still ring, and we would stop off on our return in a couple of weeks' time. In any case, I was looking forward myself to trying to forget about everything for a week, and to wandering around the islands he had first brought me to. I only called my brother once, on the second day we were there – I didn't want to be constantly bothering him, as he was having a break with his family too, a short trip to Devon. But we texted each other – he told me about a dotterel, an attractive mountain-nesting wader that neither of us had seen for years, which had turned up on the island where I was staying, and we joked about ridiculous birds that I might hope to find.

On the Monday morning I was wandering along the track beside Tresco's Great Pool, a pine-fringed stretch of brackish water that fills a dip in the island's topography, checking through a flock of goldcrests, when my phone rang. It was my sister-in-law, telling me that Chris had been rushed into hospital. His heart had stopped but he was stable now. Talking, but not making much sense.

'You need to get here,' she said.

I got hold of my partner (she'd gone for the morning to Hugh Town on the main island), before returning to our cottage and sorting out our stuff, then taking the next inter-island boat. From St Mary's we managed to catch a flight to the mainland at the end of the afternoon – passing over some of those familiar valleys in the last of the westernmost light – finally arriving where my car was parked just outside Penzance at dusk. If ever there's a time for your vehicle to decide not to start, this really wasn't the moment. But that's what happened. The breakdown man, when he eventually turned up, couldn't get it to go and it had to be towed to Dorset; we were dropped off somewhere en route to pick up a hired replacement – I can't remember where.

All of it's a shadow now.

What I do know for certain is that we finally got to Poole Hospital at around two in the morning, to find my brother largely insensible. He tried asking about my holiday, but it was an effort for him to speak, so I said I would tell him about it later when he'd rested. Now and again he attempted to pull out the oxygen tubes that were loosely fixed in his nostrils; he was being his characteristic stubborn self, at least. The nurses put him in his own small room, like the ones Mum and Dad had been in at the end.

My partner and I stayed past dawn – apparently we ate breakfast in the canteen, though I have little recollection of this – then headed briefly to Chris's house to freshen up. When we returned I fetched my youngest niece out of school; she skipped along the pavement as we arrived back at the hospital: it was devastating to watch. You don't know, do you, I thought. And I am glad that she didn't, glad that both of my nieces are today both so good and strong in spite of what they have lost.

The room was different now, because Chris was no longer speaking, his breathing measured, like my mother's had been. Later in the afternoon – some hours before the instant when the colour drained from his face and the rise and fall of his abdomen stopped – I went in with him alone, talking away in the hope he could hear me, but equally trying to cover the awful near-silence and that familiar feeling I knew from before.

'We were all right, weren't we?' I said to him.

And I swear – though it sounds like something trite I've made up – a tear glided down his cheek from the corner of his eye.

We were, weren't we Chris?

Four years have passed since I last came here with my brother. Longer, if I discount that previous bittersweet occasion when all of us – my sister-in-law, nieces, and my partner – trekked, mob-handed, in the wake of his scooter, to the beach huts at the end.

It's the middle of June and the sky is cobalt. I'm back at Hengistbury Head, the place Chris and I visited so often together – usually to look for birds that never materialised, birds that might have been.

We take the inland route to begin with, stopping to admire the vibrancy of the wild-flower meadow behind the new visitor centre, then pause to watch a whitethroat singing in the scrub beyond. We stand aside, off the tarmac, to let a teenage army on a school geography trip pass, their procession weighed down with quadrats and tape measures. Several gangling lads grin and say hello. 'Do they think we don't know they're taking the piss?' my friend

Philip asks, laughing, as they move further along the track. Once we get to the wooded gully we head right, scrambling on a dirt path up the slope onto the heathland, the sea a glinting fire before us. Up here, Chris and I once watched a pair of maroon Dartford warblers flitting between the clumps of gorse. And on the day this one most brings to mind we sat by the coastguard's lookout as waif-like storm petrels – swallow-sized black seabirds – fluttered low over the water in the fierce, warm breeze.

How can something so delicate spend its life at sea, I remember wondering.

The view from the hill could be a postcard: Christchurch Harbour's boat-filled lagoon, sheltered behind the beckoning, hut-lined finger of the spit. Like so much of Dorset, this is a site riddled with the remains of tumuli and ancient settlements, of vanished lives long gone.

We talk about books and wildlife – it feels good to be here again in the company of a friend. In this harsh light – later, when I get back, I realise my neck is red raw and burnt from the incessant sun – the area directly below the soft clay cliffs has a New England feel.

'It could be Nantucket,' Philip says.

Desert-dry clumps of succulents and desiccated grasses lay out their tendrils across the transient surface of the dunes, grasping onto what little there is to sustain them. There's a chattering above as a sand martin returns to the nest hole it's tidying, before plunging and twirling into the blinding glare. I watch its shadow pass over the exposed cliff face.

The ghost of a bird.

Plant burrs have secretly attached themselves to my shoes, and for a second, in my head, I'm back on Holy Island with Chris and Dad – back inside my earliest memory.

I'm wearing slippers. I am adamant about this, though no one else now can confirm or deny its truth. I *am* wearing slippers, and we are walking up sand dunes. Sticky burrs have adhered to the felt of my footwear and I stoop to pick them off. We are probably lost, but Chris does not seem concerned, so I'm not either. He is nearly six years older than me, making him around nine. We are on Holy Island – Lindisfarne – and the two of us have wandered from where we were having a picnic with Mum and Dad. A voice shouts in the distance. Chris ignores it, so I do too.

The dunes rise to the height of mountains, the sun is fierce. Grass needles my bare legs if I'm not super careful where I tread. The burrs poking through my slippers prickle too, hence why I've stopped to try and remove them. And now Dad is striding up over the ridge of sand that crests the hollow we're exploring. He emerges dramatically, though perhaps a little flustered.

'There you are! You mustn't go wandering off like that. Me and Mum were worried.'

'Sorry,' Chris mumbles, staring at the ground. I am still picking at my footwear, no doubt oblivious to any tension. I am not and have never been worried in the minutes (how many?) that we've been walkabout, because I'm with Chris and he is looking after the two of us and it will always be like this.

We tramp back together. We hadn't got far, just scaled seven or eight dunes before we came to the crater. Mum and Dad aren't mad for long and I wasn't ever scared – *we weren't, were we Chris* – though I am afterwards that same holiday when I meander off the path at the place where we're staying and cannot find our chalet among the rows of identically painted wooden houses. I knock on a door I hope might be the right one, only a stranger lady opens it. I don't recall the resolution of this story, the grand reunion, but do remember the incident being later repeated to me as a parable against the dangers of going off by myself. And

I do remember the dunes, and the burrs on my slippers, and my dad's white legs – a rare summer sight in shorts. My brother and me, oblivious, exploring the excitement of the world.

Looking back to that dream landscape, I suppose I might expect some foreboding to remain with me from those half-lost wanderings. In Arthur Machen's short story 'Out of the Earth' a young lad stumbles screaming from the dunes, frightened by 'funny children' who have emerged from beneath the ground to take growing delight in the chaos of the gathering Great War. I'm lucky to have escaped – for a few years, at least – what that unfortunate boy saw among the sand and swaying marram.

Perhaps instead, the experience might have offered me an early token of what it is to be alone in the world, to be adrift without purpose or direction? But I can't imagine that's what I was feeling in that moment. I was there with my brother and he was leading the pair of us onwards, and we were content beneath the baking sun. Then Dad came along, interrupting our fun, and we returned with him – though we were fine on our own anyway. Yet why did Mum look so worried when we descended the last slope to where the chequered tartan blanket lay folded on the sand, the uneaten food stacked away neatly beside in Tupperware containers?

Philip and I approach the glinting water. A charcoal-cloaked brute – an adult great black-backed gull – is hunched on the shore, nonchalantly jabbing at something in the shallows. It's a garfish, a silver-green sea serpent in miniature.

Its eye has a circular black pupil set into a pale iris – like that of a jackdaw. The gull hammers its reddened bill into the middle of the shining, floundering body, never letting up. The fish twitches, flipping itself over among the shingle and sand at the point where the waves are gently breaking.

'There's only going to be one winner,' I say, and it's not long before the bird is choking down the inert, folded-up form. The elongated head of the garfish protrudes from the gull's mouth, its staring black pupil still obscenely visible.

Like your snake and the frog in reverse, Chris.

Behind us there's a commotion among the sand martins as two crows carry out a sortie in front of the colony; the hirundines exit their holes en masse in a show of solidarity,

wisps of air chuntering around the jet-black silhouettes, irritating and annoying the larger birds until they have disappeared over the ridge.

We head back under the coolness of the oaks and birches, stopping to watch the shadows and reflections that play on the path, like flickering pictures on a screen. 'They're beautiful,' Philip says.

I *am* all right with everything now, I think. I've learned to keep my stories in reach. Learned how, when I need to, to dig beneath my skin of soil without unleashing whatever lies buried there. Without sacrificing too much of my present.

I stare down at the kaleidoscopic circles of light. For a moment I half-see my brother's face among the glimmering, shifting shapes. But only for a moment.

Always the ghosts.

Selected List of Sources

The following is a selection of the books, films, television programmes and articles that have contributed to *Ghostland*. They are arranged in alphabetical order per chapter (each source is noted only once, in the first chapter to which it pertains.)

Prologue

James, M. R. Introduction to *Ghosts and Marvels*, edited by V. H. Collins. Oxford University Press, London, 1924.

Maple, E., Humberstone, E. and Myring, L. *Usborne Guide to the Supernatural World*, Usborne, London, 1979.

Chapter 1: LOST HEART

BBC Genome Project. https://genome.ch.bbc.co.uk. (Online archive of *Radio Times* TV listings.)

British Film Institute. *The M. R. James Collection: Tales from the Master of the Ghost Story* (booklet accompanying DVD box set). BFI, London, 2012.

Boston, Lucy M. *Curfew & Other Eerie Tales*. Swan River Press, Dublin, 2014.

Boston, Lucy M. *The Children of Green Knowe*. Faber, London, 2006. (Originally pub. 1954.)

Boston, Lucy M. *Memories*. Colt Books, Cambridge, 1992.

Boston, Lucy M. *An Enemy at Green Knowe*. Puffin Books, London, 1977. (Originally pub. 1964.)

Campbell, Ramsey (introduced by). *Meddling with Ghosts*. British Library, Boston Spa & London, 2001.

Cant, Colin (Dir.). *The Children of Green Knowe*. BBC, 1986.

Cavaliero, Glen. *The Supernatural and English Fiction*. Oxford University Press, Oxford, 1995.

Clark, Lawrence Gordon. Interview on DVD extras of 'Lost Heart', featured on *The M. R. James Collection*. BFI, 2012.

Clark, Lawrence Gordon (Dir.). *The Signalman*. BBC, 1976.

Clark, Lawrence Gordon (Dir.). *Lost Hearts*. BBC, 1973.

Clarke, Roger. *A Natural History of Ghosts: 500 Years of Hunting for Proof*. Penguin, London, 2013.

Cox, Michael. *M. R. James: An Informal Portrait*. Oxford University Press, Oxford, 1983.

Dickens, Charles. *Supernatural Short Stories*. Alma Classics, Richmond, 2012.

Dunn, Clive (Dir.). *A Pleasant Terror: The Life and Ghosts of M. R. James*. Anglia TV, 1995.

Gatiss, Mark (Writer/Presenter). *M. R. James: Ghost Writer*. BBC, 2013.

Gifford, Denis. *A Pictorial History of Horror Movies*. Hamlyn, London, 1973.

Hardy, Phil (ed.). *Horror: The Aurum Film Encyclopedia*. Aurum, London, 1993 (revised ed.).

Hutchinson, Tom, and Pickard, Roy. *Horrors: A History of Horror Movies*. W H Smith, London, 1983.

James, M. R. *Curious Warnings: The Great Ghost Stories of M. R. James*. Jo Fletcher Books, London, 2012.

James, M. R. *Ghost Stories of an Antiquary*. Edward Arnold, London, 1904.

James, M. R. *Suffolk and Norfolk*. J. M. Dent and Sons, London, 1930.

Jones, Darryl (ed.). Introduction to *Collected Ghost Stories* by M. R. James. Oxford University Press, Oxford, 2011.

Kneale, Nigel. Introduction to *Ghost Stories of M. R. James* by M. R. James. Folio Society, London, 1973.

Malden, R. H. *Nine Ghosts*. Edward Arnold, London, 1943.

Murnau, F. W. (Dir.). *Nosferatu*. 1922.

Oxford University Press. *The Compact Edition of the Dictionary of National Biography*. Oxford University Press, London, 1975.

Pevsner, Nikolaus. *The Buildings of England: Suffolk*. Penguin, Harmondsworth. 2nd ed., 1974.

Pfaff, Richard William. *Montague Rhodes James*. Scholar Press, London, 1980.

Pincombe, Mike. 'Homosexual Panic and the English Ghost Story: M. R. James and others' in *The Ghosts & Scholars M. R. James Newsletter*, ed. Rosemary Pardoe. Issue 2, Sept 2002, Part 1.

Rolt, L. T. C. *Red for Danger: A History of Railway Accidents and Railway Safety Precautions*. Pan, London, 1960.

Rye, Renny (Dir.). *The Box of Delights*. BBC, 1984.

Tomalin, Claire. *Charles Dickens: A Life*. Viking, London, 2011.

Wiene, Robert (Dir.). *The Cabinet of Dr Caligari*. 1920.

Chapter 2: DARK WATERS

Abe, Naoko. *'Cherry' Ingram: The Englishman Who Saved Japan's Blossoms*. Chatto & Windus, London, 2019.

Aickman, Robert. *Know Your Waterways: Holidays on Inland Waterways*. Temprint Press, London. Fifth edition, revised *c*. 1964. (Originally pub. 1955.)

Aickman, Robert and Howard, Elizabeth Jane. *We Are for the Dark*. Jonathan Cape, London, 1951.

Barker, A. L. 'Submerged' in *The Pan Book of Horror Stories*, selected by Herbert van Thal. Pan, London, 1959.

Bewick, Thomas. *History of British Birds: Vol II containing the history and description of water birds*. Edward Walker, Newcastle, 1804.

Blanshard, Fred (ed.). *Boston Society: an illustrated monthly magazine of facts, fancies and fashions*. Vols. 1–3, 1899–1902, p. 34.

Brontë, Charlotte. *Jane Eyre: An Autobiography*. Service & Paton, London, 1897. (Originally pub. 1847.)

Cooper, Artemis. *Elizabeth Jane Howard: A Dangerous Innocence*. John Murray, London, 2016.

Cooper, Susan. *The Dark is Rising*. Aladdin, New York, 1999. (Originally pub. 1973.)

Cox, Michael (ed.). *The Oxford Book of Twentieth-Century Ghost Stories*. Oxford University Press, Oxford, 1996.

Fitzgerald, F. Scott. *The Great Gatsby*. Penguin Classics, London, 2000. (Originally pub. 1926.)

Gordon, John. *Ordinary Seaman: a teenage memoir*. Walker Books, London, 1992.

Gordon, John. *The House on the Brink*. Hutchinson, London, 1970.

Grant, Jeff (Dir.). *Lonely Water*. 1973.

Gyllenhaal, Stephen (Dir.). *Waterland*. 1992.

Harvey, Herk (Dir.). *Carnival of Souls*. 1962.

Hennels, C. E. 'The East Lighthouse at Sutton Bridge'. *East Anglian Magazine*, Vol. 38, No. 3, Jan. 1979.

Higgins, Charlotte. 'Susan Cooper: a life in writing'. *Guardian*, 21 December 2012.

Howard, Elizabeth Jane. *Slipstream: A Memoir*. Pan, London, 2003.

Illustrated London News. Articles on the sinking of the Lady Elgin and death of Herbert Ingram MP. Sept. 29, 1860 and Oct. 6, 1860.

Lockwood, W. B. *The Oxford Dictionary of Bird Names*. Oxford University Press, Oxford, 1993.

Manning, Lesley (Dir.). *Three Miles Up* (as part of the series *Ghosts*). BBC, 1995.

McNeaney, Sean. 'The Boston Bird of ill omen': https://ghostsandfolklore.blogspot.com/2013/11/the-boston-bird-of-ill-omen.html.

Pardoe, Rosemary. 'An Interview with John Gordon' in *Ghosts & Scholars*, 21, 1996.

Pim, Keiron. 'Inspired by the Fens' in *The Eastern Daily Press*, February 26, 2009.

Rolt, L. T. C. *Sleep No More*. Constable, London, 1948.

Stone, Andrew. 'Norfolk author passes away after long battle with Alzheimers'. *The Eastern Daily Press*, 21 November, 2017.

Swift, Graham. *Waterland*. William Heinemann, London, 1983.

Westwood, J. and Simpson, J. *The Lore of the Land: A Guide to England's Legends, from Spring-heeled Jack to the Witches of Warboys*. Penguin, London, 2005.

White, Adam. *John Clare's Romanticism*. Open University, Milton Keynes, 2017.

Chapter 3: WALKING IN THE WOOD

Amis, Kingsley. *Rudyard Kipling and his world*. Thames and Hudson, London. 1975.

BBC Books. *The Nation's Favourite Poems*. BBC Books, London, 1996.

Briggs, Julia. *Night Visitors: The Rise and Fall of the English Ghost Story*. Faber, London, 1977.

De la Mare, Walter. *Missing*. Hesperus Press, London, 2007.

De la Mare, Walter. *Selected Poems*. Faber, London, 1954.

De la Mare, Walter. *Best Stories of Walter de la Mare*. Faber, London, 1942.

De la Mare, Walter. *On the Edge*. Faber, London, 1930.

De la Mare, Walter. *The Listeners and other poems*. Faber, London, 1942 (new ed.).

De la Mare, Walter. *The Wind Blows Over*. Faber, London, 1936.

De la Mare, Walter. Introduction to *They Walk Again: An Anthology of Ghost Stories*, chosen by Colin de la Mare. Faber, London, 1931.

Giddings, Robert. *The War Poets*. Bloomsbury, London, 1998.

Hartley, L. P. *The Brickfield*. Hamish Hamilton, London, 1964.

Hartley, L. P. *The Go-Between*. Hamish Hamilton, London, 1954.

Hartley, L. P. *The Travelling Grave and other stories*. Arkham House, Sauk City, WI, 1948.

Kipling, Rudyard. *Puck of Pook's Hill*. Macmillan, London, 1906.

Kipling, Rudyard, *Rewards and Fairies*. Macmillan, London, 1910.

Kipling, Rudyard, *Something of Myself*. Macmillan, London, 1937.

Kipling, Rudyard. *Strange Tales*. Wordsworth Editions, Ware, 2006.

Kipling, Rudyard. *They*. Macmillan, London, 1905.

Lewis, Roger. Introductory chapter to Kipling's *Rewards and Fairies*. Penguin, London, 1987.

Losey, Joseph (Dir.). *The Go-Between*. 1971.

Lycett, Andrew. *Rudyard Kipling*. Weidenfeld & Nicholson, London, 1999.

Machen, Arthur. 'The Line of Terror'. Book review from *The New Statesman*, 11 October 1930. Re-published in *Faunus* (*The Journal of the Friends of Arthur Machen*), Autumn 2018, No. 38.

Northcote, Amyas. *In Ghostly Company*. Wordsworth Editions, Ware, 2010.

Parnell, Edward. *The Listeners*. Rethink Press, Gorleston, 2014.

St. John, Christopher. *Ellen Terry and Bernard Shaw: A Correspondence*. G. P. Putnam's Sons, New York, 1931.

Wilson, Neil. *Shadows in the Attic: A Guide to British Supernatural Fiction 1820–1950*. British Library, Boston Spa, 2000.

Wright, Adrian. *Foreign Country: The Life of L. P. Hartley*. Andre Deutsch, London, 1996.

Chapter 4: THE ROARING OF THE FOREST

Ashley, Mike. *Starlight Man: The Extraordinary Life of Algernon Blackwood*. Constable, London, 2001.

Blackwood, Algernon. *Pan's Garden: A Volume of Nature Stories*. Macmillan, London, 1912.

Blackwood, Algernon. *The Tales of Algernon Blackwood*. Martin Secker, London, 1938.

Booth, Martin. *The Doctor and the Detective: A Biography of Sir Arthur Conan Doyle*. Thomas Dunne Books, New York, 2000.

Briggs, Raymond. *When the Wind Blows*. Hamish Hamilton, London, 1982.

Carrington, C. E. *The Life of Rudyard Kipling*. Doubleday, Garden City, NY, 1955.

Cocker, Mark and Mabey, Richard. *Birds Britannica*. Chatto & Windus, London, 2005.

Doyle, Arthur Conan. *Arthur Conan Doyle on the Unexplained*. Hesperus Press, London, 2013. (Includes Doyle's essay 'The Alleged Posthumous Writings of Known Authors'.)

Doyle, Arthur Conan. *Pheneas Speaks: Direct Spirit Communications in the Family Circle reported by Arthur Conan Doyle, M.D., LL.D*. The Psychic Press, London, 1927.

Doyle, Arthur Conan. *The Coming of the Fairies*. Hodder & Stoughton, London, 1922.

Encyclopaedia Britannica (11th Edition). *Volume X*. Cambridge University Press, Cambridge, 1911. (Entry for Gustav Fechner.)

Hoare, Philip. *England's Lost Eden: Adventures in a Victorian Utopia*. Fourth Estate, London, 2005.

Hooper, Tobe (Dir.). *Salem's Lot*. 1979.

Hough, John and McEveety, Vincent (Directors). *The Watcher in the Woods*. 1981.

Le Fanu, Jospeh Sheridan. *The House by the Churchyard*. Nonsuch, Stroud, 2006. (Originally pub. 1863.)

Polidoro, Massimo. *Final Séance: The Strange Friendship Between Houdini and Conan Doyle*. Prometheus Books, New York, 2001.

Price, Lesley. 'Did Conan Doyle Haunt His Old Cottage?' in *Psypioneer Journal*, vol. 8, no. 12, December 2012.

Robertson, W. Graham. *Time Was*. Hamish Hamilton, London, 1931.

Russell, R. B. *Guide to First Edition Prices 2008/9*. Tartarus Press, Leyburn, 2007.

Stashower, Daniel. *Teller of Tales: The Life of Arthur Conan Doyle.* Henry Holt, New York, 1999.

Symons, Julian. *Conan Doyle: Portrait of an Artist.* The Mystery Press, New York, 1987.

Valentine, Mark (Ed.). *The Black Veil & Other Tales of Supernatural Sleuths.* Wordsworth Editions, Ware, 2008.

Vonnegut, Kurt. *Slaughterhouse-Five.* Vintage, London, 1991. (Originally pub. 1969.)

Chapter 5: MEMENTO MORI

Ball, Philip. *Unnatural: The Heretical Idea of Making People.* Bodley Head, London, 2011.

Bartholomey, David. 'The Wicker Man' in *Cinefantastique*, vol. 6, no. 3, 1977.

Blackburn, J., Blackburn A., and Budworth, D. 'The breeding birds of Sule Skerry and Stack Skerry' in *British Birds*, 100, May 2007.

Boulting, Roy (Dir.). *Thunder Rock.* 1942.

Bowditch, Lyndsey. 'Guide to the Robert Burns Birthplace Museum'. National Trust for Scotland, Edinburgh, 2016.

Burns, Robert. *The Complete Works of Robert Burns.* George Virtue, London, c. 1840.

Brown, Allan. *Inside The Wicker Man.* Sidgwick & Jackson, London, 2000.

Caesar, Julius. (Trans. by W. A. McDevitte and W. S. Bohn). *Caesar's Gallic War* (Book 6, Chapter 16). Harper & Brothers, New York, 1869.

Carpenter, Gary. 'About the Music' in sleeve notes to the CD soundtrack of *The Wicker Man*. Silva Screen Records, 2002.

Clarke, Alan (Dir.). *Penda's Fen.* BBC, 1974.

Gatiss, Mark (Writer/Presenter). *A History of Horror with Mark Gatiss.* BBC, 2010.

Gray, Rosemary (selected by). *Scottish Ghosts.* Lomond Books, Broxburn, 2009.

Griffin, Martin. 'The Wicker Man Pilgrim website': http://www.wickermanpilgrim.com.

Haggard, Piers (Dir.). *The Blood on Satan's Claw.* 1971.

Hardy, Robin (Dir.). *The Wicker Man.* 1973.

Hodgkinson, Will. 'Satan's all-time greatest hit: Will Hodgkinson on the devil's interval'. *Guardian*, 12 October 2007.

James, M. R. *Collected Ghost Stories.* Wordsworth, Ware, 1992.

Kingshill, Sophia and Westwood, Jennifer. *The Fabled Coast.* Random House, London, 2012.

Kingshill, Sophia and Westwood, Jennifer. *The Lore of Scotland.* Random House, London, 2009.

Mackay, James. *Burns: A Biography of Robert Burns.* Headline, London, 1993.

MacTaggart, James (Dir.). *Robin Redbreast.* BBC, 1970.

Morris, Alex. 'Come back to the village: A *Penda's Fen* pilgrimage': http://pinvin.com/tag/pendas-fen/.

Newton, Laura (ed.). *Painting at the Edge: British Coastal Art Colonies 1880–1930.* Sansom & Co., Bristol, 2005.

Nicolson, Adam. *Sea Room: An Island Life.* Harper Collins, London, 2001.

Paciorek, Andy. 'From the Forests, Fields and Furrows: An Introduction': https://folkhorrorrevival.com/about/from-the-forests-fields-and-furrows-an-introduction-by-andy-paciorek/#NoteOne.

Powell, Michael. *Edge of the World: The Making of a Film.* Faber, London, 1990. (Originally pub. in 1938 as *200,000 Feet on Foula.*)

Powell, Michael. *A Life in Movies: An Autobiography.* Heinemann, London, 1986.

Powell, Michael (Dir.). *The Edge of the World.* 1937.

Powell, Michael and Pressburger, Emeric (Directors). *I Know Where I'm Going!* 1945.

Reeves, Michael (Dir.). *Witchfinder General.* 1968.

Roscoe, I., Hardy, E., and Sullivan, M. G. *A Biographical Dictionary of Sculptors in Britain.* http://liberty.henry-moore.org/henrymoore/sculptor/browserecord.php?-action=browse&recid=2675&from_list=true&x=0.

Simpson, M. J. Transcript of 'Folk horror' interview with the film director Piers Haggard, as originally pub. in a 2003 issue of *Fangoria* magazine. http://mjsimpson-films.blogspot.com/2013/11/interview-piers-haggard.html.

Chapter 6: BORDERLAND

Baddeley, Vincent. 'The Provost and the Scroll'. Letter in *The Times*, London, June 19, 1936.

Cooper, Susan. *Silver on the Tree.* Aladdin, New York, 2000. (Originally pub. 1977.)

Cooper, Susan. *The Grey King.* Aladdin, New York, 1999. (Originally pub. 1975.)

Dalby, Richard. 'William Hope Hodgson' in *Book and Magazine Collector*, Nov 2007, no. 287.

Everts, R. Alain. 'The Life of William Hope Hodgson'. Published originally in the fanzine *Shadow*. Accessed at https:// williamhopehodgson.wordpress.com/.

Frank, Jane. *The Wandering Soul: Glimpses of a Life – A Compendium of Rare and Unpublished Works by William Hope Hodgson*. Tartarus Press, Hornsea, 2005.

Hodgson, William Hope. *Carnacki the Ghost Finder*. E-book accessed at Project Gutenberg. (Originally published 1913.)

Hodgson, William Hope. *The Collected Fiction of William Hope Hodgson, Volume 1: The Boats of the 'Glen Carrig' and Other Nautical Adventures*. Night Shade Books, San Francisco, CA, 2003.

Hodgson, William Hope. *The Collected Fiction of William Hope Hodgson, Volume 2: The House on the Borderland and Other Mysterious Places*. Night Shade Books, San Francisco, CA, 2004.

Hodgson, William Hope. *The Collected Fiction of William Hope Hodgson, Volume 5: The Dream of X and Other Fantastic Visions*. Night Shade Books, San Francisco, CA, 2009.

Hodgson, William Hope. *The Ghost Pirates*. E-book accessed at Project Gutenberg. (Originally pub. 1909.)

Hodgson, William Hope. *The Night Land*. E-book accessed at Project Gutenberg. (Originally pub. 1912.)

Honda, Ishirô (Dir.). *Matango* (aka *Attack of the Mushroom People*). 1963.

Valentine, Mark. 'A Home on the Borderland: William Hope Hodgson and Borth' in *Sargasso: The Journal of William Hope Hodgson Studies*, Vol. 1, No. 2, 2014.

West Wales War Memorial Project. https://www.wwwmp.co.uk/ ceredigion-memorials/borth-war-memorial/.

Chapter 7: GOBLIN CITY

Alain-Fournier. *The Lost Domain* (*Le Grand Meaulnes*). Centenary ed. Trans. Frank Davison, 1959 (with an introduction by Hermione Lee). Oxford University Press, Oxford, 2013.

Cavalcanti, A., Dearden, B. *et al.* (Directors). *Dead of Night*. 1945.

Dearden, Basil (Dir.). *The Halfway House*. 1944.

Lord Dunsany. Introduction to *The Hill of Dreams* by Arthur Machen. Richards Press, London, 1954.

Everett, H. D. *The Crimson Blind and Other Stories*. Wordsworth Editions, London, 2006.

Fergus, Emily. '"A Wilder Reality": Euhemerism and Arthur Machen's "Little People"' in *Faunus: The Journal of the Friends of Arthur Machen*. Autumn 2015, No. 32.

Games, Gwilym and Machin, James. 'Notes on Gawsworth's Account of Arthur Machen's Funeral' in *Faunus: The Journal of the Friends of Arthur Machen*. Spring 2014, No. 29.

Hando, Fred J. *The Pleasant Land of Gwent*. Directory Press, Newport, 1944.

Houellebecq, Michel. *H. P. Lovecraft: Against the World, Against Life*. (Trans. Dorna Khazeni, 2005.) Gollancz, London, 2008.

Ingram, Rex (Dir.). *The Magician*. 1926.

Ishiguro, Kazuo. *The Buried Giant*. Faber, London, 2015.

Knight, Jeremy K. *Caerleon Roman Fortress*. Cadw, Cardiff, 2003 (3rd ed.).

Lewis, Mark. *The Fountains of My Story: Arthur Machen and the Making of a Museum*. Three Imposters, Newport, 2017.

Lovecraft, H. P. 'Supernatural Horror in Literature' in *Dagon and Other Macabre Tales*. Panther, London, 1969. (Originally published in 1927 in the one-off magazine *The Recluse*.)

Lovecraft, H. P. *Necronomicon: The Best Weird Tales of H. P. Lovecraft*. Gollancz, London, 2008.

Maas, J., Trimpe, P. W., Gere, C. *et al*. *Victorian Fairy Painting*. Royal Academy of Arts, London, 1997.

Machen, Arthur. *Dreads and Drolls*. Martin Secker, London, 1926.

Machen, Arthur. *Tales of Horror and the Supernatural*. Richards Press, London, 1949.

Machen, Arthur. *The Autobiography of Arthur Machen*. Tartarus Press, Carlton-in-Coverdale, 2017.

Machen, Arthur. *The Bowmen and Other Legends of the War*. Simpkin, Marshall, Hamilton, Kent & Co., London, 1915.

Machen, Arthur. *The Hill of Dreams*. Alfred Knopf, New York, 1923. (Originally pub. 1907.)

Machen, Arthur. *The London Adventure*. Martin Secker, London, 1924.

Machen, Arthur. *The White People and Other Weird Stories*. Penguin, London, 2011.

Mount, Ferdinand. *English Voices: Lives, Landscapes, Laments*. Simon & Schuster, London, 2016.

Reynolds, A. and Charlton, W. *Arthur Machen: A Short Account of His Life and Work*. Richards Press, London, 1963.

Simpson, Jacqueline. *The Folklore of the Welsh Border*. Batsford, London, 1976.

Tromans, Nicholas. *Richard Dadd: The Artist and the Asylum*. Tate Publishing, London, 2011.

Valentine, Mark. *Arthur Machen*. Poetry Wales Press (seren), Bridgend, 1995.

Chapter 8: LONELIER THAN RUIN

Anonymous. 'Springfields'. Unknown magazine article, 1976. https://www.southhollandlife.com/wp-content/uploads/2014/05/AOS-D-0273-Springfields.pdf.

Argento, Dario (Dir.). *Suspiria*. 1977.

Chant, Katharine. *The History of Dunwich*. Dunwich Museum, Dunwich, 2011.

Comber, Philippa. *Ariadne's Thread: In Memory of W. G. Sebald*. Propolis, Norwich, 2014.

Cook, John (ed.). *After Sebald: Essays & Illuminations*. Full Circle Editions, Framlingham, 2014.

Griffiths, Chris. 'W. G. Sebald' in *Book and Magazine Collector*, Jan. 2009, no. 303.

Illustrated London News. Saturday 10 January 1857.

Jaggi, Maya. 'Recovered memories'. *Guardian*, 22 September 2001.

James, Henry. *English Hours*. Houghton, Mifflin and Company, Boston and New York, 1905.

Pardoe, Rosemary, and Nicholls, Jane. 'James Wilson's Secret' in *Ghosts & Scholars*, 24, 1997.

Port, M. H. 'Peto, Sir (Samuel) Morton, first baronet', in *Oxford Dictionary of National Biography*. https://doi.org/10.1093/ref:odnb/22042. Pub. online: 23 September 2004.

Sebald, W. G. *The Rings of Saturn*. (Trans. from the German by Michael Hulse.) Vintage, London, 2002.

Snæbjörnsdóttir, B. and Wilson, M. (eds). *Nanoq: Flat Out and Bluesome. A Cultural Life of Polar Bears*. Black Dog Publishing, London, 2006.

Williams, Luke. 'A Watch on Each Wrist: Twelve Seminars with W. G. Sebald' in *Body of Work: 40 Years of Creative Writing at UEA* edited by Giles Foden. Full Circle Editions, Framlingham, 2011.

Wood, James. 'An Interview with W. G. Sebald' in *Brick: A Literary Journal*, 59, spring 1998.

Chapter 9: WHO IS THIS WHO IS COMING?
Clark, Lawrence Gordon (Dir.). *A Warning to the Curious*. BBC, 1972.
Clark, Lawrence Gordon (Dir.). *The Stalls of Barchester*. BBC, 1971.
Gee, Grant (Dir.). *Patience (After Sebald)*. 2012.
Millar, Jeremy. *A Firework for Sebald*. http://www.jeremymillar.org/works-detail.php?wid=24.
Miller, Jonathan (Dir.). *Whistle and I'll Come To You*. BBC, 1968.
Pevsner, Nikolaus. *The Buildings of England. Norfolk 2: North-west and South*. Yale University Press, London, 2002.
Sebald, W. G. *The Emigrants*. (Trans. from the German by Michael Hulse.) Vintage, London, 2002. (English ed. originally pub. 1996.)

Chapter 10: NOT REALLY NOW NOT ANY MORE
Abeles, Francine F. 'Lewis Carroll's ciphers: The literary connections' in *Advances in Applied Mathematics*. No. 34, 2005.
Aldhouse-Green, Miranda. *The Celtic Myths: A Guide to the Ancient Gods and Legends*. Thames and Hudson, London, 2015.
Baines, Christopher and Dillon, Anna. 'Paul Nash and the Wittenham Clumps' website. https://www.nashclumps.org.
Chalmers, Robert. '"There is a light at the end of the tunnel": Why novelist Alan Garner's reality is tinged with mysticism'. *Independent*, 26 September 2010.
Darby, Katharine. Introductory speech given at the opening of the 'Petals and Claws' art exhibition at The Old Medicine House, Blackden, Cheshire. https://www.oriel.org.uk/docs/uploads/KatharineDarbySpeech.Ion2018.pdf.
Fimi, Dimitra. 'Alan Garner's *The Owl Service* at Fifty' in *Times Literary Supplement*, 21 August 2017.
Garner, Alan. 'A note on *Red Shift*'. (In the booklet accompanying the DVD of the 1978 BBC TV adaptation of *Red Shift*. BFI, London, 2014.)
Garner, Alan. *Boneland*. Fourth Estate, London, 2012.
Garner, Alan. *Elidor*. William Collins, London, 1965.
Garner, Alan. *Red Shift*. William Collins, London, 1973.
Garner, Alan. 'Revelations from a life of storytelling'. *New Statesman*, 2 April 2015.

Garner, Alan. *The Moon of Gomrath*. William Collins, London, 1963.

Garner, Alan. *The Owl Service*. William Collins, London, 1967.

Garner, Alan. *The Weirdstone of Brisingamen*. William Collins, London, 1960.

Garner, Alan. *Where Shall We Run To?*. 4th Estate, London, 2018.

Garner, Ellen, Adam & Katharine. *Filming The Owl Service: A Children's Diary*. William Collins, London, 1970.

Guest, Lady Charlotte (trans.). *The Mabinogion*. Longman, Brown, Green and Longmans, London, 1849.

Johnston, Trevor. 'From Beat Girl to Mad Men: the life of Gillian Hills'. BFI website, 11 July 2016. https://www.bfi.org.uk/news-opinion/sight-sound-magazine/interviews/gillian-hills-beat-girl.

Mackenzie, John (Dir.). *Apaches*. 1977.

Mackenzie, John (Dir.). *Red Shift*. BBC, 1978.

McKay, Stephen. 'The Legend Unravelled'. Sleeve notes to the DVD of the 1969 Granada TV adaptation of *The Owl Service*, Network DVD, 2008.

Plummer, Peter (Dir./Prod.). *The Owl Service*. Granada Television, 1969.

Reader's Digest. *Folklore, Myths and Legends of Britain*. Reader's Digest Association, London, 1973.

Rolinson, David. 'The boundary's undefined: *Red Shift*'. (In the booklet accompanying the DVD of the 1978 TV adaptation of *Red Shift*. BFI, London, 2014.)

The Scotsman. 'Interview: Alan Garner'. *The Scotsman*, 15 September 2012.

Thornber, Craig. 'Barthomley', part of 'A Scrapbook of Cheshire' website. https://www.thornber.net/cheshire/htmlfiles/barthomley.html.

Thurston, Herbert J. and Attwater, Donald. *Butler's Lives of the Saints: Complete Edition*. Christian Classics, Westminster, Maryland, 1990. (Second ed. pub. 1956.)

White, Donna R. *A Century of Welsh Myth in Children's Literature*. Greenwood Press, London, 1998.

Wroe, Nicholas. 'England's time lord'. *The Guardian*, 16 October 2004. https://www.theguardian.com/books/2004/oct/16/fiction.alangarner.

Chapter 11: TROUBLE OF THE ROCKS

Aarons, Sonia. *Sven Berlin: Out of the Shadows*. Millersford Press, Godshill, 2012.

Benson, E. F. *As We Were: A Victorian Peep-Show*. Longmans, Green and Co., London, 1930.

Benson, E. F. *Final Edition*. Hogarth Press, London, 1988. (Originally pub. 1940.)

Benson, E. F. *Night Terrors: The Ghost Stories of E. F. Benson*. Wordsworth, Ware, 2012.

Betjeman, John. *Cornwall: A Shell Guide*. Faber, London, 1964.

Bogle, Andrew (Dir.). *Haunters of the Deep*. Children's Film and Television Foundation, 1984.

Bolt, Rodney. *As Good as God, As Clever as the Devil: The Impossible Life of Mary Benson*. Atlantic, London, 2011.

Bord, Janet and Colin. *Mysterious Britain: Ancient Secrets of the United Kingdom and Ireland*. Paladin, London, 1974.

Bord, Janet and Colin. *A Guide to Ancient Sites in Britain*. Paladin, St Albans, 1979.

Colquhoun, Ithell. *The Living Stones*. Peter Owen, London, 2016. (Originally pub. 1957.)

Cooper, Susan. *Greenwitch*. Aladdin, New York, 2000. (Originally pub. 1974.)

Cooper, Susan. *Over Sea, Under Stone*. Aladdin, New York, 2000. (Originally pub. 1965.)

Dalby, Richard. 'The Spook Stories of E. F. Benson' in *Book and Magazine Collector*, Christmas 2010, no. 328.

Evans-Wentz, W. Y. *The Fairy-Faith in Celtic Countries*. Oxford University Press, London, 1911.

Gilling, John (Dir.). *The Plague of the Zombies*. Hammer, 1966.

Horne, Philip (ed.). *Henry James: A Life in Letters*. Allen Lane, London, 1999.

Hoskins, W. G. *The Making of the English Landscape*. Penguin, London, 1985. (Originally pub. 1955.)

Hunt, Robert. *Demons, Ghosts & Spectres in Cornish Folklore*. Tor Mark Press, Penryn, 1991.

Jackson, Shirley. *The Haunting of Hill House*. Penguin Classics, London, 2009. (Originally pub. 1959.

Kaczynski, Richard. *Perdurabo: The Life of Aleister Crowley*. North Atlantic Books, Berkeley, CA, 2010.

Kinsey, Wayne. *Hammer Films: The Bray Studios Years*. Reynolds & Hearn, Richmond, 2002.

Lawrence, D. H. *Kangaroo*. Secker, London, 1923.

Newman, Paul. *The Tregerthen Horror: Aleister Crowley, D. H. Lawrence & Peter Warlock in Cornwall*. Abraxas Editions & DGR Books, 2005.

Palmer, Geoffrey and Lloyd, Noel. *E. F. Benson: As He Was*. Lennard Publishing, Luton, 1988.

Payton, Philip. *D. H. Lawrence and Cornwall*. Truran, St Agnes, 2009.

Pevsner, Nikolaus. *The Buildings of England. Cornwall*. Penguin, London, 1951.

Thompson, Raymond H. 'Interview with Susan Cooper'. Part of The Camelot Project website. https://d.lib.rochester.edu/camelot/text/interview-with-susan-cooper.

Val Baker, Denys (ed.). *Haunted Cornwall: A Book of Supernatural Stories*. William Kimber, London, 1973.

Various. *The Dark Monarch: Magic and Modernity in British Art*. Tate St Ives, 2009.

Woolf, Virginia. *A Haunted House and Other Stories*. Penguin, Harmondsworth, 1973. (Originally pub. 1944.)

Chapter 12: ANCIENT SORCERIES

Baker, Roy Ward (Dir.). *Quatermass and the Pit*. Hammer, 1967.

Bradbury, Ray. *The Halloween Tree*. Yearling Books, New York, 1999. (Originally pub. 1972.)

Cartier, Rudolph (Dir.) *Quatermass and the Pit*. BBC, 1958–59.

Chambers, Emma (ed.). *Paul Nash*. Tate Publishing, London, 2016.

Clark, Lawrence Gordon (Dir.). *Stigma*. BBC, 1977.

Fisher, Terence (Dir.). *Night of the Big Heat*. 1967.

Fryer, Ian. *The Quatermass History* (booklet accompanying DVD box set). Clear Vision Ltd, Enfield, 2003.

Grant, Simon. *Informal Beauty: The Photographs of Paul Nash*. Tate, London, 2016.

Haggard, Piers (Dir.). *Quatermass*. 1979.

Hardy, Thomas. *The Return of the Native*. Oxford University Press, Oxford, 2005. (Originally pub. 1878.)

Hardy, Thomas. *The Withered Arm and Other Stories*. Penguin Classics, London, 1999.

Hardy, Thomas. 'A Tryst in an Ancient Earthwork'. Electronic version accessed at The Thomas Hardy Society website. (Originally pub. in *A Changed Man* in 1913.)

Harris, Alexandra. *Romantic Moderns: English Writers, Artists and the Imagination from Virginia Woolf to John Piper*. Thames & Hudson, London, 2010.

Jarman, Derek. *Derek Jarman's Garden*. Thames and Hudson, London, 1995.

Jarman, Derek (Dir.). *Journey to Avebury*. 1971

Johnston, Derek. *Haunted Seasons: Television Ghost Stories for Christmas and Horror for Halloween*. Palgrave, Basingstoke, 2015.

King, Stephen. *Danse Macabre*. Sphere, London, 1982.

Lister, Derek (Dir.). *The Ice House*. BBC, 1978.

Losey, Joseph (Dir.). *The Damned*. Hammer, 1963 (UK release).

Kubrick, Stanley (Dir.). *The Shining*. 1980.

Marshall, Steve. *Exploring Avebury: The Essential Guide*. The History Press, Stroud, 2016.

Montagu, Jemima (ed.). *Paul Nash: Modern Artist, Ancient Landscape*. Tate Publishing, London, 2003.

Nash, Paul. *Fertile Image*. Faber, London, 1975 (2nd ed.). (Originally pub. 1951.)

Pitt-Rivers, Michael. *Dorset: A Shell Guide*. Faber, London, 1966. (Contains the intro Nash wrote to his original 1935 ed. of the guide.)

Schlesinger, John (Dir.). *Far from the Madding Crowd*. 1967.

Scott, Peter Graham (Dir.). *Children of the Stones*. HTV, 1977.

Smiles, Sam. *British Art: Ancient Landscapes*. Paul Holberton Publishing, London, 2017.

Tomalin, Claire. *Thomas Hardy: The Time-torn Man*. Viking, London, 2006.

Tourneur, Jacques (Dir.). *Night of the Demon*. 1957.

Various. *Derek Jarman: A Portrait*. Thames and Hudson, London, 1996.

Wheeler, Sir Mortimer. *Maiden Castle*. HMSO, London, 1972.

Young, Rob. *Electric Eden*. Faber, London, 2011.

Image Credits

13, photo (M. R. James) Hulton Archive/Stringer via Getty Images; 14, photo by the author, reproduction by permission of the Syndics of The Fitzwilliam Museum, Cambridge; 17, *Illustrated London News*, 1865 (Wikimedia Commons); 18, 275, 279, original illustrations by James McBryde (1874–1904) from the first edition of *Ghost Stories of an Antiquary* by M. R. James; 20, detail from *Dulle Griet* by Pieter Bruegel the Elder (Wikimedia Commons); 23, ullstein bild Dtl./Contributor via Getty Images; 27, illustration ('Watery Arrival') by Peter Boston from *The Children of Green Knowe*, reproduced here by kind permission of Diana Boston; 77, photo *c*. 1900 by William Henry Jackson (1843–1942) (Wikimedia Commons); 83, photo (Walter de la Mare) Hulton Deutsch/Contributor via Getty Images; 91, H. R. Millar (1869–1942), illustration from *Puck of Pook's Hill* (1906) by Rudyard Kipling (Wikimedia Commons); 107, Glenn Hill/Contributor via Getty Images; 111, LMPC/Contributor via Getty Images; 119, photo

(Algernon Blackwood) Hulton Deutsch/Contributor via Getty Images; 182, Hope Hodgson and his sister on Borth Beach. Image supplied by Ray Russell via Jane Frank (photographer unknown); 214, photo (Arthur Machen) Hulton Archive/ Stringer via Getty Images; 222, Hulton Archive/Stringer via Getty Images; Richard Dadd photographed in the act of painting *Contradiction: Oberon and Titania, c.* 1856 (Wikimedia Commons); 249, photo (W. G. Sebald) Ulf Andersen/ Contributor via Getty Images; 251, Joergens.mi/Wikipedia (https://creativecommons.org/licenses/by-sa/3.0/de/legal-code); 296, reproduced by kind permission of C. Buckton; 302, wood engraving of a merman by the sea. Wellcome Collection. CC BY; 352, Dorothy Pentreath, a Cornish-speaking fish seller, line engraving by R. Scaddan. Wellcome Collection. CC BY; 360, photo (Ithell Colquhoun) Reg Speller/Stringer via Getty Images; 370, photo (E. F. Benson) Hulton Archive/Stringer via Getty Images; 404, 'Stone Henge, Wiltshire' from *Picturesque views in England and Wales, London* (1838) by J. M. W. Turner, engraved by R. Wallis. Typ 805 38.8530, Houghton Library, Harvard University.

All chapter initial illustrations are by Richard Wells (www.richardwellsgraphics.com).

All other images are by the author, or from the author's own collection. While every effort has been made to trace the owners of copyright material, in some cases this has proved impossible. The publishers would be grateful for any information that would allow any omissions to be rectified in future editions of this book.

Acknowledgements

Many people helped and encouraged me during the writing of *Ghostland*, and I am obliged to all of them, including those who assisted with visits or queries that didn't make it into the finished book. I'd like to express my gratitude to Ray Russell at Tartarus Press for answering my enquiry about William Hope Hodgson, and to James Machin and Mark Valentine at the excellent Friends of Arthur Machen. Many thanks are due to Anthony Morris, for letting a complete stranger inside the house on the borderland. Equally, to my friend Christine, for the story of the real Dr Selwyn and of the place where Max Sebald first lived in Norfolk. To Janette Mullett, for showing me E. F. Benson's Lis Escop. And to Diana Boston, for her warm welcome to Hemingford Grey Manor and allowing her late husband's wonderful illustration of Tolly arriving at Green Knowe to be reproduced here. In addition, thanks to Dr Suzanne Reynolds and Nicholas Robinson at the Fitzwilliam

Museum for giving me permission to look around MRJ's former office. I'm also grateful for the questions answered by Dave Rogers at RSPB Lakenheath Fen, as well as to Lesley Manning for digging up her old notes about the Wash filming of her adaptation of Elizabeth Jane Howard's *Three Miles Up*. And to Frank Gordon for sharing memories of his brother Jack, author of *The House on the Brink*. All these travels in *Ghostland* were assisted by a grant from the Authors' Foundation, which is administered by The Society of Authors.

I received useful early editorial comments from Elizabeth Ferretti, as well as design feedback from Ian Claxton and Simon Brooke. Thanks also to James Wilson, who gave me initial encouragement about the idea, and who put me back in touch with Anna Power, now my agent at Johnson & Alcock – thank you Anna for all your assistance and hard work.

I'm particularly indebted to Paul Willetts for his invaluable knowledge of how to approach a book proposal, and for his help throughout. And to my friend Philip for his support and suggestions, and for revisiting Hengistbury Head with me on that sun-blasted morning. A special thank you to Clive Dunn, who accompanied me on my first visit to Great Livermere, when I was merely interested in seeing where M. R. James grew up and any ideas of a non-fiction narrative in which MRJ would feature had not even crossed my mind. The day led to me writing a serendipitous blog post that was seen by my soon-to-be editor Tom Killingbeck, and out of our initial bonding over folk horror films (and the cult 1970s schlock of *Psychomania*) this book was born; with his surname, I'd like to think that Tom was predestined for the job ... Thanks to everyone at William Collins who has helped to produce *Ghostland* – and to Richard Wells, a fellow devotee of vintage movies, whose wonderful cover and illustrations really make it stand out.

Finally, I'm grateful to my sister-in-law Karen's patient attempts to answer my questions about which year a particular half-remembered family event might have occurred in, and to my late Aunt Pat who performed a similar role at the start of the research process. Also to Hardy, my feline companion during the days spent working on *Ghostland*, who chased away the phantom chimes of the Westminster Quarters.

Above all, however, this book wouldn't have happened without Kirsty and her unflinching support for my writing, and for helping me to see past the ghosts.

Index